T0259934

S-BPM in the Production Industry

Matthias Neubauer · Christian Stary
Editors

S-BPM in the Production Industry

Industry

A Stakeholder Approach

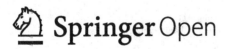

Springer Open

Editors
Matthias Neubauer
Johannes Kepler Universität Linz
Linz
Austria

Christian Stary
Johannes Kepler Universität Linz
Linz
Austria

ISBN 978-3-319-83949-3   ISBN 978-3-319-48466-2   (eBook)
DOI 10.1007/978-3-319-48466-2

© The Editor(s) (if applicable) and the Author(s) 2017. This book is published open access.
Softcover reprint of the hardcover 1st edition 2016
Open Access This book is distributed under the terms of the Creative Commons Attribution-NonCommercial 4.0 International License (http://creativecommons.org/licenses/by-nc/4.0/), which permits any noncommercial use, duplication, adaptation, distribution and reproduction in any medium or format, as long as you give appropriate credit to the original author(s) and the source, provide a link to the Creative Commons license and any changes made are indicated.
The images or other third party material in this book are included in the work's Creative Commons license, unless indicated otherwise in the credit line; if such material is not included in the work's Creative Commons license and the respective action is not permitted by statutory regulation, users will need to obtain permission from the license holder to duplicate, adapt or reproduce the material.
This work is subject to copyright. All *commercial* rights are reserved by the Publisher, whether the whole or part of the material is concerned, specifically the rights of translation, reprinting, reuse of illustrations, recitation, broadcasting, reproduction on microfilms or in any other physical way, and transmission or information storage and retrieval, electronic adaptation, computer software, or by similar or dissimilar methodology now known or hereafter developed.
The use of general descriptive names, registered names, trademarks, service marks, etc. in this publication does not imply, even in the absence of a specific statement, that such names are exempt from the relevant protective laws and regulations and therefore free for general use.
The publisher, the authors and the editors are safe to assume that the advice and information in this book are believed to be true and accurate at the date of publication. Neither the publisher nor the authors or the editors give a warranty, express or implied, with respect to the material contained herein or for any errors or omissions that may have been made.

Printed on acid-free paper

This Springer imprint is published by Springer Nature
The registered company is Springer International Publishing AG
The registered company address is: Gewerbestrasse 11, 6330 Cham, Switzerland

Preface

More than 100 years ago, Frederick Taylor moved forward applying scientific methods to the engineering of processes. Analyzing and synthesizing workflows in order to improve economic efficiency is a challenge we are facing again today when digitizing production processes. However, this time labour force plays a dual role. Besides being the affected, due to its knowledge and market pressure, it is required for designing work, thus, redefining the role of management.

S-BPM has received attention for digitizing processes, while aiming to empower stakeholders developing their organization. However, its application in managing production processes still challenges management and operation. Several case studies, presented in this volume, helped exploring the potential and experiencing the limits of engineering a company from a communication-centred perspective. It is not only about demonstrating capabilities and implementation, but also letting people design their workplace while running the business operation.

In this volume, we have structured the latest findings in Industry 4.0 projects utilizing S-BPM features. Developers, educators, and practitioners will find some conceptual background and results from the field indicating the state of the art in vertical and horizontal process integration.

The chapters have been carefully selected and thoroughly peer-reviewed by at least two experts in the field. In order to get such job done, many people have been actively involved, in particular,

- The authors of the various contributions documenting their findings for sharing experiences,
- The project team supporting the developments and reviews, and
- The European Commission funding this SO-PC-Pro[1] outreach activity

Finally, we cordially thank Ralf Gerstner and Eleonore Samklu from Springer for their continuous support and assistance when publishing this volume.

Linz, Austria
Matthias Neubauer
Christian Stary

[1]SO-PC-Pro is a European FP 7 project on subject orientation for people-centred production supported under grant agreement no. 609 190 (Theme FoF.NMP-2013-3 Workplaces of the future: the new people-centred production site "Factories of the Future")—see also www.so-pc-pro.eu.

Acknowledgements

The work reported in this book received funding in part from the European SO-PC-Pro project. SO-PC-Pro represents a collaborative research project in the Seventh Framework Programme (FP7/2007–2013) of the European Union under the grant agreement no 609190. The authors would like to gratefully acknowledge the contribution of the SO-PC-Pro project to this book.

Both the industrial cases reported in this book aimed to involve workers and provide worker-centred solutions. We gratefully acknowledge the valuable contributions of the workers and the management commitment allowing to take sufficient time for in-depth investigations. In Company A, we would like to especially thank Mr. Marek Baris for his strong commitment to the project and the support of the SO-PC-Pro project team as well as his support for the workers. Besides, we would like to acknowledge Tatiana Telecká and Tibor Telecky for providing a testbed.

In Company B, we would like to acknowledge the valuable feedback from shop floor workers and their encouragement to contribute to workplace redesign. Especially, we would like to thank Davide Tiziani, Ricardo de Bon, Giovanni Bassotto and Massimiliano Ruffo.

Aside from the industrial cases, laboratory testing related to stress measurement has been performed at Johannes Kepler University Linz, Austria. These activities were strongly supported by students in terms of test design, implementation and evaluation. We gratefully acknowledge the test persons for volunteering to be part of this research as well as the students for enabling and conducting the test.

Contents

Editors and Contributors

About the Editors

Matthias Neubauer is researcher and project manager of the SO-PC-Pro project. He has deep knowledge both in S-BPM and in all case studies performed in the project and presented in the book. He received his Ph.D. in Business Information Systems in 2013. He teaches in the fields of BPM, distributed systems, and knowledge management, and is involved in other funded international projects.

Christian Stary is Full Professor in the Department of Business Information Systems—Communications Engineering. He also leads the Competence Centre on Knowledge Management located at the University in Linz. Christian received his Ph.D. in Conceptual Modelling of Human–Computer Interaction at Vienna University of Technology in 1988 and was promoted to Associate Professor in 1993 there before becoming Full Professor in 1995 in Linz. He has held several visiting professorships in Europe and the US. He has been and still is principal investigator of several national and international projects. He has authored several articles and books on interactive systems and usability engineering, and modelling and learning support for complex socio-technical systems.

Contributors

Lubomir Billy is a graduate of the International Economic Relations' doctoral study programme at the University of Economics in Bratislava. His research interest includes migration, management and the EU Structural funds. He has participated in preparation of international projects within cross-border cooperation programmes, 7th Framework Programme, LLP, Horizon 2020 and Erasmus+. Lately, his interest in the topic of social innovations has augmented and he has participated in several projects containing the social innovation aspects at the national level, such as Development of the Action Plan of the Culture Development Strategy,

Universities as the driving forces of a knowledge-based society, as well as at the international level such as the LEGEND project focused on the intellectual capital methodology.

David Bonaldi is the Managing Director of ByElement. He holds a Masters' degree in Business Administration (University of Zurich). He has broad experiences in international project management, ERP/SAP implementations for production companies and usability/user experience engineering and human-centred design for ICT solutions.

Franco Cesaro is the owner of Cesaro&Associati. He specializes in uniting business and family values and dynamics. The focus of his studies is the individuals who work in organizations. In order to grow, these organizations must decide to invest in culture which is a prerequisite for autonomy, development of talent and the solution of problems. At present, he teaches at the University of Milan. He is the author of Non ne posso più dei venditori (2003), Piccoli e Scatenati (2004) and Racconti di Fabbrica, with M. Bini (2011).

Chiara Di Francescomarino is a researcher at Fondazione Bruno Kessler (FBK), Trento, Italy, in the Shape and Evolve Living Knowledge (SHELL) unit. She received her Ph.D. in Information and Communication Technologies from the University of Trento, working on business process modelling and reverse engineering from execution logs. Her current research interests include business process modelling, collaborative modelling and the evaluation of tools and techniques for its support, as well as business process monitoring and mining. She has been involved in local (e.g. FESR), and international (e.g. Euregio and EU) research projects. She serves as PC member in international conferences and workshops and as a peer reviewer in international journals in the field of knowledge and process management.

Mauro Dragoni is a researcher at Fondazione Bruno Kessler within the Shape and Evolve Living Knowledge research unit (SHELL). He received his Ph.D. in Computer Science from the University of Milan in 2010. His main research topics concern knowledge management, information retrieval, and sentiment analysis by focusing on the development of real-world prototypes as outcome of his research activities. He has been involved in a number of international research projects, including Organic.Lingua (FP7), SO-PC-Pro (FP7), Medical CPS (EIT), PROMO (FESR), and Presto (FESR). He co-authored more than 50 scientific publications in international journals, conferences, and workshop.

Nicola Flores is a psychologist specialized in organizational and work psychology. He gained his Bachelor's degree in Working and Organizational Psychology at Padua University and his Master's in in Human Resources Management and Organizational Development at University of California Los Angeles (UCLA). He is a trainer in different work-related training and positive psychology courses. He is also project manager in different EU funded projects and research programmes. Since 2010, he has supported the Psychology and Educational Psychology classes at Milan University—Statale.

Chiara Ghidini is a senior Research Scientist at Fondazione Bruno Kessler (FBK), Trento, Italy, where she now heads the Shape and Evolve Living Knowledge (SHELL) research unit. She obtained her Ph.D. in Computer Science Engineering in a joint programme between the Università "La Sapienza" of Rome and the University of Trento. Before joining FBK in 2003, she has worked as a postdoc at the Centre for Agent Research and Development, Manchester Metropolitan University (1998–2000), and as a lecturer at the Department of Computer Science, University of Liverpool (2000–2003). Her scientific work in the areas of Semantic Web, knowledge engineering and representation, and multi-agent systems is internationally well known and recognised.

Chiara has actively been organizing workshops and conferences on multi-agent systems (EUMAS'04), context-based representations (Context-03, 05 and 07), knowledge engineering and capturing (K-CAP 2013, EKAW 2014), and Semantic Web (ESWC 2012 and 2016, ISWC 2014 and 2016). In addition, she has served as a programme committee member for most of the top international conferences in these areas.

She has been, and still is, involved in a number of international research projects, as well as industrial projects in collaboration with companies in the Trentino area.

Richard Heininger works at Metasonic and conducts applied research in the field of S-BPM. He holds a Master's degree in Business Informatics from Johannes Kepler University Linz (Austria) and currently attends a course, Applied Knowledge Management, at the Center for Knowledge Management Linz. He was involved in many customer and research projects in which he was responsible among others for process elicitation, training or prototype development.

Udo Kannengiesser is a researcher in the fields of business process management, Industry 4.0, multi-agent systems, and design science. He worked for Metasonic GmbH and National ICT Australia, and served as a research consultant for several universities in Australia and the United States. He holds a Ph.D. in Design Computing and Cognition from the University of Sydney (Australia), where he developed an extension of the function–behaviour–structure (FBS) ontology, which is one of the most highly cited models of designing. He also holds a Master's degree in Production Engineering from Karlsruhe Institute of Technology (Germany).

Florian Krenn is a researcher in the field of business process management. He received his Master in Business Information Systems in 2013 and is working at the Department of Business Information Systems—Communications Engineering at Johannes Kepler University, Linz, Austria. Currently, he is working on his Ph.D. thesis about process decomposition and workflow execution. Florian has been involved in national and international research projects on articulation, learning and workflow supports.

Dennis Majoe is the Chief Technical Officer of MA Systems and Control Limited. He has over 20 years experience in product and systems design in the development of physiological sensors and low-power SMART wearable systems. He has a B.Sc. in Electronics, a Master's in Cybernetics and a Ph.D. in Signal Processing. He has also a Master's in Business Administrations.

Ioan-Alexandru Schärfl is currently studying Business Informatics (Master's) with a focus on security aspects of information systems at the Johannes Kepler University of Linz. He worked as a student assistant for the Data and Knowledge Engineering Institute, before he got involved in the SO-PC-Pro project at the Communications Engineering department. His research area is the vertical integration in future manufacturing companies.

Pavol Terpak is a graduate of the Slovak University of Technology in Bratislava in the area of modelling and simulation of event systems in the field of applied informatics. He participated in several development and advisory projects for customers from both public and private sectors. In custom development area, he was member of analytical team that built the eGovernment service portal which enables provision of electronic services for citizens and organizations in several municipalities in Slovakia. Regarding advisory projects, he has been focused on business transformation projects and responsible for their delivery and their profit and loss. In addition, he has been involved in the knowledge discovery R&D project with a goal of discovering new processes for extracting knowledge from data.

Alexandra Totter holds a Masters' degree in Occupational Psychology from the University of Vienna (Austria). She has worked in the field of work stress, task appropriateness, computer-supported collaborative work, technology-enhanced learning and empirical evaluation research. She has participated in a number of EU supported R&D projects and programmes (e.g. AVANTI, lab@future).

Introduction

Matthias Neubauer and Christian Stary

Abstract

This chapter frames the developments described in this book and gives an overview of its structure. The background is provided with respect to the difficulties of introducing innovation on technical and organization level in well-established fields such as production industry. The nature of disruptiveness is explained in light of the applied subject-oriented modelling and execution approach. Thereby, disruptiveness motivates the process that guided the developments, both on the conceptual layer, and in practice, aiming to establish stakeholders as informed work place and process designers.

New digital technologies start changing production processes substantially. Self-controlled vehicles, additive manufacturing, and semantic technologies open up opportunities in business operation, which industry has never experienced so far. Although in the industrialized countries labour force has increased due to such possibilities so far, this time the role of all stakeholders needs to be revisited due to the disruptive nature of technologies and their exponential rate penetrating the market.

In "The Innovator's Dilemma" Christensen (1997) has analyzed how companies can be blindsided by high-end products from competing organizations. In "The Innovator's Solution" Christensen et al. (2003a) reveal how organizations can create disruptions themselves rather than being blindsided by them. "Disruptive innovations do not attempt to bring better products to established customers in

M. Neubauer (✉) · C. Stary
Department of Business Information Systems – Communications Engineering,
Johannes Kepler University Linz, Linz, Austria
e-mail: matthias.neubauer@jku.at

© The Author(s) 2017

M. Neubauer and C. Stary (eds.), *S-BPM in the Production Industry*,
DOI 10.1007/978-3-319-48466-2_1

existing markets. Instead, they introduce products and services that are not as good as existing products, but which are simpler, more convenient, and less expensive than existing items" (Christensen et al. 2003b). These findings match digitization today, since utilizing innovative digital technologies and their capabilities requires an adjusted sequence of changes in customer, product and organizational management.

Starting with either low- or high-end disruption, processes and all related (re-) engineering tasks will be affected. Managing them has become crucial for operating a production business: "Processes are defined or evolve to address specific tasks, and the efficiency of a given process is determined by how well these tasks are performed. Processes that define capabilities in executing certain tasks concurrently define disabilities in executing others. Consistency is key—processes are not as flexible as resources, and must be applied in a consistent manner, time after time" (Christensen et al. 2003b, p. 7). In that way, a learning organization is defined, as business- and the knowledge-processing environment affected through these iterative changes (cf. Firestone and McElroy 2003).

Due to technology capabilities, in particular the automated execution of business process models, changes can be propagated directly to operation, while humans take responsibility for organizing their own work tasks in the respective organizational context. First estimates on the effects of automation in Switzerland reveal that nearly 50 % of employees could be replaced by automation in the next few years or decades (Jensen and Koch 2016). With the increase in total number of jobs created in the past 25 years, automation is expected to open opportunities across all skill levels, in particular with respect to creativity, social interaction, and quality customer service. However, adaptation of business processes at an early stage seems to be the key (*ibid.*).

As customers, network partners, management and workers are involved, processes concern all stakeholders. Given the potential of subject-oriented business process management (S-BPM) (Fleischmann et al. 2012, 2015) it involves them not only according to their mutually interacting functional roles or in terms of networked organizational units, but also as designers, and more particularly, engineers. The engineering part is required since ad hoc dynamics of change are becoming common due to concepts like demand-driven excellence (Aronow et al. 2016). Such concepts shift organizational change management to the level of business operation. Hence, management and workers need to have proper skills, techniques, and tools to adjust or adapt business processes on the fly.

How should stakeholders develop these multifaceted skills? In a recent study Pfeiffer (2016) demonstrated how the vocational system contributes to specific economic strengths like innovativeness and exporting capability that are not only relevant for production and manufacturing sectors but are also an essential asset for the transformation towards Industry 4.0. Hereby, the key asset is e-skills as they refer to a fundamental understanding of IT regardless of the domain (Bliem et al.

2014). Hence, the qualification profile in 2025 is expected to be a mix of domain and cross-domain competencies (Pfeiffer and Suphan 2015; Pfeifer et al. 2016):

- Domain competencies:
  - Cyber-physical systems/Internet of Things
  - Additive manufacturing
  - Robotics
  - Web 2.0
  - Wearables

- Cross-domain competencies:
  - Data security/privacy
  - Big Data handling
  - Interdisciplinary collaboration
  - Innovation design

The latter, interdisciplinary collaboration, and innovation design, are considered methodological skills, challenging the means of communication and documentation. With respect to process design and engineering activities, both the notation and modelling process, including stakeholder validation, need to be supported in a human-centred way. Otherwise, stakeholder participation is likely to lead to re-specifying existing patterns and behaviour rather than letting novel designs to emerge (cf. Allmer et al. 2015). The chapters of this volume set the stage for stakeholder-centred work redesign and process engineering, providing relevant background in current Industry 4.0 and S-BPM, before reporting on various findings from case studies performed in the field of production. The case studies reveal various opportunities on how to trigger and perform people-centred production projects aiming to digitize processes.

In Chap. 2, industrial challenges driven by the German "Industry 4.0" are condensed, in order to document a concrete vision for future production industries. The vision becomes manifest in terms of understanding production companies as socio-technical systems. When redesigning production processes, humans and organizational structures are of equal importance to technology. The digital production of the future requires humans as drivers and carriers of further automation steps. Concepts, such as digital readiness and digital literacy of involved stakeholders, need to be practically implemented, in order to create value from Industry 4.0 developments. On the process level, restructuring production processes in terms of vertical and horizontal adjustment needs be tackled.

In Chap. 3, we introduce the basic concepts of S-BPM and its capabilities, in particular for supporting the restructuring of processes mentioned above. One of its particularities is the claim to be usable by non-BPM experts in a straightforward way when representing process knowledge. Thereby, a stakeholder perspective encapsulating specific behaviour, e.g. evaluating a customer change request, is followed. Besides technical task accomplishment, all interactions with other stakeholders are considered with equal importance in the course of modelling. For digitizing production processes, stakeholder behaviour can be instantiated by technological systems. Each representation can be executed in its networked environment, thus allowing stakeholders to experience process designs immediately after validating models. This capability is useful to integrate processes on different automation levels, including planning, monitoring and real-time execution (changing processes on the fly).

In Chap. 4, we report about the case implemented at an SME offering the production of atypical, unique and special-purpose machinery, equipment and technologically complex units useful particularly in the automotive and electronic industries. The proposed subject-oriented solution targets to increase the worker's autonomy, the worker's involvement and information transparency as well as integration across organizational control layers. In this respect, subject orientation is applied to integrate real-time information from the shop floor (e.g. location information of parts, power consumption of machines) and business processes (e.g. customer order). Within the design and implementation, a novel S-BPM modelling approach has been developed that seeks to model subjects rather as fine-grained behaviours of actors than roles. The revealed behaviours may be assigned to actors (i.e. humans, machines) depending on their capabilities and skills. This allows for dynamic allocation of tasks to humans and machines and process execution support based on skill levels, revealing performed behaviours of actors and (de-)constructing organizational behaviours.

In Chap. 5, we report on a worldwide operating SME producing floor cleaning machines. The SME distinguishes itself from its competitors by providing highly customizable high-quality products. Employees are considered one of the "most valuable resources" of the management. However, the initial situation reveals significant improvement opportunities related to the employee involvement and empowerment concerning workplace redesign.

The proposed subject-oriented solution aims to involve shop floor workers in workplace (re)design by providing them structural empowerment means such as social media for suggestion proposals, discussions, and negotiations. Furthermore, the solutions are designed to allow for context-sensitive reporting of suggestions and errors. In addition, this context-sensitive elicitation provides the basis for analyzing the impacts of changes (e.g. the affected location, worker) and visualizing potential improvement areas within the shop floor. The subject-oriented solution represents a generic suggestions and error-handling process that can be tailored to different organizations. Furthermore, the S-BPM process has been integrated with a semantic wiki allowing for context-sensitive workplace improvement elicitation and change propagation analysis.

In Chap. 6, we address the well-being of workers in the factory of the future from a situation-awareness perspective. Recognizing latest developments in the area of wearable sensors well-being data can be captured by sensors in manufacturing settings. These data can be used to adapt production systems behaviour. Existing findings from adaptive systems design allow identifying triggers for adaptations and dimensions for intervention. The latter enrich the design space of S-BPM based process settings. In a laboratory setting, a respective system architecture and S-BPM process design have been developed and evaluated in stressful situations.

The final chapters wrap up the achievements and experiences in terms of learnings and envisioned actions in the future. It draws a realistic picture from the existing findings to future activities to be set when aiming to establish stakeholder-centred digital production systems.

In line with Adam Smith who was looking for a balance of opposing forces (Smith 2009), we need to look for balancing capabilities of digital process techniques and technologies with human needs when engineering organizations. Striving for a balance means to look beyond "training the troops" (formulated by Christensen et al. (2003a, b) as part of the innovator's solution), since such an approach might not lead to people-centred digital production processes. The following contributions are intended not only to provide a realistic picture from actual settings in organizations, but also to open up space for promoting discussions on how to actively engage stakeholders when developing digital production processes with skills beyond engineering, namely socio-technical design skills.

References

Aronow, St., Burkett, M., Nilles, K., & Romano, J. (2016). *The Gartner Supply Chain top 25 for 2016*. Stamford, CT: Gartner.

Allmer, T., Sevignani, S., & Prodnik, J. A. (2015). Mapping approaches to user participation and digital labour: A critical perspective. In *Reconsidering value and labour in the digital age* (pp. 153–171). London: Palgrave Macmillan.

Bliem, W., Van den Nest, E., Weiß, S., & Grün, G. (2014). *AMS Standing Committee on New Skills*. AMS report 105. Arbeitsmarktservice, Vienna. Austria.

Christensen, C. (1997). *The innovator's dilemma: When new technologies cause great firms to fail*. Brighton, MA: Harvard Business Review Press.

Christensen, C., & Raynor, M. (2003a). *The innovator's solution: Creating and sustaining successful growth*. Boston, MA: Harvard Business Review Press.

Christensen, C., & Raynor, M. (2003b). Creating and sustaining successful growth. The innovator's solution. In *Soundview Executive Book Summaries, 25(11) Part I, 1–8*. Boston, MA: Harvard Business Review Press.

Firestone, J. M., & McElroy, M. W. (2003). *Key issues in the new knowledge management*. London: Routledge.

Fleischmann, A., Schmidt, W., Stary, C., Obermeier, S., & Börger, E. (2012). *Subject-oriented business process management*. Berlin: Springer Publishing Company.

Fleischmann, A., Schmidt, W., & Stary, C. (Eds). (2015). *S-BPM in the Wild. Practical value creation*. Berlin: Springer Publishing Company.

Jensen, B., & Koch, M. (2016). *Mensch und Maschine: Roboter auf dem Vormarsch*. Deloitte AG, Zurich: Folgen der Automatisierung für den Schweizer Arbeitsmarkt.

Pfeiffer, S. (2016). Berufliche Bildung 4.0? Überlegungen zur Arbeitsmarkt-und Innovationsfähigkeit. *Industrielle Beziehungen, 23*(1), 25–44.

Pfeiffer, S., & Suphan, A. (2015). *The labouring capacity index: Living labouring capacity and experience as resources on the road to industry 4.0*. Retrieved January 30, 2016, from http://www.sabine-pfeiffer.de/files/downloads/2015-Pfeiffer-Suphan-EN.pdf.

Pfeiffer, S., Lee, Ch., Zirnig, H., & Suphan, A. (2016). *Industrie 4.0 - Qualifizierung 2015*. Frankfurt: VDMA.

Smith, A. (2009). *The theory of moral sentiments*. New York: Pengiun.

Open Access This chapter is distributed under the terms of the Creative Commons Attribution-NonCommercial 4.0 International License (http://creativecommons.org/licenses/by-nc/4.0/), which permits any noncommercial use, duplication, adaptation, distribution and reproduction in any medium or format, as long as you give appropriate credit to the original author(s) and the source, provide a link to the Creative Commons license and indicate if changes were made.

The images or other third party material in this chapter are included in the work's Creative Commons license, unless indicated otherwise in the credit line; if such material is not included in the work's Creative Commons license and the respective action is not permitted by statutory regulation, users will need to obtain permission from the license holder to duplicate, adapt or reproduce the material.

Industrial Challenges

2

Christian Stary and Matthias Neubauer

Abstract

Recently, the German "Industry 4.0" initiative gained momentum, and sketches a vision for future production industries. This chapter reviews industrial challenges in the area of "Industry 4.0". The findings are structured along the fundamental understanding of production companies as socio-technical systems. Socio-technical systems consist of three important aspects—(i) human, (ii) organizational structures and technology—and, most importantly their mutual relations, and thus, the interdependencies of these aspects. The review reveals that humans need to remain a vital element of future production and need to drive organizational development efforts and continuous workplace improvement. Organizational structures are challenged by changing business models of production companies. Enabling organizational change requires an open organizational culture (e.g., in terms of digital readiness), learning support and digital literacy of all involved stakeholders. In order to create value from Industry 4.0 developments, still technical challenges, in particular vertical and horizontal process integration need be resolved.

2.1 Introduction

Today's industry needs to survive in a volatile environment. Changing customer demands, high degree of product individualization, increasing digitalization and system integration, effective and efficient manufacturing operations to meet high

C. Stary (✉) · M. Neubauer
Department of Business Information Systems Communications Engineering, Johannes Kepler University Linz, Linz, Austria
e-mail: christian.stary@jku.at

© The Author(s) 2017
M. Neubauer and C. Stary (eds.), *S-BPM in the Production Industry*,
DOI 10.1007/978-3-319-48466-2_2

quality at low cost, well-being of employees, etc., are just some factors that challenge daily work in industry. In general, an **industry** refers to the production of certain goods or services within an economy (e.g., automotive industry in Germany). Different Industry classification systems like the ISIC (2008), NAICS (2012) or NACE exist that organize companies with respect to production processes or similar products. (cf. https://en.wikipedia.org/wiki/Industry_classification). According to the NAICS (2012) **Manufacturing** *"comprises establishments primarily engaged in the chemical, mechanical or physical transformation of materials or substances into new products. These products may be finished, in the sense that they are ready to be used or consumed, or semi-finished, in the sense of becoming a raw material for an establishment to use in further manufacturing. Related activities, such as the assembly of the component parts of manufactured goods; the blending of materials; and the finishing of manufactured products by dyeing, heat-treating, plating and similar operations are also treated as manufacturing activities. Manufacturing establishments are known by a variety of trade designations, such as plants, factories or mills"*. Compared to the definition of manufacturing, the understanding of "**Production**" is more generic in terms of any conversion from input to output. This also includes intangible products like the delivery of services in areas as government and health care or even knowledge production.

In this book, production companies are understood as complex, socio-technical systems of people, processes and machines that flexibly interact within a certain context when generating goods. A "workplace" is defined as a physically or conceptually distinguishable set of interactions between people, machines and processes within their contexts. For example, workplaces may include the interactions of individual workers in their immediate physical surroundings, and the interactions of teams of workers that are distributed across different departments. Taking a socio-technical systems point of view includes the consideration of three different perspectives—human, organization and technology—as well as their interdependencies (cf. Botthof and Hartmann 2015—Industry 4.0 as socio-technical system). In the subsequent section, industrial challenges for each of the given perspectives are identified. They form the basis for describing the S-BPM potential to support Industry 4.0 designs and implementation in Chap. 3.

2.2 The Vital Role of Humans in Production Industries

With the advent of initiatives like Industry 4.0, industrial internet, internet of things, cyber-physical systems or smart factories a vision of a tightly connected real and digital world has been evangelized in order to open new avenues for production and workplace design. In addition to the development of technological enablers, the vital role of the human beings for factories of the future has been emphasized by research and industry (cf. EFFRA 2013). Humans remain an integral and essential part of future production, since humans are of utmost importance for the overall production system flexibility and intelligence (Kärcher 2015, p. 49). However, the range of activity will change for people in future production situations. Human-centred workplace design has been an important aspect since the beginning of the "Industry 4.0" project development. Fundamental design issues refer to the elements of socio-technical systems and comprise aspects such as:

- Central or decentral decision-making; process and information transparency across organizational layers [Organization]
- The role of humans and technology—does technology serve humans as support means? Or do humans merely represent machine operators? [Human]
- Technology design—will technology substitute or support human work? [Technology]

(cf. Kärcher 2015, p. 50).

Lüdtke (2015, p. 125) highlights the explicit and systematic recognition of humans when designing and implementing automation support. He stresses that automation may not be successful in cases where humans are neglected and argues for a flexible assignment of tasks either to machines or humans. In his vision, the optimal task sharing should not be determined a priori. Instead, at each point in time task sharing shall be evaluated based on distribution strategies and situated requirements. Thereby, Lüdtke (2015) takes a "Human-Machine Team" (HMT) perspective leading to a collaborative task solving attempt between humans and machines. Taking such a perspective requires shifting focus to a team perspective rather than to the mere automation perspective. Thus, aspects such as communication among team members (H2H, H2 M, M2H, M2 M), knowledge about abilities, skills, activities, roles and plans of team members are vital for situation awareness and alignment between the team members.

Lüdtke (2015) proposes a procedural model for developing human-machine teams. This model structures development activities along four human-machine team dimensions:

- **Composition**
  describes the purpose of a HMT, the typical number and types of involved actors as well as the number and types of required resources.
- **Cooperation**
  describes who works with whom on a certain task and who might substitute the required behaviour; also defines handover behaviour between machines and humans vice versa.
- **Interaction**
  defines the communication and modality among actors.
- **Interface**
  defines the dedicated user interface for humans.

For each dimension Lüdtke (2015) suggests to follow the traditional development phases (1) requirements definition, (2) specification, (3) implementation and (4) evaluation. However, he stresses the importance of people involvement by participatory design techniques to meet human expectations and requirements. Furthermore, Lüdtke (2015) recommends a model-based approach to support these phases. Thereby, he proposes to apply different kinds of models which cover tasks, the work domain, humans, machines and user interfaces.

The **Involvement of people in the development of human–system interactions** represents an important aspect for any development attempt. System design always serves a certain purpose, aims to reach certain objectives and addresses actual user groups. Research and developments in the field of human computer interaction (HCI) promote human-centric design processes to meet user's expectations and requirements. Standards such as ISO 9241-210:2010 promote approaches and guidelines to integrate users in the design and evaluation of IT solutions in order to improve adequate system design and adaptation. ISO 9241-210:2010 Ergonomics of human–system interaction—Part 210: Human-centred design for interactive systems promotes the following key principles:

- The design is based upon an explicit understanding of users, tasks and environments
- Users are involved throughout design and development
- The design is driven and refined by user-centred evaluation
- The process is iterative
- The design addresses the whole user experience
- The design team includes multidisciplinary skills and perspectives

Besides the explicit recognition of humans in design specifications and their active involvement in development initiatives, **humans** themselves represent an essential **enabler for organizational improvement**. Employees are considered to be domain experts in their field of activity within a company. As such, employees pose a valuable source for improvement ideas (Setiawan et al. 2011; Fairbank and Williams 2001). Nevertheless, employees are often not involved in the innovation process (Setiawan et al. 2011; Fairbank and Williams 2001). The idea of employee participation in innovation processes is well-proven. Since the late eighteenth century employee suggestion systems (ESS) provide means for *employee engagement* and have been used to collect suggestions and ideas for improvements (Fairbank and Williams 2001). Integrating employees in the innovation process has the potential to lead to important improvements and financial benefits (Fairbank and Williams 2001). However, empowering employees to take part in innovation and improvement processes requires *organizational structures* facilitating employee involvement as well as *adequate tools* supporting employee commitment (Fairbank and Williams 2001). Considering the design of organizational structures enabling employee involvement, requirements and principles have already been defined (cf. Lawler 1986). Taking into account such design principles for organizational structures, the provision of adequate tool support to facilitate employee empowerment is still challenging organizational development.

Basically, two complementary views on empowerment at work and employee involvement have emerged in literature: a *sociostructural* and *psychological* perspective (Liden et al. 2000; Spreitzer 2007). The *sociostructural* perspective focuses on "conditions that enable empowerment in the workplace", whereas the *psychological* perspective focuses "on the psychological experience of empowerment at work" (Spreitzer 2007, p. 54). In general, sociostructural empowerment can be subsumed as the sharing of decision-making power between superiors and subordinates (Liden et al. 2000; Spreitzer 2007).

Parallel aspects of structural empowerment can be found in *high-involvement management* (cf. Spreitzer 2007; Konrad 2006; Lawler 1986). High-involvement management as well as structural empowerment focus on the sharing of decision-making power within different levels in the organizational hierarchy. Lawler (1986) identified that by providing *power, information, knowledge* and *rewards* the building of a high-involvement work system is enabled. These enablers are in line with Spreitzers' understanding of facilitators for structural empowerment (cf. Spreitzer 2007).

Providing *power* refers to sharing decision-making power between superiors and subordinates (Konrad 2006; Lawler 1986; Spreitzer 2007). Sharing decision-making power is not exclusively limited to granting final authority and accountability for decisions but already starts at giving employees the possibility to provide input and contribute to decision-making processes (Konrad 2006; Lawler 1986).

As Spreitzer (2007, p. 55) states: *"relevance is key", the focus lies on enabling employees to make and influence decisions concerning their day-to-day work.* Transferred to the context of workplace improvement, the goal is to enable employees to take part in improving processes, tools and artefacts and interactions in which they are involved in their everyday work (Lawler 2008).

Sharing decision-making power is necessary but not sufficient to facilitate employee involvement (Lawler 2008; Macduffie 1995). In order to contribute to improvement and innovation processes, employees need to know how their actions influence their environment and affect the organization's performance (Gibson et al. 2007; Konrad 2006; Spreitzer 2007). This can be done by explicitly providing *information* on performance indicators (e.g., output/throughput, revenues, costs) relevant for the particular work process (Konrad 2006). This information allows employees to reveal how their actions or planned changes in their workplace affect the organization. Furthermore, the provision of additional information supports employees when making decisions and suggestions (Spreitzer 2007).

Knowledge, in terms of an employee's skills and abilities, is essential when it comes to making right decisions and taking action (Lawler 2008; Konrad 2006). This includes not only knowledge about a certain work task but also interdependences and economical aspects within the organization (Lawler 2008).

Additionally, financial *rewards* are seen as a compensation for additional involvement beside the day-to-day work (Spreitzer 2007) and, furthermore, are seen as a method to ensure that employees use the given power and information for the organization's advantage (Konrad 2006).

Taking into account the importance of humans within socio-technical development as well as their empowerment in organizations, a context sensitive understanding of workplaces is essential. There has been considerable research in the notion of context in business processes and context awareness of business process management systems (Rosemann et al. 2008; Saidani and Nurcan 2007; Wieland et al. 2007). Context can be generally defined as "any information that can be used to characterize the situation of an entity. An entity is a person, place or object that is considered relevant to the interaction between a user and an application, including the user and applications themselves" (Dey 2001). Context in the domain of business processes has been more narrowly defined as "the minimum set of variables containing all relevant information that impact the design and execution of a business process" (Rosemann et al. 2008). In accordance with this definition, most work on developing context-aware systems in business process management focuses on the adaptation of processes to changes in the context (Rosemann et al. 2008; Saidani and Nurcan 2007). This aims at increasing the effectiveness and efficiency of processes, by reducing the gap between desired process behaviour and the workers' interactions afforded by specific contextual conditions.

Including the views of human workers in context-aware systems requires a dynamic, people-centred notion of context. Based on Dourish (2004), Kannengiesser et al. (2014) define interactional context as "a process that generates subjective views of a workplace. The workplace is the environment a process participant interacts with; it can include the technophysical environment (tools, business objects, physical layout, etc.) and the sociocultural environment (values, norms, organizational structures, etc.)". The subjective perspective of interactional context provides a suitable basis for developing context-aware process applications that are adaptive to the individual psychological and physiological needs of human actors. For context-aware processes to be labelled people-centred, it is not so much the specific information dimensions (e.g., technophysical, sociocultural etc.) of context that matter but the way in which context information is captured and used for the benefit of workers.

In this book *people-centred context awareness* is understood as the ability to adapt workplaces to the workers' needs so that the changes are perceived as beneficial by the workers. Thereby two important aspects are differentiated:

- Capturing context

    - Direct sensing by workers
    - Indirect sensing via facilitators (Observer, Contextual Inquiry, Contextual Design)
    - Physiological Sensor systems

- Adapting Processes to context:

  – Process instances
  – Process models

Summarizing, requires a novel, integrative perspective on system design. Although the fundamental understanding of can be applied, the constituents, relations and contextual factors of these systems need to be revisited. In particular, the roles need to be redefined in terms of active actors operating on concrete work tasks as well while at the same time rethink the structure and arrangement of these work tasks. Dynamic development of processes seems to be crucial for meeting the demands of today's production companies. Since management can only represent regulative power in terms of standards and legal frameworks, workers need to be empowered to develop design force. Adapting and designing production and business processes across organizational layers requires interactive tool support. It needs aligning previously isolated areas to enable novel concepts such as servitization delivering value to customers.

2.3 Organizational Challenges of Future Production—"Servitization"

Digitization is driving many organizations, both in service and manufacturing industry. The impact of digital technologies on services and products are so severe that organizations in all sectors have started revisiting their business models and production processes. In manufacturing industries, traditionally developing and producing tangible goods, providing customers with services such as maintenance and repair, have not played a significant role in business strategies. When taking them into account these services as part of value-driven operation, "servitization" conceptualizes the idea of manufacturers becoming service providers (Lay et al. 2014). Thereby, the role of IT as an enabler for digitization has to be recognized (Abolhassan 2016). Since the integrated digitization of manufacturing and service industries is likely to have similarly far-reaching impact as the industrial revolution in the nineteenth century, a crucial question for manufacturing companies is not only how products are going to change in a digital world, but also what challenges arise from those developments for organizing work and production processes (Baines et al. 2013).

Products in a digital world are likely to become hybrid as physical goods increasingly integrate digital elements. Entire sectors, such as automotive heavily rely on digital components embedded in physical products. The benefit of such a shift are intelligent functions for customers affecting essential areas of human living, such as in case of healthcare through networked medical devices. Digital systems facilitate the development of hybrid products, so-called "digicals". Their effective use depends on high connectivity and real-time data processing capabilities enabling situation awareness.

Although digital information systems have formed the backbone of business operations now over several decades, many manufacturing and production organizations are still reluctant to digital integration tasks (see also two of the case studies in this volume—Chaps. 4 and 6). However, such an endeavour requires rethinking their organizational structure and processes (cf. Rigby 2014). While customers increasingly become digitally literate, organizations still are trying to cope with transformation tasks due to the socio-technical nature of that process and its adjacent challenges (cf. Rigby et al. 2015).

2.3.1 Changing the Business Model

For organizations a chance to compete in the realm of increasing digitization is cooperation with customers and companies outside the sector, and competition, as it brings about opportunities for them to design a digital business model in the realm of innovating it (cf. Roos 2015). Business indicators reveal growing technology sectors, see, e.g. TechCity et al. (2016) for the UK. Stakeholders are interacting with multi-sided platforms going beyond B2B and B2C, and proliferated rapidly with the Internet. They lead to the development of new business models to monetize innovative value propositions in digital markets. Internet intermediaries are considered as resource integrators, involving consumers and business partners in a process of co-creation of value, thus establishing an integrated, two-sided business model (Muzellec et al. 2015). Business models of respective Internet ventures reveal a clear pattern of evolution from inception to an integrated combination, B2B&C and B2C&B. This development can be accounted to a shift in the relative influence of different business stakeholders (ibid.).

The emerging concept of servitization has been recognized as trigger for changing business models of production companies. However, the expected benefits from servitization have not been measured so far on the business model level. As Cai et al. (2014) point out when analysing empirical evidence, manufacturing companies still encounter challenges when implementing servitization concepts. They could identify risks for each element of the business mode, in particular service strategy, -offering, -process and a variety of environmental factors. Today's managers still need guidance for service business development, in order to handle the process of introducing servitization and to develop respective organizational capabilities (cf. Paiola et al. 2012). For instance, organizations selling through distributors (indirectly) to customers, with functional structuring, are likely to achieve servitization "through four distinct phases: (1) rearranging collaboration with distributors, (2) enlarging the service competence of distributors, (3) modifying potential distributors into subsidiaries and (4) job enlargements in subsidiaries" (ibid.).

Recently, Tsou et al. (2015) could show that openness of organizations accelerates changes of business models. It concerns (i) the technological context (openness of technology) when adopting systems, (ii) the organizational context (i.e., openness of corporate culture) triggering innovation, and (iii) the environmental context (i.e., openness to the external environment) when opening boundaries to the external environment. In particular, openness to service co-production fosters organizational performance. In addition, knowledge reach/richness, and also process reach/richness plays a crucial role (see Fig. 2.1). Greater process reach/richness significantly increases the effects of service co-production on organizational performance. Process reach/richness is an explanatory variable that accounts for important differences in organizational performance. The latter clearly indicate that the process design is crucial for implementing servitization in manufacturing industries Fig. 2.2.

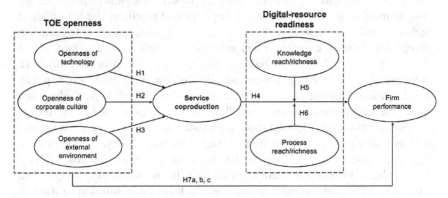

Fig. 2.1 Service co-production increasing organizational performance (adapted from Tsou et al. 2015, © Elsevier Ltd. All rights reserved)

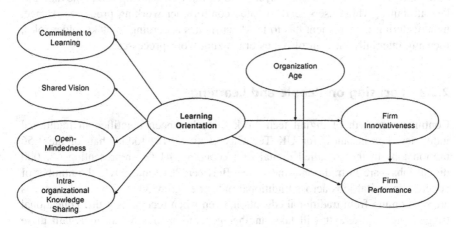

Fig. 2.2 Learning orientation (adapted from Calantone et al. 2002, © 2002 Elsevier Science Inc. All rights reserved)

The study has revealed several practical implications for managing business models:

- Top management needs to actively transform an organization's business models to an open model, in order to stimulate its ability to manage collaboration.
- Managers should remain highly sensitive to competition and the macro-environment while encouraging service co-production with partners.
- "With regard to IT service co-production project managers need to ensure that (1) project objectives are clearly defined in terms of openness aspects from both the market (i.e., external environment) and the organization's (corporate culture) perspectives, (2) the involvement and support of top management (i.e., the chief executive officer) are secured, (3) standard project management processes are used to mitigate the failure of service co-production practices, and (4) sufficient technological resources and capacity (i.e., digital resources) are dedicated to completing the service co-production project in the time allotted. This sequence of resource picking and capability building may serve as an effective roadmap for IT firms that are contemplating service co-production implementation" (ibid., p. 11).
- Digital process management for service operation is crucial, in particular when managing the increased amount and flow of knowledge related to customers. Moreover, "customers demand more information and knowledge about organizations with which they co-produce products or services". Digital process management is thus necessary to ensure that this need can be fulfilled (ibid., p. 12).
- Open collaboration channels are required for value networks supporting digital innovation. They are essential membranes for knowledge diffusion to partners and customers and vice versa.

As Raja et al. (2015) have found, value from servitized offerings will be derived differently by buyers and users. Buyers tend to value cost savings and innovation as key attributes, whilst users tend to value control over working processes. Hence, manufacturing management has to tackle attributes according to stakeholder roles, focusing internally on control issues organizing work processes.

2.3.2 Focusing on People and Learning

Continuous growth of digital tech work force has been identified in traditional industries. For instance, for UK TechCity et al. (2016) found that, of the 1.56 million jobs in the so-called digital tech economy, 41 %—representing 648,000 digital jobs—are in traditional industries. Between 2012 and 2015, the number of adverts for digital jobs across traditional industries grew 34 %. The skills it needs are not coming from traditional education, even when recognizing that educational triggers are required. It will take another generation of scholars to regain these skills. For instance, the recent "Computer Science for All" initiative in the US, enacted by the Every Student Succeeds Act (ESSA) into law, is a fundamental step forward for K-12 education, as computer science needs to be considered a new basic skill required for economic opportunity and social mobility.

In addition, there is the need to link technical skills with business skills. In particular, for product and service innovation, up-to-date technical skills need to be complemented with business know-how (TechCity et al. 2016). Technical skill development to that respect may require dedicated learning formats (cf. Willett 2007), as industrial product-service systems for lasting customer retention require new development methods). Herzog et al. (2013) identified cross-domain thinking to be essential for the developer's mind setting. Thereby, gamification can help engineers not to think in separate service and product domains.

Calantone et al. (2002) findings revealed, based on in-depth interviews with senior executives and a review of the literature, four components relevant for learning orientation: commitment to learning, shared vision, open-mindedness and intra-organizational knowledge sharing. Learning orientation affects the innovativeness of organizations, which in turn affects their performance.

Picot et al. (2013) have detailed skills required for organizing work in digitized societies. According to their findings the potential of digitization can only be leveraged when content, process, organization of work and collaboration are considered as design entities. Such an understanding goes beyond the provision of digital systems for organizations and their stakeholders. It requires rethinking processes and the technological infrastructure. They lay ground for increasing flexibility in work design, with respect to locality, time, connectivity and distribution of knowledge. The authors identified a set of competences that need to become part of qualification schemes:

- Networking skills to form communities and units in a more self-organized way
- Leadership based on social skills, such as conflict resolution in real time
- Comprehensive digital literacy, even leading to first time users
- Dynamic adaptation of regulations including business rules and decision-making procedures, in order to meet requirements from an organizational perspective, such as letting robots control production lines, and letting customers change orders up to production time
- Value responsiveness revisiting work-life balance

Finally, the involvement of employees in digital workflows leads to a higher visibility of the work activities. A flood of employee-related data needs to be screened with respect to preserving workforce protection. Transmitting workforce data requires approval when measuring performance or dispatching resources in real time. A gain in flexibility can be accompanied with the trade-off of self-control for workers.

2.3.3 Digital Service Provision

Traditionally, manufacturers use services to differentiate their products and trigger sales. Although they have different service strategies, three categories of service offerings were identified by Raddats et al. (2014): product-attached services, operations services on own products, and vendor independent operations services. Consequently, manufacturers follow different service strategies. The service offerings refer either to customers, products or services themselves, and can be differentiated further (ibid.):

- Services supporting the supplier's product versus services supporting the customer's processes
- Transactional services versus relational services
- Individual services versus bundled and/or integrated services
- Standardized offerings versus customized offerings
- Input-based services versus output-based services
- Product-attached services versus product-independent services
- Services on own products versus services on multivendor products

The relationships between categories of services are additionally depicted in Fig. 2.3.

Of particular interest for process design are all links to operational issues on the organization's value creation activities. "Despite the high level of interest in how organizational structures facilitate service orientation in capital goods manufacturing companies, researchers have neglected this field" (Gebauer et al. 2009). They have explored distinct categories of organizational approaches contributing to service orientation:

- Product-strategic business unit
- Product-service strategic business unit
- Service-product strategic business unit
- Service strategic business unit and product strategic business unit

Although each organizational approach reflects a unique degree of service orientation and thus, leads to different levels of performance outcome, it can be noted that of main interest has been the static anchoring of service orientation rather than the dynamics of business operation in relation to organizational structuring.

Organizational considerations so far seem to focus on either the integration or the separation of product and service business. However, manufacturing is shifted increasingly towards distribution and cloud-based services. Hence, not only core processes of production, but rather business model and architectures need to be revisited and restructured, emphasizing service orientation, high degree of collaboration, knowledge management, eco-efficiency. Current manufacturing involves all activities ranging from product design, production, fabrication, testing, maintenance and all other stages of a product life cycle (Li et al. 2010, 2011).

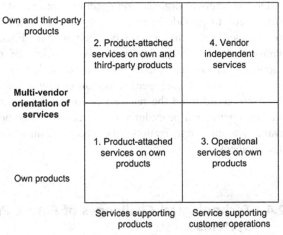

Fig. 2.3 Framework of service categories (adapted from Raddats et al. 2014, © Taylor & Francis Group)

While not evident from its beginning collaboration and service orientation are playing fundamental roles in becoming agile and stay in business (Tsou et al. 2015). From empirical evidence it can be concluded that is positively linked with increasing service networking activities of manufacturing companies (Bikfalvi et al. 2013), however, depending on the servitization strategy of an organization (see above). Consequently, interaction between organizations or business unit plays a crucial role in digital production. Manufacturers establish inter-firm collaboration for service operations. However, the results indicate that the mere existence of service networks does not guarantee success in servitizing (Bikfalvi et al. 2013) "Despite the existence of a parsimonious set of standardization efforts addressing product-related services, manufacturing firms have not reached a common understanding of the product-service system and the corresponding business processes and IT systems" (Neff et al. 2013, p. 1).

Servitization needs to rely on an intelligent and collaborative manufacturing service model. Distributed resources, such machines, computer-aided design and engineering tools, models repositories, and capabilities for design, fabrication, assembling, simulation, and testing need to be interconnected through process specifications and workflows for operation support (cf. Alexopoulos et al. 2011). They form a shared pool in servitized manufacturing, establishing a platform which can itself be considered as a service. Stakeholders (including customers) need access to services which are part cloud settings, in particular, encapsulating.

- Design as a service (Wu et al. 2012)
- Social networking as a service (Wu et al. 2013)
- Simulation as a service (Ren et al. 2011)
- Production, test and assembling as a service (Cohen et al. 2015)
- Logistics as a service (Holmborm et al. 2014)

Due to actor- or organization-specific requirements service manufacturing platforms need to provide intelligent service composition facilities. They allow customized settings including collaboration support. Finally, a service manufacturing platform should encapsulate not only a variety of physical resources but also knowledge categories in terms of operationalizing aggregated information, such as broker services or intelligent information agents (cf. Wu et al. 2013). Business processes could build the relevant boundary for building such platforms, as they provide operational procedures which can be embodied into various contexts relevant for an organization, including manufacturing and business model development.

2.4 Technological Challenges of Future Production Systems

With the advent of the Internet of Things (IoT) and its application in the industry sector (cf. Kagermann et al. 2012), not only the communication among technical IoT devices (e.g., sensors, actuators) and humans became vital to reach organizational goals but also the integration of different organizational levels (i.e., vertical integration of business processes with production planning systems and production control systems) has become an important aspect (cf. Meyer et al. 2013; Schüller and Elger 2013; Bassi et al. 2013; Kagermann et al. 2012). The vertical integration of business processes and technical manufacturing processes targets towards the need of production companies to be able to flexibly change requirements, reconfigure processes, get immediate feedback about the current state of production processes for the management, and to reach information integration between all process levels (Schüller and Elger 2013; Kannengiesser and Müller 2013). Accordingly, Haller et al. (2009) identify two paradigms from which business value out of IoT can be derived. First, real-world visibility which addresses the increased information on what is going on within the real world and thus allows to increase accuracy of timeliness of information and to support the identification of optimization opportunities. Second, business process decomposition is identified as a paradigm to gain added value out of IoT. The benefit of business process decomposition is described as following by Haller et al. (2009):

> The decomposition and decentralization of existing business processes increases scalability and performance, allows better decision making and could even lead to new revenue streams through entitlement management of software products deployed on smart items... Edge processing and business process decomposition allows applications to make (part of their) decisions locally in a decentralized manner and act accordingly. It thereby extends the real world visibility concept with real world interaction.

To implement such decomposed, distributed systems a design environment is required which allows to take into account "all business objects, business processes, services, as well as processing, sensing and communication capabilities of smart items" (Haller et al. 2009, p. 17). Such an environment should allow for modelling and executing organizational processes in an integrated and distributed way. Furthermore, it should support the adaptability of a model during deployment to support self-organization and optimization during runtime (Haller et al. 2009).

However, even if a vision of future production systems is well established, the design and implementation of such systems remains a challenging task. Subsequently, further characteristics, challenges and requirements related to future production systems are summarized based on literature findings.

Vogel-Heuser (2014, p. 37ff) describe the following fundamental technical characteristics of CPS:

- (Reference) Architectures allowing for the integration of diverse, heterogeneous system architectures
- Communication and integrated data flow among diverse stakeholders in terms of heterogeneous systems as well as different human target groups
- Intelligent products and production units, e.g. flexible units that may be adapted, products know where to go and consider changes in production environment, this typically requires a modular product structure and a model-based engineering approach which allows to adapt products at runtime. Thus, a specification of required (product) and offered (machine) capabilities is necessary
- Human-centred system design in terms of understandable data aggregation and integration and assistance.

In addition, Bauernhansl (2014, p. 26) envision a shift from the hierarchical automation pyramid to a service-oriented network. It will lead to encapsulating services within the different traditional automation layers and their provision in a service network. In such an environment, software, infrastructures, platforms may be offered as services which can be flexibly combined, e.g. software services to apps which may be used to support the value chain. In the context of modelling cyber-physical systems Derler et al. (2012) identify challenges like:

- Modelling interactions of functionality and implementation
- Modelling distributed behaviours
- System heterogeneity requiring the combination of multiple models
- Methodologies bridging the gaps between the disciplines involved (e.g., control engineering, software engineering, sensor networks) (Derler et al. 2013)
- Modelling service semantics

From the technological requirements given above, the following design challenges of future production systems can be derived:

- Handling the heterogeneity of system components
- Loose coupling of system components
- Case-based, flexible application composition
- Late binding of system components

- Providing means for modelling decomposed, distributed behaviours of organizational processes
- Modelling (message) semantics

2.5 Conclusive Summary Industrial Challenges

The aim of this chapter was to review industrial challenges in the area of "Industry 4.0". The review has been structured along the fundamental understanding of production companies as socio-technical systems. Socio-technical systems consist of three important aspects—(i) human, (ii) organizational structures and technology—and the interdependencies of these aspects.

The review reveals that humans will remain a vital element of future production situations and need to become involved in organizational development efforts and continuous workplace improvement. Organizational structures are challenged by changing business models of production companies. Enabling organizational change requires openness to adaptation and innovation, digital readiness), learning support and digital literacy of all involved stakeholders. In terms of adequate technology design for people in organizations, technical challenges have still to be tackled, in particular, developing adequate design and implementation environments for vertical and horizontal process integration to generate value from the Industry 4.0 concept.

The contents of this chapter frame the description of the S-BPM potential in the area of "Industry 4.0". In the following chapter this potential will be discussed and current developments from the S-BPM community will be summarized.

References

Abolhassan, F. (Ed.). (2016). *Was treibt die Digitalisierung?* Wiesbaden: Springer.

Alexopoulos, K., Makris, S., Xanthakis, V., & Chryssolouris, G. (2011). A web-services oriented workflow management system for integrated digital production engineering. *CIRP Journal of Manufacturing Science and Technology, 4*(3), 290–295.

Baines, T., & Lightfoot, H. (2013). *Made to serve: How manufacturers can compete through servitization and product service systems.* Wiley.

Bassi, A., Bauer, M., Fiedler, M., Kramp, T., Kranenburg, R., Lange, S., et al. (Eds.). (2013). *Enabling things to talk: Designing IoT solutions with the IoT architectural reference model.* Springer Open.

Bauernhansl, T. (2014). Die Vierte Industrielle Revolution - Der Weg in ein wertschaffendes Produktionsparadigma. In T. Bauernhansl, M. ten Hompel, & B. Vogel-Heuser (Eds.), *Industrie 4.0 in Produktion, Automatisierung und Logistik* (pp. 5–35). Wiesbaden: Springer. http://dx.doi.org/10.1007/978-3-658-04682-8_1.

Bikfalvi, A., Lay, G., Maloca, S., & Waser, B. R. (2013). Servitization and networking: Large-scale survey findings on product-related services. *Service Business, 7*(1), 61–82.

Botthof, A., & Hartmann, E. A. (Eds.). (2015). *Zukunft der Arbeit in Industrie 4.0*. Berlin: Springer.

Cai, S., & Shen, N. (2014). Risk management model of servitization: A business model perspective. In J. Zhang, X. Zhang, P. Yi, & K. Wang (Eds.), *ASCE Proceedings International Conference of Logistics Engineering and Management ICLEM 2014* (pp. 815–822). American Society of Civil Engineers.

Calantone, R. J., Cavusgil, S. T., & Zhao, Y. (2002). Learning orientation, firm innovation capability, and firm performance. *Industrial Marketing Management, 31*(6), 515–524.

Cohen, Y. (2015). A technique for integrated modelling of manual and automatic assembly. *Journal of Manufacturing Technology Management, 26*(2), 164–181.

Derler, P., Lee, E. A., & Vincentelli, A. S. (2012). Modeling cyber physical systems. *Proceedings of the IEEE, 100*(1), 13–28.

Derler, P., Lee, E. A., Tripakis, S., & Törngren, M. (2013). Cyber-physical system design contracts. In *Proceedings of the ACM/IEEE 4th International Conference on Cyber-Physical Systems, ICCPS '13* (109–118). New York, NY: ACM Digital Library. http://doi.acm.org/10.1145/2502524.2502540.

Dey, A. K. (2001). Understanding and using context. *Personal Ubiquitous Computing, 5*(1), 4–7. doi:10.1007/s007790170019.

Dourish, P. (2004). What we talk about when we talk about context. *Personal Ubiquitous Computing, 8*(1), 19–30. doi:10.1007/s00779-003-0253-8.

EFFRA—European Factories of the Future Research Association. (2013). *Factories of the future: Multi-annual roadmap for the contractual PPP under horizon 2020*. Brussels, Belgium: Publications Office of the European Union.

Fairbank, J. F., & Williams, S. D. (2001). Motivating creativity and enhancing innovation through employee suggestion system technology. *Creativity and Innovation Management, 10*(2), 68–74. doi:10.1111/1467-8691.00204.

Gebauer, H., Puetz, F., Fischer, T., & Fleisch, E. (2009). Service orientation of organizational structures. *Journal of Relationship Marketing, 8*(2), 103–126.

Gibson, C. B., Porath, C. L., Benson, G. S., & Lawler, E. E. (2007). What results when firms implement practices: The differential relationship between specific practices, firm financial performance, customer service, and quality. *Journal of Applied Psychology, 92*(6), 1467–1480.

Haller, S., Karnouskos, S., & Schroth, C. (2009). The internet of things in an enterprise context. In J. Domingue, D. Fensel, & P. Traverso (Eds.), *Future internet—FIS 2008* (Vol. 5468, pp. 14–28). Lecture notes in computer science. Berlin: Springer.

Herzog, M., Köster, M., Meuris, D., & Sadek, T. (2013). Battleships: An industrial use-case of 'playful' teaching IPS^2 concept generation. In H. Meier (Ed.), *Product-service integration for sustainable solutions—Proceedings of the 5th CIRP International Conference on Industrial Product-Service Systems* (pp. 53–62). Lecture notes in production engineering. Berlin: Springer.

Holmbom, M., Bergquist, B., & Vanhatalo, E. (2014). Performance-based logistics–an illusive panacea or a concept for the future? *Journal of Manufacturing Technology Management, 25* (7), 958–979.

ISO. (2009). *9241-210: 2010. Ergonomics of human system interaction-Part 210: Human-centred design for interactive systems*. Switzerland: International Standardization Organization (ISO).

Kagermann, H., Wahlster, W., & Helbig, J. (Eds.). (2012). *Umsetzungsempfehlungen für das Zukunftsprojekt Industrie 4.0*. Berlin: Forschungsunion im Stifterverband für die Deutsche Wirtschaft.

Kannengiesser, U., & Müller, H. (2013). Towards agent-based smart factories: A subject-oriented modeling approach. In *Web Intelligence (WI) and Intelligent Agent Technologies (IAT), 2013 IEEE/WIC/ACM International Joint Conferences* on (Vol. 3, pp. 83–86). IEEE Computer Society, Washington, DC, USA, 83-86. http://dx.doi.org/10.1109/WI-IAT.2013.155.

Kannengiesser, U., Totter, A., & Bonaldi, D. (2014). An interactional view of context in business processes. In C. Zehbold (Ed.), *S-BPM ONE 2014, CCIS 422* (pp. 42–54). Springer.

Kärcher, B. (2015). Alternative Wege in die Industrie 4.0–Möglichkeiten und Grenzen. In A. Botthof, & E. A. Hartmann (Eds.), *Zukunft der Arbeit in Industrie 4.0* (pp. 47–58). Berlin: Springer.

Konrad, B. A. M. (2006). Engaging employees through high-involvement work practices. *Ivey Business Journal*. Retrieved August 11, 2016, from http://iveybusinessjournal.com/publication/engaging-employees-through-high-involvement-work-practices/.

Lawler, E. E. (1986). *High involvement management*. Jossey Bass business and management series. San Francisco, California: Jossey-Bass Inc.

Lawler, E. E. (2008). *From the ground up: Six principles for building the new logic corporation*. San Francisco, California: Jossey Bass Business and Management Series. Jossey-Bass Inc.

Lay, G. (Ed.). (2014). *Servitization in industry*. Switzerland: Springer International Publishing.

Li, B. H., Zhang, L., Wang, S., Tao, F., Cao, J., Jiang, X., et al. (2010). Cloud manufacturing: A new service-oriented networked manufacturing model. *Computer-Integrated Manufacturing Systems CIMS, 16*(1), 1–7.

Li, B. H., Zhang, L., Ren, L., Chai, X., Tao, F., Luo, Y., et al. (2011). Further discussion on cloud manufacturing. *Computer Integrated Manufacturing Systems CIMS, 17*(3), 449–457.

Liden, R. C., Wayne, S. J., & Sparrowe, R. T. (2000) An examination of the mediating role of psychological empowerment on the relations between the job, interpersonal relationships, and work outcomes. *Journal of Applied Psychology, 85*(3), 407–416.

Lüdtke, A. (2015). Wege aus der Ironie in Richtung ernsthafter Automatisierung. In A. Botthof, & E. A. Hartmann (Eds.), *Zukunft der Arbeit in Industrie 4.0* (pp 125–146). Berlin: Springer.

Macduffie, J. P. (1995). Human resource bundles and manufacturing performance: Organizational logic and flexible production systems in the world auto industry. *Industrial and Labor Relations Review, 48*(2), 197–221.

Meyer, S., Ruppen, A., & Magerkurth, C. (2013). Internet of things-aware process modeling: integrating IoT devices as business process resources. In C. Salinesi, M. C. Norrie, & O. Pastor (Eds.), *CAiSE 2013* (Vol. 7908, pp. 84–98). Springer lecture notes in computer science. Springer.

Muzellec, L., Ronteau, S., & Lambkin, M. (2015). Two-sided Internet platforms: A business model lifecycle perspective. *Industrial Marketing Management, 45*(2), 139–150.

NAICS—North American Industry Classification System. (2012). 31–33 Manufacturing. Retrieved July 18, 2016, from http://www23.statcan.gc.ca/imdb/p3VD.pl?Function=getVD&TVD=118464&CVD=118465&CPV=31-33&CST=01012012&CLV=1&MLV=5.

Neff, A. A., Hamel, F., Uebernickel, F., & Brenner, W. (2013). Information systems in the industrial service business. Analyzing unaddressed requirements in a multiple case study. In *Proceedings CONF-IRM 2013*, paper 35. http://aisel.aisnet.org/confirm2013/35.

Paiola, M., Gebauer, H., & Edvardsson, B. (2012). Service business development in small-to medium-sized equipment manufacturers. *Journal of Business-to-Business Marketing, 19*(1), 33–66.

Picot, A., & Neuburger, R. (2013) *Arbeit in der digitalen Welt. Zusammenfassung der AG1-Projektgruppe anlässlich der IT-Gipfels Prozesses 2013* (13 pp.). München: Münchner Kreis.

Raddats, Ch., & Kowalkowski, Ch. (2014). A reconceptualization of manufacturer's service strategies. *Journal of Business-to-Business Marketing, 21*(1), 19–34.

Raja, J. Z., Johnson, M., & Goffin, K. (2015). Uncovering the competitive priorities for servitization: A repertory grid study. *Academy of Management Proceedings. Academy of Management, 2015*(1), 11988.

Ren, L., Zhang, L., Zhang, Y., Tao, F., & Luo, Y. (2011). Resource virtualization in cloud manufacturing. *Computer-Integrated Manufacturing Systems CIMS, 17*(3), 511–518.

Rigby, D. K. (2014). Digital-physical mashups. *Harvard Business Review, 92*(9), 84–92.

Rigby, D., & Bilodeau, B. (2015). *Management tools & trends 2015*. London: Bain & Company.

Roos, G. (2015). *Servitization as innovation in manufacturing—a review of the literature* (pp. 403–435). The handbook of service innovation. London: Springer.

Rosemann, M., Recker, J. C., & Flender, C. (2008). Contextualisation of business processes. *International Journal of Business Process Integration and Management, 3*(1), 47–60.

Saidani, O., & Nurcan, S. (2007) Towards context aware business process modelling. In *8th Workshop on Business Process Modeling, Development, and Support (BPMDS'07), CAiSE* (Vol. 7, p. 1).

Schüller, A., & Elger, J. (2013). Business processes and technical processes a comprehensive meta model for execution and development. In *INDIN '13* (pp. 30–35). Bochum: IEEE.

Setiawan, M. A., Sadiq, S., & Kirkman, R. (2011). Facilitating business process improvement through personalized recommendation. In *Business information systems* (Vol. 87, pp. 136–147). Lecture notes in business information processing. Berlin: Springer.

Spreitzer, G. (2007) *Toward the integration of two perspectives: A review of social-structural and psychological* (Vol. 1, pp. 54–72). The SAGE handbook of organizational behavior: Volume one: Micro approaches ch. 3. London, UK: Sage Publications.

TechCity, Nesta. (2016). TechNation 2016. Transforming UK Industries, 65 pp. Retrieved July 18, 2016, from http://www.techcityuk.com/wp-content/uploads/2016/02/Tech-Nation-2016_FINAL-ONLINE-1.pdf.

Tsou, H. T., & Hsu, S. H. Y. (2015). Performance effects of technology–organization–environment openness, service co-production, and digital-resource readiness: The case of the IT industry. *International Journal of Information Management, 35*(1), 1–14.

Vogel-Heuser, B. (2014). Herausforderungen und Anforderungen aus Sicht der IT und der Automatisierungstechnik. In T. Bauernhansl, M. ten Hompel, & B. Vogel-Heuser (Eds.), *Industrie 4.0 in Produktion, Automatisierung und Logistik* (pp. 37–48). Wiesbaden: Springer. http://dx.doi.org/10.1007/978-3-658-04682-8_1.

Wieland, M., Kopp, O., Nicklas, D., & Leymann, F. (2007). Towards context-aware workflows. In *CAiSE07 Proceedings of the Workshops and Doctoral Consortium* (Vol. 2, p. 25).

Willett, R. (2007). Technology, pedagogy and digital production: A case study of children learning new media skills. *Learning, Media and Technology, 32*(2), 167–181.

Wu, D., Thames, J. L, Rosen, D. W., & Schaefer, D. (2012). Towards a Cloud-based design and manufacturing paradigm: Looking backward, looking forward. In *Proceedings of the ASME 2012 International Design Engineering Technical Conference & Computers and Information in Engineering Conference* (IDETC/CIE12), Paper number DETC2012-70780.

Wu, D., Greer, M. J., Rosen, D. W., & Schaefer, D. (2013). Cloud manufacturing: Strategic vision and state-of-the-art. *Journal of Manufacturing Systems, 32*(4), 564–579.

Open Access This chapter is distributed under the terms of the Creative Commons Attribution-NonCommercial 4.0 International License (http://creativecommons.org/licenses/by-nc/4.0/), which permits any noncommercial use, duplication, adaptation, distribution and reproduction in any medium or format, as long as you give appropriate credit to the original author(s) and the source, provide a link to the Creative Commons license and indicate if changes were made.

The images or other third party material in this chapter are included in the work's Creative Commons license, unless indicated otherwise in the credit line; if such material is not included in the work's Creative Commons license and the respective action is not permitted by statutory regulation, users will need to obtain permission from the license holder to duplicate, adapt or reproduce the material.

S-BPM's Industrial Capabilities

Matthias Neubauer, Christian Stary, Udo Kannengiesser,
Richard Heininger, Alexandra Totter and David Bonaldi

Abstract

S-BPM targets Business Process Management and has been applied in various business domains to model business processes and implement workflow support. This chapter investigates S-BPM's capabilities to support workplace and process design as well as process execution in production companies. Thereby, industrial capabilities of S-BPM are structured along the three dimensions of socio-technical systems which need to be considered for Industry 4.0 developments. Technological capabilities address the ability to integrate processes on different automation levels (planning, monitoring, real-time execution, etc.). Organizational capabilities discuss the potential of subject orientation for organizational development, and human capability development investigates how humans in production companies could be supported when involving them in workplace (re)design.

M. Neubauer (✉) · C. Stary
Department of Business Information Systems – Communications Engineering, Johannes Kepler University, Linz, Austria
e-mail: matthias.neubauer@jku.at

U. Kannengiesser · R. Heininger
Metsonic GmbH, Pfaffenhofen, Germany

A. Totter · D. Bonaldi
ByElement, Schindellegi, Switzerland

© The Author(s) 2017
M. Neubauer and C. Stary (eds.), *S-BPM in the Production Industry*,
DOI 10.1007/978-3-319-48466-2_3

3.1   S-BPM's Technological Capabilities

Subject-oriented Business Process Management (S-BPM) represents a generic approach to modelling, execution and improvement of business processes, with a particular focus on the involvement and empowerment of the people in the process. S-BPM has been applied in many business domains for a variety of process applications, such as "service order and delivery in the banking area", "management of the development and maintenance of complex processes" or "incident management" (Konjack 2010; Nakamura et al. 2011; Walke et al. 2013). These application cases have focused on providing workflow support for SMEs and large companies.

However, business processes are just one part of the process landscape in production companies; and while business processes are certainly important for these companies, they are not considered to be "core" processes. It is the physical processing and movement of materials on the shop floor, with associated manual or automated activities, representing the predominant concern of production managers and production workers alike. Therefore, the application of S-BPM in the production domain requires expanding the scope of process management. Thereby, not only business, planning and logistics but also shop-floor activities need to be captured.

Processes in production enterprises have traditionally been represented at different levels of abstraction and granularity. A well-known framework defining these levels is the IEC 62264 control hierarchy depicted in Fig. 3.1. It comprises four levels: Field Instrumentation Control (Level 1), Process Control (Level 2), Manufacturing Operations Management (Level 3) and Business Planning and Logistics (Level 4).

As these levels impose distinct requirements on processes with respect to real-time processing, data storage, safety and security, the development of models and systems at each level has been undertaken rather independently. This has resulted in poorly integrated applications especially between Low-Level Control (LLC, i.e. Levels 1 and 2) operating in real-time and High-Level Control (HLC, i.e. Levels 3 and 4) operating in non-real time. Systems developed for LLC include Programmable Logic Controllers (PLCs), and systems for HLC include ERP, MES and BPM systems. The vertical integration of processes across the different levels and systems has been considered essential, since none of the processes of an enterprise operates in isolation. It is rather triggered by others and, vice versa, other processes rely on the output of another process. For planning, executing and monitoring this network of processes effectively and efficiently, all processes need to be seamlessly integrated.

A major objective of the EU-funded project "Subject-Orientation for People-Centred Production" (SO-PC-Pro) has been seamless process integration via S-BPM. The SO-PC-Pro approach for vertical integration is depicted in Fig. 3.2. It is based on using subject-oriented process models as a uniform representation of processes at all levels of the IEC 62264 control hierarchy, including HLC and LLC processes. The theoretical feasibility of this approach has already been demonstrated by Müller (2012). Data between processes at the different levels may be

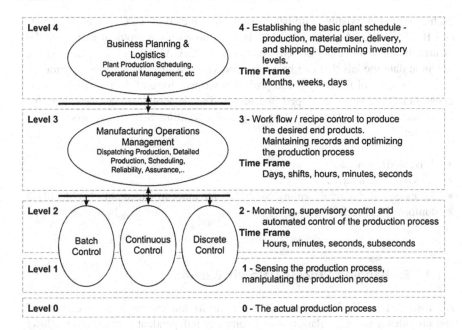

Fig. 3.1 The IEC 62264 control hierarchy (adapted from IEC 62264-3 © 2007 IEC—All rights reserved)

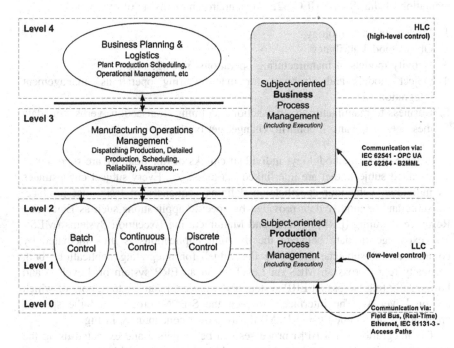

Fig. 3.2 Vertical integration of processes based on S-BPM and existing data standards including OPC UA (extended based on IEC 62264-3)

exchanged using existing automation standards, including OPC UA (IEC 62541) and B2MML (IEC 62264). OPC UA is a communication protocol that is implemented in most modern PLC environments. OPC UA includes specifications of semantic data models that can be exchanged via web services or binary protocols.

In the course of the SO-PC-Pro project, interfaces for an S-BPM-based process integration have been developed and tested. The developments are based on the Metasonic Suite software for modelling and executing S-BPM processes. They comprise:

- A B2MML interface
- An OPC UA interface
- An extension for transforming S-BPM behaviours to executable IEC 61131-3 conform PLC code

3.1.1 Exchanging Process Data via B2MML

B2MML (MESA 2013) stands for "Business-to-Manufacturing Markup Language" and provides a vendor-, platform- and company-independent format which allows handling the data of a process to be exchanged between Level-3 and Level-4 applications (Scholten 2007; Gifford 2011). B2MML represents an XML implementation of the ISA-95 (IEC 62264) standard and consists of five parts:

1. Models and terminology
2. Object model attributes
3. Activity models of manufacturing operations' management
4. Object models and attributes for manufacturing operations' management integration
5. Business-to-manufacturing transactions defining transaction verbs for data messages, e.g. cancel, confirm, change, get or show

In the S-BPM methodology, individual chunks of functionality are represented as so-called subjects that are interlinked via messages. Every subject encapsulates its individual behaviour specification defining sequences of tasks that produce, consume and/or modify data provided by specific applications such as Enterprise Resource Planning (ERP) systems and Manufacturing Execution Systems (MES). The exchange of data between the different applications is thus mediated by communicating subjects, providing the "glue" for integrating applications both vertically (e.g. across an MES on Level 3 and an ERP system on Level 4) and horizontally (e.g. across an ERP system and a project planning tool, both of which are on Level 4). The interfaces between the S-BPM process and the specific applications are defined using B2MML, as shown conceptually in Fig. 3.3.

The integration via S-BPM processes can be modelled and executed using the Metasonic Suite. This tool provides a number of ways to establish and configure

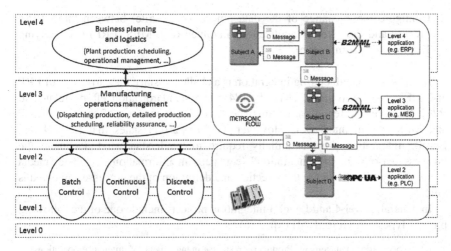

Fig. 3.3 S-BPM as the glue for integrating processes across Levels 2 and 3 (OPC UA interface) and Levels 3 and 4 (B2MML interface) in the IEC 62264 control hierarchy

mappings between the data objects stored in the Metasonic Suite and the data structures provided by external applications. However, as currently there is no support for common data standards, the definition and maintenance of these mappings is usually a tedious effort. This hampers the agility needed in modern factories, as the mappings need to be reconfigured every time a new application is integrated or a change occurs in its data requirements. Using the B2MML standard as a basis for defining the mappings of the Metasonic Suite and B2MML-compliant applications helps overcoming this challenge.

On a technical level, a B2MML interface has been implemented in Metasonic's S-BPM process modelling suite by means of two extensions:

Ext 1. An import wizard for selecting the B2MML schemas needed in a particular process model and transforming them into data objects

Ext 2. A graphical user interface (called "refinement template") for configuring the exchange of data objects with B2MML-compliant external applications

These features support a best practice related to the B2MML application for Level-3 and Level-4 data integration. This best practice means to first "identify[…] the context and content of the information that needs to be exchanged" (Pipero and Manjunath 2006). These aspects are commonly provided by process models, in terms of task structures, communication between process participants and the data objects handled in the process. Thus, connecting B2MML with an S-BPM process (and workflow engine) requires the following two steps:

1. Generate S-BPM data objects (called "business objects") according to the B2MML schemas relevant in the respective process (by applying Extension 1 given above)

2. Configure the exchange of the data objects (read/write) between the S-BPM
   process and the external applications involved (e.g. MES, ERP) (by applying
   Extension 2 given above)

Business-to-manufacturing integration is a challenge since the early days of ERP
and MES systems (Gifford 2011, p. 184). The standardization efforts related to
B2MML target the reduction of time spent, costs and increase of successful ERP
and MES system integration. However, Gifford (2011) states that Level-4 and
Level-3 integration projects initially require to "understand and document the
business reasons for the integration" (e.g. gaps in information exchange, media
discontinuity). Furthermore, the selection and definition of the processes involved is
vital.

In general, Level-4 and Level-3 integration projects include one of the following
process types (cf. Gifford 2011, p. 186):

> Production order management; Production response management; Maintenance operations
> management; Laboratory operations management; Warehouse, tank farm, and other
> inventory operations management; Operations capacity management; Receiving manage-
> ment; Shipping management; Manufacturing master data management (MDM); Key per-
> formance indicators (KPI) and overall equipment effectiveness (OEE) calculation,
> monitoring and management.

The implementation of such integration projects typically requires a middleware
that enables the interaction, for example through schema conversion, data conversion or intelligent routing (cf. Scholten 2007, p. 190). The developed B2MML
prototype for S-BPM enables case-based modelling and execution of the behaviour
of such an S-BPM based middleware. The middleware behaviour can be shown
using the S-BPM interaction diagram in Fig. 3.4.

Depending on the individual application case the integration solution may differ
in terms of relevant B2MML data structures to be exchanged, and internal subject
behaviours of the ERP/MES subjects. Sample cases for enabling the interoperability
of different existing ERP systems and MES are (cf. Vieille 2012):

- Case 1: ERP and MES are not IEC 62264 compliant
- Case 2: ERP is IEC 62264 compliant
- Case 3: MES is IEC 62264 compliant

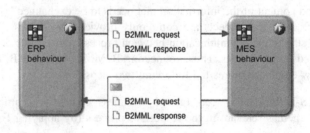

Fig. 3.4 Generic S-BPM model for ERP and MES behaviour integration via B2MML

- Case 4: ERP and MES speak B2MML
- Case 5: B2MML mapping

For each of the cases relevant processes and data need to be defined at first. Based on the selection further integration steps can be taken. In *Case 1* neither the ERP system nor the MES apply B2MML. However, B2MML may act in this case as intermediary language between given ERP and MES elements. In such a situation, the modelling approach could be structured as follows:

1. Select relevant B2MML elements for actual integration case and create a corresponding intermediary business object (BO) in the Metasonic Suite.
2. Model the ERP behaviour in Metasonic Build and fill the defined B2MML object with the corresponding information from the ERP system (ERP -> B2MML mapping), e.g. fill the B2MML BO via Metasonic's existing "DBReader" refinement template with data from the ERP database, fill via data requested from a web service
3. Model the MES behaviour in Metasonic Build and apply the B2MML business object when exchanging data with the MES, e.g. via a MES web service, MES specific messages. Since the MES is not B2MML enabled in this case, additionally, a transformation is required from B2MML to a MES interpretable format

In *Case 2 and 3*, either the ERP or the MES is able to receive/send B2MML messages. For the system not being B2MML compliant, a transformation needs to be implemented within the S-BPM middleware (compare Step 2 and 3 of Case1).

Case 4 describes a situation in which both systems are B2MML compliant and could exchange B2MML data directly. In such a case S-BPM might act as an intelligent router. However, due to possible, custom B2MML extensions or supported transaction, errors might occur in the communication. Therefore, *Case 5* is a more convenient solution, which considers individual XML extensions and maps the custom XML extensions to B2MML messages. Here the mapping functionality needs to be implemented by the subject (ERP or MES) providing the extensions. In general, the mapping may be defined in S-BPM within refinements of function states by writing Java code to be executed at runtime.

In addition to Level-4 and Level-3 integration support, S-BPM can be applied to support the integration of processes across the Levels 3 (Manufacturing Operations Management) and 2 (Process Control) via the OPC Unified Architecture (UA).

3.1.2 Process Communication via OPC UA

OPC UA represents a standardized communication protocol (cf. IEC 62541) enabling the vendor- and platform-independent communication within and between Level-1 and Level-2 processes executed by Programmable Logic Controllers (PLCs). To enable runtime communication among Level-3 and Level-2 processes, the data exchanged need to be defined according to the OPC UA standard. As this needs to be done at design time (i.e. before the actual execution of the processes), the process modelling editor Metasonic Build has been used as a basis for a OPC UA data definition prototype. Specifically, a graphical user interface as part of this editor has been developed to guide the S-BPM process modeller through the steps required when specifying OPC UA interfaces.

The basic features of the interface have been derived from the structure of the OPC UA standard (IEC 2008). OPC UA applies the client–server concept to implement the interaction between different communication partners, e.g. a work-flow engine and a shop-floor PLC. To allow requesting services provided by an OPC UA server or within a network of OPC UA servers, OPC UA defines an Address Space model. In such an Address Space an OPC UA server defines which contents (i.e. nodes representing objects, variables, methods etc. related to dedi-cated objects) are visible/editable for clients. Servers also allow clients to monitor attributes and events on the server. Each client can subscribe to the attributes and events it is interested in and will then be notified accordingly.

Figure 3.5 shows the basic functions of the OPC UA refinement template using a schematic representation for the interplay between the behaviour of the "PLC" subject in the Metasonic Suite and a PLC addressable via an OPC UA server. The refinement template allows (1) configuring the endpoint of the server, (2) config-uring the relevant node (e.g. variable, method and event), (3) reading/writing variables from/to business objects, (4) invoking methods on the server and (5) subscribing to data changes or events provided by the server.

The concrete OPC UA refinement template shown in Fig. 3.6 allows (i) reading values from a PLC and storing them in a business object, and (ii) writing concrete values of a business object to variables of a PLC. The template thus facilitates configuring the concrete OPC UA server endpoint that provides the desired

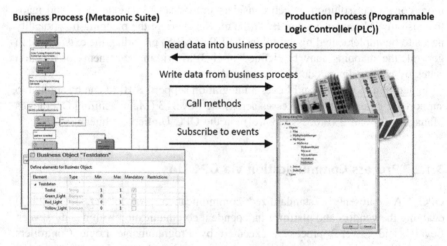

Fig. 3.5 Basic functions of the OPC UA refinement template

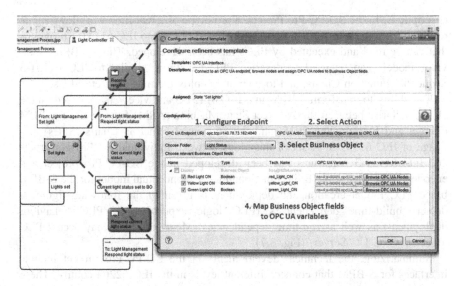

Fig. 3.6 Refinement template for reading/writing values from/to an OPC UA server variable

variables. Furthermore, one needs to choose the action and the relevant business object before mapping variables to each other. The refinement template shown in Fig. 3.6 allows mapping multiple PLC variables to different fields of business objects. It is associated with the function state "Set lights" within the SBD of the "Light Controller" subject in a lighting control process.

3.1.3 Executing S-BPM Models in Real Time via IEC 61131-3

The B2MML and OPC UA interfaces allow using S-BPM as the glue for integrating processes at any location of the vertical control hierarchy. This is depicted conceptually in Fig. 3.3. Current implementations of this approach are based on using Metasonic Flow as the workflow engine that controls the execution of all subjects in the process. This has an important limitation: The execution times of subjects located at Levels 1 and 2 are too slow to meet the "hard" real time constraints of many control tasks, because Metasonic Flow was designed for office-based processes where time is usually measured in days, hours and minutes—not in milliseconds or microseconds, as typically being the case in automated factory processes. To fully apply the S-BPM approach to production processes, a different workflow engine is needed that is capable to execute real-time behaviours of S-BPM processes.

Today only Programmable Logic Controllers (PLCs) can execute real-time control tasks on the shopfloor. However, PLCs are not commonly thought of as "workflow" engines because they deploy specialized programs (often based on automation standards defined in IEC 61131-3) rather than general workflow descriptions. In the SO-PC-Pro Project, a prototype of a real-time workflow engine resulting from the transformation of S-BPM workflows into IEC 61131-3 programs that can be read and executed by PLCs has been developed. Thus, S-BPM behaviour models can be used to describe PLC behaviour similar to IEC 61131-3 Sequential Function Charts, and to map and deploy them to concrete PLCs.

The ability to transform S-BPM into IEC 61131-3 and vice versa is based on the close similarity between the Abstract State Machine (ASM) formalism of S-BPM (Börger and Fleischmann 2015) and the Sequential Function Charts (SFCs) language of IEC 61131-3. A set of mappings between individual S-BPM constructs and IEC 61131-3 constructs has been developed in the SO-PC-Pro project and encoded in the Metasonic Build functionalities. A conceptual model for the S-BPM based PLC model creation and deployment is given in the following figure. It depicts build-time dependencies (PLC logic export/import; PLC behaviour deployment) as well as run-time dependencies (Metasonic flow may access PLC logic via OPC UC Server) (Fig. 3.7).

Summarizing, the technical developments in the SO-PC-Pro project include interfaces for S-BPM that connect different levels in the IEC 62264 control. These interfaces comprise:

- OPC UA interface for integrating processes across Levels 2 and 3
- B2MML interface for integrating processes across Levels 3 and 4
- Mapping S-BPM onto IEC 61131-3 to reuse S-BPM behaviours and deploy them on PLCs for real-time execution

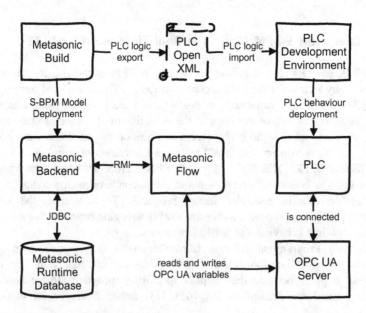

Fig. 3.7 Conceptual mapping architecture

The application of the above given technical developments will be illustrated within the case studies presented in the subsequent chapters. Especially, within the lot-size 1 case the focus has been seamless integration. Thus, this case will describe the application of the interfaces.

3.1.4 S-BPM as Communication Model for Process Integration

Aside to structuring the developments along the ISA 95 automation pyramid, an alternative point of view may be taken as described below. The shape of the IEC 62264 model reflects two distinguishing characteristics. First, this automation architecture is strictly hierarchical. Systems at the same hierarchical level share similar functions and need to satisfy similar constraints regarding real-time processing, data storage, safety and security. Second, the automation pyramid reflects the amount of data being processed at the different levels. Towards the bottom end (or wider end) of the pyramid large amounts of raw (sensor) data are produced and handled, while towards the top end (or narrower end) of the pyramid the data become more condensed and less frequently exchanged (Vogel-Heuser et al. 2009).

The strictly hierarchical structure with clearly defined concerns at each level had a strong impact on the vertical connectivity of many automation systems, in that, individual components within one level were developed to exchange data only with components of adjacent levels. A number of standard protocols were defined to establish the necessary communication layers for these exchanges.

Over the past 25–30 years, a number of changes in technology and production organization have occurred that break with the foundational assumptions of the traditional automation pyramid (Vogel-Heuser et al. 2009). At the bottom end of the pyramid, field devices became computationally more powerful and intelligent, with a new range of communication capabilities that allow for modular organization and decentralized control of production processes (Vogel-Heuser et al. 2009; Mendes et al. 2012). Such smart devices are today called cyber-physical systems (Kagermann et al. 2013) and compose what is often called the industrial Internet of Things (IoT) (Haller et al. 2009). Communication between devices is no longer restricted to adjacent levels but can occur anywhere across the hierarchy. A similar trend can be observed towards the top end of the automation pyramid, where there is increasing interest in decentralized approaches to business process management such as agent-based and service-oriented architectures (Sinur et al. 2013; Cummins 2009).

To account for these changes in the production industry, more recently a new model for automation was proposed (Vogel-Heuser et al. 2009): the "diabolo" model, as shown in Fig. 3.8. Diabolo is an acronym for "Distributed Information Architecture to Bolster Lifecycle Optimization". It also reflects the double-cone shape of the model.

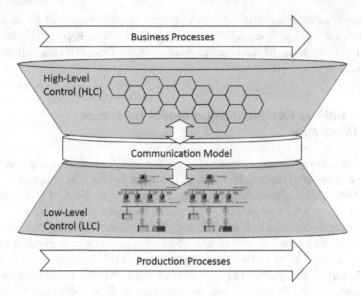

Fig. 3.8 The diabolo model of modern automation systems (adapted from Vogel-Heuser et al. 2009)

In the diabolo model, the four hierarchical levels are collapsed into just two:

- *High-level control* (HLC, upper cone in Fig. 3.8) is composed of Levels 3 and 4 in the traditional automation pyramid. The hexagons in the figure represent the interconnected process functionalities typically found in production management, including common Level-3 functions such as work order management, quality management and maintenance management (McClellan 1997; Vogel-Heuser et al. 2009), and Level-4 functions such as planning, logistics and business process management.
- *Low-level control* (LLC, lower cone in Fig. 3.8) is composed of Levels 1 and 2 in the traditional automation pyramid. As indicated in the figure, the various field devices and PLCs remain hierarchically structured to meet real-time and other requirements specific to process control in physical production environments.

The two levels are vertically integrated by a communication model that provides a central interface for all cross-level exchanges of information. These exchanges may involve any field device within the LLC level, including sensors and actuators. Having a central interface is convenient, as it avoids having to maintain potentially large numbers of point-to-point interfaces.

The increasing modularization and distribution of processes at both HLC and LLC levels can be conceptualized using the idea of partial diabolos (Vogel-Heuser et al. 2009). Every diabolo represents a "module" (that may be composed of other modules) that is functionally and/or structurally (i.e. by implementation as a

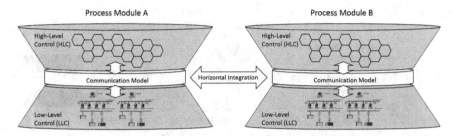

Fig. 3.9 Horizontal integration of multiple diabolos via the communication model

separate component) distinct from other modules. As shown in Fig. 3.9, partial diabolos are interconnected via the horizontal integration of their communication models. This is the foundation of the notion of "plug-and-produce": the model-based reconfiguration of automation software to adapt to changes in products and production processes (Niggemann et al. 2015).

Subject-oriented business process management fulfils essential criteria for such a communication model stated in recent literature (Vogel-Heuser and Feiz-Marzoughi 2013; Keddis et al. 2014):

- S-BPM includes modelling data structures in terms of so-called business objects (Fleischmann et al. 2012)
- S-BPM allows mapping data objects between different external systems by means of refinements (Fleischmann et al. 2012; Kannengiesser et al. 2016)
- S-BPM describes process logic together with the data mappings (Fleischmann et al. 2012; Kannengiesser et al. 2016)
- S-BPM has a well-defined formalism that allows instant execution by a run-time environment (Fleischmann et al. 2012; Börger and Fleischmann 2015)
- S-BPM provides generic constructs that enable modelling business processes as well as physical production processes (Müller 2012)
- S-BPM supports the creation of individual views for different systems and users (Fleischmann et al. 2012)
- S-BPM uses a data-centric coordination concept that allows for loosely coupled, flexible system architectures (Meyer et al. 2011; Kannengiesser 2015)
- S-BPM has a minimal set of modelling constructs, facilitating understanding by stakeholders with different educational backgrounds (Fleischmann et al. 2013)

The overall concept of using S-BPM as the basis of a communication model in the automation diabolo is shown in Fig. 3.10. Every system is represented as a subject that encapsulates its behaviour and data structures. Subjects coordinate the execution of their behaviours through message passing, establishing a decentralized process architecture. Subjects may encapsulate not only individual systems but also systems of systems. For instance, "Subject F" in Fig. 3.10 represents a whole process module ("Process Module C"). As indicated in the figure, that module may use a non-S-BPM based communication model, such as one based on UML

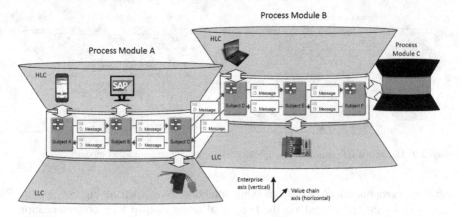

Fig. 3.10 S-BPM as a basis for horizontal and vertical communication in the automation diabolo

(Vogel-Heuser and Feiz-Marzoughi 2013). The S-BPM based approach allows this module to be integrated as a "black box", using the encapsulation concept enabled by subjects.

S-BPM facilitates changes in the communication model at design time and at runtime. This capability is enabled by the notational simplicity and modular composition of S-BPM models: Individual behaviours and data structures in a subject can be changed as long as the messages exchanged with the neighbouring subjects (and the business objects associated to these messages) remain the same. Messages can be viewed as interfaces between two subjects. There needs to be a realignment of the two subjects about the particular message, only if a change in a subject affects its message structure with another subject. Such a realignment may require further changes and realignments with other subjects. Yet, it can usually be expected that changes do not propagate to all the subjects of a model.

3.2 S-BPM's Organizational Development Capabilities

Thinking in subject-oriented terms and modelling business processes in a subject-oriented notation aim to support overcoming the disruptive pressure organizations are currently facing (cf. Lorenz et al. 2015). In particular, it enables tackling how organizations should be dealing with changes at the same time when operating it. Transforming while performing requires a digital infrastructure, both in terms of human resources and technology, as the table from work practice reveals (Table 3.1).

Neither digitizing nor servitizing an organization through process integration can be handled simply by providing respective technologies. While technology is an indispensable enabler, such change processes require a human-centred approach, driven by management, one that takes the people who have to implement changes

Table 3.1 Shifts through digitization

	Traditional	Digital
Strategy	Efficiency	Innovation
Culture	Hierarchy	Collaboration
Talent	Low cost	High skill
Technology	Legacy	Cloud, mobile, apps
User experience	"Who cares?"	Mission critical
IT Philosophy	Waterfall	Iterative (agile)
Business model	Service and support	Relationship and partner

Source Michael Krigsman www.cxotalk.com. Available at: http://techcrunch.com/2016/01/31/digital-transformation-requires-total-organizational-commitment/

into account. So-called dynamic capabilities should enable building and reconfiguring internal and external resources including competencies (Eisenhardt and Martin 2000). The goal is resilient behaviour based on organizational agility (cf. Worley and Lawler 2010; Kirchmer 2011).

In change management projects IT-affinity tend to dominate (cf. Sambamurthy et al. 2003; Overby et al. 2006; Ngai et al. 2011; Kim and Suh 2012) although stakeholders[1] and their communities play a crucial role for succeeding in those projects. Korpelainen and Kira (2013) revealed "that most of the problems were identified in the social context and only one fifth of the problems were related to the employees' experiences of a lack of skills and competencies in using the IT-systems". Apparently, it still holds what Hammer (1996, 1999) found out already in the context of Business Process Re-Engineering when revisiting the original, model-centric concept of Hammer and Champy (1993).

Moving from adopting IT systems to organizational design involving human-centred work models and semantic process analysis (cf. Prilla et al. 2012) can be facilitated by business process modelling notations. Such a stakeholder-centred procedure needs to include the opportunity to transfer human experience and ideas into a process model for effective work support (Aschoff et al. 2003). Capturing work knowledge requires a context-sensitive BPM approach (cf. Ates and Bititci 2011; Silva and Rosemann 2012).

Following the human-centred approach for organizational development has a cognitive, a content-oriented and social perspective. From the cognitive perspective, a semantically valid representation of work knowledge is required when stakeholders create models and when eliciting/documenting work processes. From the content perspective, models represent the baseline of organizational development. From the social perspective, an intelligible and executable version of models is required. They allow sharing, reflecting and experiencing processes through different roles and stakeholders (Fig. 3.11).

---

[1]Stakeholder denote humans directly or indirectly (e.g., being responsible) involved in business operations.

Fig. 3.11 Organizational
development leveraging
stakeholder knowledge

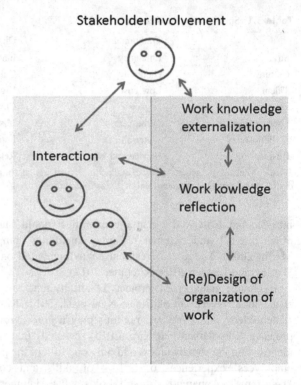

3.2.1 Creating Semantically Valid Representations

In this section, the acquisition of work knowledge from a stakeholder perspective, and its mapping to diagrammatic models is discussed. Existing concepts, stemming from Business Process Management (BPM) and Knowledge Management (KM) are reviewed. A conclusive summary wraps up the findings.

3.2.1.1 Work Analysis

Modelling principles and conventions (cf. GoM—Becker et al. 2008) traditionally set the stage for representing work knowledge in terms of process models. As in practice, modelling standards often comprise 100 and more pages, they may not be understood or accepted by stakeholders—a modelling notation should rather serve as a means for communication and sharing work knowledge than requiring technical mastery. The organizational aspect of work should be considered primarily from work profiles of stakeholders in the operational business, and the roles that need to be supported by information technology.

Often, stakeholders ask "What do I need an analysis for?" as they know their organization like their own pocket. However, process analysis moves beyond accumulating existing facts. Hence, it needs to involve all who could contribute to a work process. Analysis is an overarching process, which needs to involve a large part of the organization, as it denotes a purposeful representation of relevant process information in preparation for transforming an organization (cf. Weske 2012).

Analysis may start with particular elements, e.g. with actors in S-BPM (Fleischmann et al. 2012) or functions as in ARIS (Scheer 1999). The context is framed by elements stemming from system analysis, knowledge management and organizational learning. Representations refer to a certain system, as they allow describing phenomena of various complexity (cf. Von Bertalanffy 1968). A major characteristic of a system is the set of mutual relationships as constitutive element. System thinking has been elaborated with respect to causal relationships and associative ones (cf. Senge 1990), as analysis targets identifying and describing besides the elements of a system their major effective relationships. The acquisition of work-relevant knowledge might include leveraging tacit or implicit knowledge (Nonaka and Von Krogh 2009). Explicit knowledge is already documented information whereas tacit knowledge is not available in documented form. It resides with people and can be elicited to explain the rationale of behaviours or processes.

In the course of analyses, performance-relevant processes among work force are put into mutual context. Traditionally, when the dynamic view of an organization is the focus, tasks rather than roles move to the centre of interest (cf. Scheer 1999). The essential question is how organizational units need to be mutually related to accomplish work objectives in a correct temporal order when executing tasks. Such arrangements should then be mapped to workflow specifications which are at least partially automated.

According to Fischermann (2006) purely task-centred approaches are likely to lead to some deficiencies with respect to stakeholder orientation: Positions located in managerial parts of the hierarchy are traditionally handling tasks with less cooperation, such as deciding on requests from the operational staff. However, running processes even in expert organizations, such as hospitals, requires effective and efficient collaboration. In addition, thinking in terms of processes is generally more difficult than thinking in familiar structures of a static organization of work.

A work process analysis is therefore a special form of organizational analysis. This means, conversely, that it should take into account the organizational structure in an appropriate way. The processes have to be aligned to the organization and to be embedded in existing hierarchical structures, leading to a process-oriented organizational hierarchy (Fischermann 2006).

S-BPM provides a twofold approach when analysing work procedures. One could either start taking a role-perspective and relevant communication acts among roles, or alternatively start to describe a certain encapsulated task behaviour and the communication interfaces to other behaviours (performed by certain roles).

3.2.1.2 Top-Down Versus Bottom-Up Modelling

In traditional process analysis basically two approaches can be followed, top-down and bottom-up: The top-down approach puts the corporate strategy and vision of an organization to the centre. Processes at the top level, such as customer service routines, are progressively detailed and structured. Process analysis is correspondingly understood as a stepwise refinement of the processes of a high-level representation, such as value chains, to a more detailed description level, such as sequences of operational activities (Gaitanides 1983).

Both approaches to detailing a process, decomposition and refinement, leave open, at what level of detail processes need to be specified before starting refinements, and how to design the interface between different levels of detail. Different stakeholders will approach this issue in a different way (Fischermann 2006), thus, developing systematic guidelines is difficult. The analyst and the stakeholders involved in the collection and evaluation of data may interpret differently for each case, at what level of abstraction a process needs to be positioned.

In the bottom-up approach, however, processes are constructed from actions performed at a workplace upwards. As individual actions are linked to processes and procedures they propagate to various levels of abstraction. A survey could start identifying elementary actions involved in task accomplishment, and be followed by composing those actions to a process specification. The advantage of a bottom-up approach when involving operative stakeholders concerns the initial selection of an abstraction level, as it corresponds to their perception. Analysis will consequently lead to collecting and describing only those processes that match the perceived reality.

S-BPM promotes a bottom-up approach for eliciting and representing work knowledge. Bottom-up modelling in S-BPM may start with the definition of individual behaviours and their interfaces to inter-dependent behaviours. A next step could be the definition of exchanged data or the aggregation of subject behaviours to roles in organizations. The resulting models may be validated by domain experts in a role-play fashion supported via IT tools. The validation allows checking whether a created model meets the intended objectives or needs to be reworked.

3.2.1.3 Emergent Semantics

Most of the modelling approaches for work knowledge analysis provide a notation, which might be more or less oriented towards execution, such as CommonKADS (Schreiber et al. 2002) focusing on representation and analysis, and FRODO (Aschoff et al. 2003) interleaving modelling and execution of knowledge-intense processes. Emergent semantic approaches allow dynamic development of semantic process representations. For instance, Cohn and Hull (2009) use (business) artefacts combining data and the manipulation process as basic building blocks of modelling. Artefacts are key business entities (business-relevant objects) evolving when passing through a business's operation. They can be created, modified and stored. As a result business, operations can be decomposed along various levels of abstraction. Artefacts are typed using both an information model for data about the business objects during their lifetime, and a lifecycle model, describing the possible ways and timings that tasks can be invoked on these objects.

According to the approach, such an artefact could be a knowledge claim. Its information model could include attributes, such as claimID, originator, elaboration time, duration of validity, and operating information. The lifecycle model could include the multiple ways that the knowledge claim could be handled. Artefacts define a useful way to understand and track operations, such as the stations that a claim has passed through, typically being of relevance for involved stakeholders. The information model's attributes are filled with information elements over the life cycle time of the artefact. In Cohn et al.'s approach (2009), artefact instances can be generated in state-based way, as instances interact through message passing as they transition between states. The artefact-based business operation model is thus being termed actionable. Specifications can be used to automatically generate an executable system based on various, accumulated kinds of data corresponding to the stages in a business entity's lifecycle. Clustering data based on a dynamic entity that moves through a business's operations is in contrast to decomposing business entities, as it avoids isolated data manipulations.

Moreover, it facilitates the use of representations, as the authors state "it enables strong communication between a business's stakeholders in ways that traditional approaches do not. Experience has shown that once the key artefacts are identified, even at a preliminary level, they become the basis of a stakeholder vocabulary. Artefacts enable communication along three dimensions" (Cohn and Hull 2009):

- Lifecycle dimension, as "stakeholders who focus on one part of a lifecycle are better equipped to communicate with stakeholders focused on another part. All are talking about the same overall artefact and can confidently discuss attributes that are shared or produced in one part of the lifecycle and consumed in another" (ibid.)
- Variations' dimension, as "stakeholders from multiple geographies could understand similarities and differences between their respective operations by comparing them to the commonly held artefact model" (ibid.)
- Management dimension: "Communication between stakeholders at different management levels is enhanced because the artefact approach naturally lends itself to a hierarchical perspective" (ibid)

Hence, we can conclude that evolving element and relation categories are of benefit for developing a stakeholder-oriented modelling and analysis approach (cf. also Salovaara and Tamminen 2009). The presented approach of Cohn and Hull (2009) may be mapped to S-BPM as follows: Data and their manipulation process map in S-BPM onto business objects and within certain subject behaviours. In S-BPM, there is not an overall defined data manipulation process, instead data may be changed by different subjects depending on the defined "create-read-update-delete" operations for the dedicated subject (operation). Finally, an S-BPM model defines the exchange sequence of data embodied in certain message exchanges.

3.2.1.4   Semantic Business Process Management

Semantic Business Process Management (S-BPM) relies on ontological concepts in order to capture process-relevant items, however, targeting at automated processing and reasoning (Ciuciu et al. 2011; de Castro et al. 2010; Hoang et al. 2010). While striving for consistency by relying on a common terminology, "the main challenge here lays in the availability and existence of the common domain description that would be accepted by the process participants. Not only obtaining process participants' acceptances to use the proposed ontology that constitutes a problem, but also development of domain ontologies that would be a specialization of already delivered solutions is a challenging and time consuming task" (Filipowska et al. 2011).

It a first phase in S-BPM a business analyst models a business process. As a result of this phase, semantically annotated business process models exist. They should not only capture explicitly the functionality of tasks and decisions in the process flow, but also actors, roles, resources that are involved in the process. This process content is revisited in terms of not only modelling, but also with support of ontologies in terms of additional functionalities taking advantage of the ontological process descriptions (e.g. ontology-based searching for process fragments matching business criteria, process fragments reuse or compliance checking). This design reflects a set of activities supporting stakeholder needs in analysis, which have to be captured methodologically (cf. Mendling et al. 2010).

3.2.1.5 Conclusive Summary

What kind of support could stakeholders need when getting involved actively in organizational development based on work processes? The current findings indicate that

- Eliciting knowledge requires an open format for articulation and collaborative reflection (semantic openness). Hence, predefined notations could direct articulating work knowledge and inputs for change in a certain direction, e.g. functional representations, role-based representation
- Knowledge codification needs to be accompanied by sharing knowledge. It needs to be accessed and reflected by others—representations, such as concepts or business process models serve as baseline for discussion and discourse
- Middle-out as well as top-down analysis should be performed on models, depending on the type of granularity and encapsulation
- Intertwining the functional perspective on accomplishing tasks with interaction processes helps not only for reflecting a situation "as-it-is" to come up with ideas "as-it-could-be", but also for setting the context of work procedures in terms of relevant factors for task accomplishment

3.2.2 Process-Based Organizational Development

Both developers and stakeholders need to be qualified for effectively participating in work (re)design, in particular when innovative concepts need to be handled (cf. Lorenz et al. 2015 for industry 4.0). As indicated also above, openness for content generation and sharing seems to be crucial for stakeholder-driven organizational development: "Incremental innovations and organizational learning processes are of growing importance for the competitiveness of firms" (Strambach 2001, p. 56). For flexible operation, stakeholders have to work on their work processes (Herrmann 2000; Herrmann et al. 2004), rather than being qualified to adapt (cf. Pütz and Lüger 2003).

The more stakeholders are informed about their organization of work, the more they become connected personally to their performance, and finally, willing to change (cf. McGregor 2006). It has been observed that people react to situations based on context rather than fixed behaviour patterns, such as process specifications they need to follow (cf. Meyrowitz 1985). Hence, even roles as functional or social entities evolve over time (Castells 2010). Stakeholders may change roles dynamically, driven by their personal identities triggering their behaviour (cf. Montague 2012). Such observations manifest individuals as self-regulated subjects. As such, they decide according to the construction of their reality on goals and the arrangement of activities. Based on their conscious reflection, they learn to select from a variety of options to act, and finally, to solve problems (cf. Edelmann 2000).

Consequently, any approach to organizational development should allow active design when organizing work and be on some characteristic particularities, according to Ulich (1991) (cf. Arnold 1996; Sennett 2008): (i) holistic, (ii) challenging, (ii) possibility of social interaction, (iii) featuring autonomy, (iv) facilities to learn and develop. Organizational development driven by actively engaged actors mainly concerns work and business processes (cf. Fischer 1989). Once stakeholders reflect work practices, self-transforming of organizations is enabled (Geißler 1995; Seidl 2005). Thereby, the direct access of actors to organizational development knowledge, including the business processes stakeholders are actually involved in, seems to be essential (cf. Schwaninger 2000).

From management theory, timely organization of work has already been recognized as learning endeavour, depending on highly engaged stakeholders (cf. Rieckmann 1997). However, few implementations of organizational development concepts exist focusing on the highly dynamic nature of business structures and learning facilities that need to be provided for engaging stakeholders in the above mentioned sense. Although a variety of frameworks exist for systemic organizational change (cf. Senge 1990; Kim 1993; Haeckel 1999) they mostly lack operational support (cf. Zhu 2009).

According to Chen et al. (2003) systems supporting organizational change should comprise the following: (i) an integrated Organizational Memory, (ii) individual learning support on the operational and conceptual level, (iii) lower and higher level organizational learning, (iv) an organization-wide Knowledge Management System (KMS). In case of BPM-driven organizations business process models are part of the organizational knowledge that needs to be kept as organizational asset. In addition, information about process analysis, validation, implementation (workflow management) and optimization needs to be kept.

Operational learning by individual stakeholders should be supported enabling direct access to the Organizational Memory, while individual conceptual learning requires integrated ICT-support for communication, content management and dissemination. Lower level organizational learning refers to adjustments of processes to their environment, e.g. through establishing additional lines of dissemination, whereas higher level organizational learning affects mental models, and as such underlying assumptions and beliefs influencing thinking and behaviour in work processes. These assumptions rely on fundamentals, such as knowledge about BPM and its practical implementation through Workflow Management Systems.

Individual learning support on both levels requires education qualifying stakeholders for their engagement in (BPM-based) organizational change. Besides *epistemological* connections, *personal* connections to BPM knowledge need to be provided for stakeholders actively engaging in learning processes (cf. Resnick et al. 1996). Facilitators to this respect are personalized learning environments (cf. Dabbagh and Kitsantas 2012), social technologies integrated in BPM lifecycle support systems (cf. Matthiesen et al. 2011), and agility support features (Bruno et al. 2011).

For S-BPM the main qualification need is given for modelling. The qualified participation in S-BPM organizational development projects to fully utilize S-BPM's human support capabilities is twofold.

- *Diagrammatic skills*: On one hand Subject-Interaction Diagrams need to be understood as primary means of abstracting from behaviour in a certain situation, e.g. state of organizational development. On the other hand, each subject needs to be refined to concrete actions.
- *Perspective skills*: Subject-specific activities comprises two perspectives on the same behaviour abstraction: first, functional role behaviour, and second interaction with other subjects (sending and receiving messages). The latter is substantially important to accomplish a model of how to run an organization.

For executing S-BPM specifications, the validation phase reveals semantic and syntactic correctness. The subsequent execution allows for direct user experience before freezing procedures for the actual business operation until the next cycle of organizational development is triggered.

3.3 S-BPM's Human Support Capabilities

Chapter 2 revealed that humans will remain a vital element of future production situations and need to be involved in organizational development efforts and continuous workplace improvement. Thereby, human-centred design techniques and the involvement of domain experts contribute to people-centred workplace design. Furthermore, organizational structures and workflows shall be designed to support the empowerment of organizational actors and high involvement in workplace redesign and continuous improvement. With respect to human support capabilities, S-BPM offers different potentials such as:

- Eliciting process knowledge of domain experts
- Involvement of domain experts in process design
- Development of a shared process understanding between domain experts

- Workflow execution support
- Workflow monitoring and analysis (e.g. via KPIs, reporting).

The first three bullets target designing work practices. The last two bullets aim at run-time support for actors (manager, worker, etc.) of organizations. Subsequently, the potential of S-BPM and a possible enrichment for designing industrial workplaces in a human-centred manner will be illustrated. Beyond, run-time support that can be offered by S-BPM implementations will be discussed.

3.3.1 Designing Industrial Workplaces in a Subject-Oriented Way

Subject-oriented business process management (S-BPM) aims to provide simple tools for people when designing and improving their own workflows. As it has been successfully used in many office-based business processes such as credit applications and order processing (Konjack 2010; Nakamura et al. 2011; Walke et al. 2013), the addressed processes are predominantly virtual—they are executed almost entirely within IT-based environments using various software tools such as SAP, Microsoft Office and email programs. As a result, business processes can be specified without much information related to the physical, cultural or social environment in which they occur—they can often be executed independently of the spatiotemporal location of the involved or concerned people.

However, more detailed information about the context is crucial in the physical world of production processes where the spatial layout of workplaces in the factory, the artefacts and tools available, the work culture and the company values embody a specific way of working that may be different from the desired processes. Successful factory and workplace development creates a way of working that employees want to adopt. This can only be achieved once there is no mismatch between the planned interactions people are to perform to achieve their personal and company goals, and the actual interactions afforded by the people's work context (Vilpola et al. 2006).

What could an enhanced S-BPM methodology look like for improving workplaces considering both people-centred and economic aspects? One way to derive such a methodology is to examine existing approaches for each aspect and check whether they could contribute extending the current S-BPM methodology (cf. Table 3.2). Typical approaches for the two aspects include contextual design (emphasizing people-centred aspects) and value stream design (emphasizing economic aspects). However, we first look at the existing S-BPM methodology. Its steps include (Fleischmann et al. 2012, p. 29ff):

1. Analysis: defines the scope and goals of process improvement and sets up a project structure
2. Modelling: represents the process in terms of the subjects (i.e. the active entities in the process), their interactions and behaviours, and the data handled by them

3. Validation: checks whether the process is effective
4. Optimization: checks whether the process is efficient
5. Organization-specific implementation: integrates the process in the organization by assigning people and departments to subjects
6. IT implementation: integrates the process in the organization's existing IT infrastructure
7. Monitoring: executes the process and collects data from it for evaluation and, potentially, a further cycle of improvement

Contextual design is based on observing how the work unfolds, directly at the workplace. This allows gathering ongoing experience about the people's work, how processes are managed and systems are used, rather than relying on abstract information. While contextual observation or inquiry aims at capturing the workers' subjective views of their context (Kannengiesser et al. 2014), this method uses an external consultant who observes and asks questions related to the reasoning behind some of their actions. The consultant documents these observations using notes, sketches and sometimes photos to facilitate the identification and documentation of problems or "disturbances" from the perspective of the worker. The detailed steps of contextual design are described in (Beyer and Holtzblatt 1998; Bonaldi et al. 2011) and include:

1. Contextual Inquiry is conducted with users in their workplace while they work, observing and inquiring into the structure of the users' own work practice. Data is collected through observations and interviews and is validated through team interpretation sessions.
2. Work Modelling: Five work models capture the work of individuals and organizations in diagrams. Each model provides a different perspective on how the work is done.
3. Consolidation refers to the process of defining a common pattern and structure without losing individual variation.
4. Work Redesign uses the consolidated data to focus the conversation on how technology can help people accomplish their tasks. The redesigned work is captured in scenarios embodied and elaborated upon in storyboards.
5. User Environment Design captures the "floor plan" and design of a new system, how each part of the system supports the users' work – along with what functions are available in it – and how to access each of these parts.
6. Mock-up and Prototype Testing are important to system development in ensuring functionality and usability. Furthermore, continuous iterations of prototyping and testing have the potential to bring incremental improvement to the system and drive detailed design (Bonaldi et al. 2011, p. 99).

Scoping typically comprises all activities related to the definition and qualification of the object (e.g. workplace, tool, process) to be (re-)designed. Scoping comprises collecting data, gathering requirements and defining the scope based on the collected information. In order to collect information (*Collecting*) different elicitation techniques such as workshops, focus groups, creativity techniques, interviews, document analysis or product analysis may be applied. In SO-PC-Pro, the focus on collecting data from the people involved has been considered vital.

Table 3.2 Methodological design framework synthesis based on S-BPM, contextual design and value stream design (output-oriented mapping)

Extended methodology	S-BPM	Contextual design
1. Scoping	**Analysis** Goal of process analysis, initial information	Involved processes, people, customers, products, timeframe, available resources
2. Collecting workplace information	**Monitoring and analysis** AS-IS situation described in terms of: Who acts? What is done? What is edited? Process metrics, AS-IS: Existing process models, process instances, key performance indicators	Workplace observation data, Interview data revealing relevant aspects of the workplace
3. Representing workplace information	**Modelling** Subject Interaction Diagram, Subject Behaviour Diagram, Business Objects	Flow Model, Sequence Model, Physical Model, Artefact Model, Cultural Model -> revealing relevant aspects of work that matter for the design and existing disturbances
4. Consolidating workplace information	**Modelling** views, remarks of process participants related to process models	Individual views, remarks of stakeholder (customer, user) related to work-relevant dimensions
5. Synthesizing improved workplaces	**Validation, optimization** To-be model, validation results, adapted to-be model	Vision statement, storyboard
6. Prototyping	**Integration** UI-prototypes, process prototypes	Paper prototypes, documentation of user interface ideas
7. Implementation	**Integration** Actor definition, role specification, assignment of actors to roles, integration with existing IT-systems	NA

However, in order to be able to communicate and align different views on workplaces representations are required.

Representing Workplace Information depends on the scope and may include contextual models, value streams or subject-oriented process models as means for communication, *consolidation* and *alignment* of different views on a workplace. The structured and aligned representation of workplace information provides the basis for *Synthesizing Improved Workplaces*. Synthesizing comprises the design and validation of (new) solutions ideas (e.g. new process design and immediate validation via IT-supported role-play; design of to-be physical model and validation of the model with workers; to-be value stream map; Storyboard).

For selected design solutions prototypes should be built, in order to allow to get feedback from involved users at an early stage of development. *Prototyping* can comprise process prototypes, UI-Prototypes, tool prototypes or even workplace prototypes to test real-life work settings. Prototyping results inform the (organizational and technical) *implementation* of desired solutions.

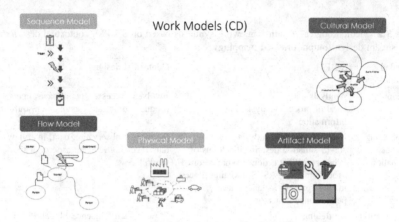

Fig. 3.12 Work models used in Contextual Design

An enrichment of S-BPM models with context information to be able to support contextual design has been presented in Bonaldi et al. (2011). In the contextual design approach, this information is captured in five "work models" showing different aspects or dimensions of the work context (Beyer and Holtzblatt 1998; Holtzblatt and Beyer 2014). Conceptual depictions of the five Contextual Design work models are shown in Fig. 3.12.

The different models have been described in the literature (Beyer and Holtzblatt 1998; Holtzblatt and Beyer 2014). Various information elements could be derived from published examples (Beyer and Holtzblatt 1998; Holtzblatt 2001; Holtzblatt et al. 2005; Vilpola et al. 2006), and enriched with work on modelling context in business process management (Saidani and Nurcan 2007; Rosemann et al. 2008; Heravizadeh and Edmond 2008). The SO-PC-Pro development team derived several information elements for each model:

1. Flow model: This model captures the *communication/information* dimension of workplace context. It includes the following information elements:

- Role (formal or informal), e.g. assembly line worker, care-taker
- Task (to describe responsibilities of a role, e.g. assemble part, discuss safety issues)
- Object (e.g. work bench, shipping document, receipt)
- Communication/collaboration relation (between roles)
- Generic relation (between roles, objects)
- Disturbances (problems, e.g. related to communication, tasks, objects)

2. Sequence model: This model captures *activity* dimension of workplace context. It includes the following information elements:

- Organizational role
- Activities and their sequence

- Intent of activities
- Trigger
- Event
- Time/duration
- Disturbances (problems)

3. Physical model: This model captures the *environment* dimension of workplace context. It includes the following information elements:

- Movements (e.g. direction, speed, route)
- Places/locations
- Physical objects in the environment
- Environment characteristics (e.g. light, humidity, noise)
- Map/floorplan
- Disturbances (problems)

4. Artefact model: This model captures the *tool/document* dimension of workplace context. It includes the following information elements:

- Documents
- Structure of documents
- Tools (incl. physical and software tools)
- Information structure
- Disturbances (problems)

5. Cultural model: This model captures the *social/cultural* dimension of workplace context. It includes the following information elements:

- Dependencies (e.g. hierarchical relations, perceived influences/expectations)
- Stakeholders
- Personal factors (e.g. physiological, mental, mood, expertise, stress, health, cultural and personal values)
- Disturbances (problems)

Some of the information elements contained in the Contextual Design work models can be associated as annotations with specific modelling elements of S-BPM, thus enriching process information with context. Furthermore, information elements from Contextual Design work models may be (partially) mapped to S-BPM modelling elements as described in the subsequent sections.

S-BPM modelling elements partly overlap with Contextual Design work models and may be used in order to represent Flow models and Sequence models. Following, a mapping for both model types to S-BPM elements is given in Table 3.3. In this table, a checkmark indicates the overlapping of the constructs in S-BPM diagrams and the Contextual Design Flow Model.

Roles of Flow Models may be represented in Subject Interaction Diagrams as subjects. Subjects represent a behaviour in a process and can be executed by a person or technical system (i.e. actor). S-BPM also defines "role" as basic modelling construct. In S-BPM, a role aggregates multiple subject behaviours and links concrete actors with subject behaviours. However, existing modelling support tools do not aim to graphically depict roles in Subject Interaction Diagrams. Roles are configured separately as properties of subjects. The representation of tasks for a role in Flow models may be depicted in a Subject Interaction Diagram as textual annotation for a subject. Tasks of a role within a concrete process could also be represented as functions (do, send, receive) in Subject Behaviour Diagrams. However, for an initial high-level model comprising roles, their interaction and tasks of a role, it is recommended to model tasks as textual annotations.

Objects (e.g. shipping document, receipt) of Flow models may be represented using the corresponding S-BPM modelling element "business object". Communication Relations of Flow models may be represented in Subject Interaction Diagrams as message flows. Regarding message flows, S-BPM offers the possibility to depict the message name and the objects (e.g. documents, forms) that are exchanged between subjects. Generic Relations between subjects are not part of the language definition. In order to include this information in S-BPM models, the respective subjects can be annotated with reference to the according Contextual Design work model showing these generic relations.

In Flow models flash symbols are used to indicate disturbances related to roles, tasks, relations or objects. Equivalently, a modeller may use yellow or red flags to indicate such disturbances related to the given modelling elements. Subsequently, a Flow model created with Metasonic Suite is depicted in Fig. 3.13 to illustrate the defined mapping given in Table 3.3. The model comprises four different subjects: Technologist, Production manager, Worker, Quality Control. The Technologist handles customer orders and defines required operations, estimated times for each production step and the required blueprint. In case a CNC programme is required, the technologist writes the programme after a request from the worker. Problems for the Technologist arise related to the time estimations for certain operations. They are considered unrealistic by the workers. This disturbance is indicated through the red flag number 1 in Fig. 3.13. Further disturbances are indicated related to the task "prepare workplace" which is performed by the worker (cf. flag number 2). In this case required tools and materials are regularly not available. A third disturbance is depicted related to the object "produced part" (cf. flag number 3)—some parts are lost in the shop floor and the reason has not been identified so far.

Sequence models from Contextual Design focus on the *activity* dimension of workplaces. Activities and their sequences are depicted in S-BPM for each subject separately within a Subject Behaviour Diagram. In the following, Table 3.4 depicts a mapping of modelling constructs defined in Sequence Models and Subject Behaviour Diagrams.

Table 3.3 Mapping Flow Model elements to S-BPM Subject Interactions Diagram constructs

S-BPM constructs	Contextual design—Flow model					
	Role	Task	Object	Communication relation	Generic relation	Disturbance
Subject Interaction Diagram						
Internal subject	✓					
External subject	✓					
Message flow				✓	✓	
Message				✓	✓	
Business object			✓	✓	✓	
Additional (semantically open) annotation elements						
Flag						✓
Rectangle						✓
Circle						✓
Triangle		✓				✓
Text annotation						✓

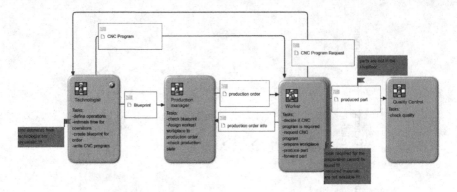

Fig. 3.13 Example mapping of a Flow model to a Subject Interaction Diagram

Sequences in Subject Behaviour Diagrams are either triggered by specific states (start states) or receive states. To indicate the intention or purpose of an action, textual annotations on states or flows may be defined. Events may be modelled as receive or send states. Activities are equally to function states in Subject Behaviour diagrams. The sequence of activities may be represented as sequence or message flows. Regarding disturbances, a modeller may use annotation elements to indicate problems related to the modelling elements. Following, the behaviour of the technologist represented in the Flow model in Fig. 3.13 is depicted in Fig. 3.14. The internal behaviour is enriched using textual annotations for INTENT and TRIGGER. Furthermore, red flags are used to indicate disturbances.

The mapping of both, flow models and sequence models from Contextual Design to S-BPM modelling constructs is intended to show the feasibility of using S-BPM as alternative for these models. As an advantage S-BPM models provide the capability to immediately validate the communication and coordination among subjects via IT-supported role-plays. Furthermore, the modelling and implementation effort related to an executable workflow can be significantly reduced, since S-BPM models can serve as basis for generating the required software.

As described above, Flow models and Sequence models from Contextual Design can be mapped to Subject Interaction and Subject Behaviour Diagrams. For the remaining diagrams a direct mapping requires additional effort, since Artefact models, Physical models and Cultural models focus on different information categories. Some information elements within these models can be modelled as attributes of existing S-BPM modelling elements, adding valuable contextual details. Other information elements can be seen as being subsumed in existing S-BPM modelling elements. An overview of S-BPM elements and their definitions, and the subsumption and extension relationships with contextual information elements is shown below (Tables 3.5, 3.6, 3.7, 3.8, 3.9 and 3.10).

Table 3.4 Mapping Sequence Model elements to S-BPM Subject Behaviour Diagram constructs

S-BPM constructs		Intent and purpose of action	Contextual design—*Sequence model*				
			Trigger	Event	Activity	Sequence	Disturbance
Subject Behaviour Diagram	Start state		✓				
	End state						
	Function state				✓		
	Receiving state			✓			
	Sending state			✓			
	Sequence flow					✓	
	Message flow					✓	
Additional (semantically open) annotation elements	Flag						✓
	Rectangle						✓
	Circle						✓
	Triangle						✓
	Text annotation	✓					✓

INTENT: Create a feasible blueprint for a production
order from a customer which can be effectively and
efficiently produced on the shopfloor

TRIGGER: Customer order

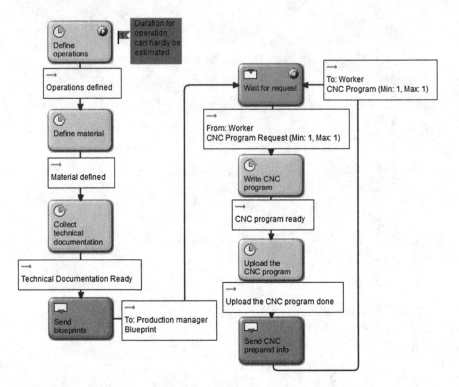

Fig. 3.14 Example mapping of a Sequence Model to a Subject Behaviour Diagram

Table 3.5 Subject definition and contextual information subsumption/extension

A **subject** is a process-related functionality to be executed by an actor	
subsumes: • Responsibility • Intent (in a sequence model: what is the overall goal/functionality of the set of activities)	is extended by: N/A

Table 3.6 Role definition and contextual information subsumption/extension

A **role** is an organizational position aggregating multiple process-related functionalities (similar to a "job description")	
subsumes: • Role	is extended by: N/A

Table 3.7   Actor definition and contextual information subsumption/extension

An **actor** is the person or technical system executing a subject	
subsumes: • Individual	is extended by: • Expectations, needs, values, wishes, strategies • Influences between actors (cultural/social) Disturbances

Table 3.8   Message definition and contextual information subsumption/extension

A **message** is a piece of information exchanged between subjects	
subsumes: • Communication	is extended by: • Location of the communication • Disturbances, disruptions

Table 3.9   Business object definition and contextual information subsumption/extension

A **business object** is a data structure that is created or edited by a subject. It can be associated with a message to be passed from one subject to another	
subsumes: • Artefact (as abstract, virtual representation of information)	is extended by: • Physical representation of the business object: structure, layout, texture, colour etc. of documents or other objects • Physical interaction with the artefact (affordances) • History of affordances (How was it used previously? How is it used now?) • Disturbances

Table 3.10   State (being part of subject behaviours) definition and contextual information subsumption/extension

A **state** is the activity in which a subject can engage. There are three types of states: function states ("what do I need to do"), receive states ("what do I receive from another subject"), and send states ("what do I provide to another subject"). States are interconnected by transitions	
subsumes: • Steps • Sequence, loops, branches • Trigger/event (subsumed by a message being received)	is extended by: • Intent of individual states • Location of the behaviour and its physical environment • Physical description of activities and interactions with objects • Tools used for carrying out the activities (hardware, software) • Disturbances

3.3.2 Designing and Executing Organizational Structures for Active Involvement and Empowerment of Organizational Actors

Aside from applying S-BPM as means to elicit context-sensitive workplace knowledge and to develop a shared understanding and alignment among workplaces, S-BPM models can be developed fostering the involvement and empowerment of people in organizations.

The notion of people-centeredness is generally viewed as a particular characteristic or quality of a production workplace, describing a state in which the physical, sociocultural, operational and economic workplace environment is closely aligned with the needs of the people working in that environment. Striving for such a state is the goal of any production company concerned about the well-being of its workers. Thus, people-centred technologies should aim to support this quest based on a view of people-centeredness as a process rather than a state of affairs. Such a view takes into account the dynamics of both the production environment and the worker's needs. Workplaces need to be continuously adapted to make people-centeredness truly sustainable rather than the result of a one-off improvement project.

One effect of this view is that changes need to be considered as first-order citizens of a people-centred workplace. Changes can be related to various aspects (e.g. the physical work environment, work procedures and instruments) and may occur at different levels, e.g.:

- The requirements level: relating to changes in the environment impacting the company, including external (e.g. new legislation or competitive environment) and internal influences (e.g. novel company policies)
- The model level: relating to changes in (normative) descriptions of workplaces, including process models and (possibly) associated contextual information
- The instance level: changes in resources or running instances of a process

Changes rarely occur in isolation. A single change can trigger a set of other changes (at model and instance level) that need to be taken into account. *Change propagation analysis* aims to investigate how a local change (occurring at requirement, model or instance level) can lead to other changes and to checks whether existing constraints, rules or the structural and behavioural soundness of processes are violated (Rinderle et al. 2004; Fdhila et al. 2015). For instance, many workplace improvement suggestions provided by workers are not limited to a single workplace or worker. When sharing information about the work context, tools and interactions with other workers, it is often the case that a suggestion made by a worker also affects his/her co-workers. Similarly, when changes occur in real-life process executions, it is very likely that the model has to be adapted as a consequence, e.g. to avoid the violation of constraints such as norms for quality assurance.

A prerequisite for change propagation analysis is the identification (or "acquisition") of initial local changes. For the purpose of suggestion and idea collection, people in a company pose a valuable source of information as they can be considered domain experts in their field of activity (cf. Fairbank and Williams 2001; Setiawan et al. 2011). Research in the fields of employee involvement and empowerment suggests that the involvement of people in organizational innovation processes has the potential to lead to substantial improvements and financial benefits (cf. Fairbank and Williams 2001). However, adequate organizational structures and tool support for collecting suggestions and evaluating them is required (cf. Fairbank and Williams 2001).

Collecting local changes, suggestions or errors require a collective effort engaging workers who contribute their suggestions for workplace enhancement, as well as collaboration when keeping track of the actual data to be analysed for detecting changes. Collecting input for change propagation and impact localization analysis thus need a *collaborative environment* in which issues, suggestions and process data can be collected, shared and discussed with others. In this regard, S-BPM processes may be designed to digitize "Suggestion making processes", "Error reporting processes" and to provide basis for change propagation analysis. The case presented in Chap. 5 will describe the design and implementation of such an endeavour at an Italian SME.

3.4 Conclusive Summary

The aim of this chapter was to investigate capabilities and potentials of the S-BPM application within the context of future production systems. Thereby, taking the socio-technical system perspectives (introduced in Chap. 2) has been continued and the potentials and capabilities are structured along the dimensions technology, organization and human.

Recent technological developments in the field of S-BPM target towards process integration among different levels of control. Section 3.1 presents the traditional automation pyramid and S-BPM prototypes that allow for integration across different levels of control. Aside, this section presents an innovative approach to system integration in production companies based on the so-called automation diabolo. In this context, S-BPM can act as middleware exhibiting the communication model between different system participants.

Since technology only serves as enabler for better workplace design, additionally, requirements stemming from organizational development have been revisited and discussed with respect to the S-BPM approach in Sect. 3.2. In this regard, S-BPM may serve to represent and (partially) automate work practices in a bottom-up manner. Thereby, the involvement of domain experts/users is emphasized in order to empower people to become active workplace redesigners and tailor solutions to dedicated workplace requirements.

The potential of S-BPM to support humans in organizations has been discussed twofold. On the one hand, the enrichment of the S-BPM approach with contextual design elements aims to provide a comprehensive approach to capturing and designing work practices in production industries. On the other hand, S-BPM enables designing organizational structures that foster active involvement and the empowerment of people as discussed in Sect. 3.3.2.

References

Ates, A., & Bititci, U. (2011). Change process: A key enabler for building resilient SMEs. *International Journal of Production Research, 49*(18), 5601–5618.

Arnold, R. (1996). *Weiterbildung - Ermöglichungsdidaktische Grundlagen.* München: Vahlen.

Aschoff, F.-R., Bernardi, A., & Schwarz, S. (2003). Weakly-structured workflows for knowledge-intensive tasks: An experimental evaluation. In *Proceedings IEEE International Workshops on Enabling Technologies: Infrastructure for Collaborative Enterprises (WETICE'03)* (pp. 340–345).

Becker, J., Kugeler, M., & Rosemann, M. (Eds.). (2008). *Prozessmanagement* (6th ed.). Berlin: Springer.

Beyer, H., & Holtzblatt, K. (1998). *Contextual design: Defining customer-centered systems.* San Francisco: Morgan Kaufmann Publishers.

Bonaldi, D., Totter, A., & Pinter, E. (2011). Towards contextual S-BPM—method and case study. In W. Schmidt (Ed.), *S-PBM ONE—Learning by Doing—Doing by Learning. 3rd International Conference S-BPM ONE 2011, Ingolstadt, Germany, September 29–30, 2011 Proceedings* (pp. 98–108). Heidelberg: Springer.

Börger, E., & Fleischmann, A. (2015). Abstract state machine nets: Closing the gap between business process models and their implementation. In J. Ehlers, & B. Thalheim (Eds.), *S-BPM ONE'15 Proceedings of the 7th International Conference on Subject-Oriented Business Process Management.* New York: ACM Press. doi:10.1145/2723839.2723840.

Bruno, G., Dengler, F., Jennings, B. K., Khalaf, R., Nurcan, S., Prilla, M., et al. (2011). Key challenges for enabling agile BPM with social software. *Journal of Software Maintenance and Evolution: Research and Practice, 23*(4), 297–326. doi:10.1002/smr.523.

Castells, M. (2010). *The power of identity. The information age: Economy, society, and culture* (2nd ed.). Chicester: Wiley-Blackwell.

Chen, J. Q., Lee, T. E., Zhang, R., & Zhang, Y. J. (2003). System requirements for organizational learning. *Communications of the ACM, 46*(12), 73–78.

Ciuciu, I., Zhao, G., Mülle, J., von Stackelberg, S., Vasquez, C., Haberecht, T., et al. (2011). Semantic support for security-annotated business process models. *Enterprise, business-process and information systems modeling* (pp. 284–298). Berlin: Springer.

Cohn, D., & Hull, R. (2009). Business artifacts: A data-centric approach to modeling business operations and processes. *Bulletin of the IEEE Computer Society Technical Committee on Data Engineering, 32*(3), 3–9.

Cummins, F. A. (2009). *Building the agile enterprise: With SOA, BPM and MBM.* Burlington: Morgan Kaufmann Publishers.

Dabbagh, N., & Kitsantas, A. (2012). Personal learning environments, social media, and self-regulated learning: A natural formula for connecting formal and informal learning. *The Internet and Higher Education, 15*(1), 3–8.

de Castro, R. P. L., Armayor, D. P., Gómez, J. M., Mosquera, I. S., & Batista, J. A. D. (2010). Semantic supported modeling and orchestration of logistic integrated processes, with focus on supply chain: Framework design. *ICT Innovations 2009* (pp. 285–294). Berlin: Springer.

Edelmann, W. (2000). *Lernpsychologie*. Weinheim: Beltz.

Eisenhardt, K. M., & Martin, J. A. (2000). Dynamic capabilities: What are they? *Strategic Management Journal, 21*, 1105–1121.

Fairbank, J. F., & Williams, S. D. (2001). Motivating creativity and enhancing innovation through employee suggestion system technology. *Creativity and Innovation Management, 10*(2), 68–74.

Fdhila, W., Indiono, C., Rinderle-Ma, S., & Reichert, M. (2015). Dealing with change in process choreographies: Design and implementation of propagation algorithms. *Information Systems, 49*(4), 1–24.

Filipowska, A., Kaczmarek, M., Koschmider, A., Stein, S., Wecel, K., & Abramowicz, W. (2011). Social software and semantics for business process management-alternative or synergy? *Journal of Systems Integration, 2*(3), 54–69.

Fischer, H.-P. (1989). Die Arbeit des Sisyphus oder unsere Mission als Bildungsbereich in einer Automobilfabrik. In T. Sattelberger (Ed.), *Innovative Personalentwicklung* (pp. 42–53). Konzepte, Erfahrungen, Gabler, Wiesbaden: Grundlagen.

Fischermann, G. (2006). Praxishandbuch Prozessmanagement, ibo Schriftenreihe Band 9, Gießen.

Fleischmann, A., Schmidt, W., Stary, C., Obermeier, S., & Börger, E. (2012). *Subject-oriented business process management*. Berlin: Springer.

Fleischmann, A., Schmidt, W., & Stary C. (2013). Subject-oriented BPM = socially executable BPM. In *2013 IEEE International Conference on Business Informatics, Vienna, Austria* (pp. 399–406).

Gaitanides, M. (1983). *Prozessorganisation. Entwicklung, Ansätze und Programme prozessorientierter Organisationsgestaltung*. München: Hanser.

Geißler, H. (Ed.). (1995). *Organisationslernen und Weiterbildung. Die strategische Antwort auf Herausforderungen der Zukunft*. Neuwied/Berlin: Luchterhand.

Gifford, C. (2011). *When worlds collide in manufacturing operations: ISA-95 Best Practices Book 2.0*. International Society of Automation, Research Triangle Park, NC.

Haeckel, S. S. (1999). *Adaptive enterprise: Creating and leading sense-and-respond organizations*. Cambridge, MA: Harvard Business School Press.

Haller, S., Karnouskos, S., & Schroth, C. (2009). The internet of things in an enterprise context. In J. Domingue, D. Fensel, & P. Traverso (Eds.), *FIS 2008* (Vol. 5468, pp. 14–28). Lecture notes in computer science. Berlin: Springer.

Hammer, M. (1996). *Beyond reengineering: How the process-centered organization is changing our lives*. New York: Harper Business.

Hammer, M. (1999). How process enterprises really work. *Harvard Business Review, 77*(6), 108–118.

Hammer, M., & Champy, J. (1993). *Reengineering the corporation: A manifesto for business revolution*. New York: Harper Business.

Heravizadeh, M., & Edmond, D. (2008). Making workflows context-aware: A way to support knowledge-intensive tasks. In *Proceedings of the Fifth Asia-Pacific Conference on Conceptual Modelling, Wollongong, Australia*, (Vol. 79, pp. 79–88).

Herrmann, T. (2000). Lernendes workflow. In *Verbesserung von Geschäftsprozessen mit flexiblen Workflow-Management-Systemen* (Band 4). Heidelberg: Physica-Verlag.

Herrmann, T., Hoffmann, M., Kunau, G., & Loser, K. U. (2004). A modelling method for the development of groupware applications as socio-technical systems. *Behaviour & Information Technology, 23*(2), 119–135.

Hoang, H. H., Tran, P. C. T., & Le, T. M. (2010). State of the art of semantic business process management: An investigation on approaches for business-to-business integration. *Intelligent Information and Database Systems* (pp. 154–165). Berlin: Springer.

Holtzblatt, K. (2001). *Contextual design: Experience in real life*, In H. Oberquelle, R. Oppermann & J. Krause (Eds.), Mensch & Computer, B.G. Teuber, Stuttgart, pp. 19–22.

Holtzblatt, K., Burns Wendell, J., & Wood, S. (2005). *Rapid Contextual Design: A How-to Guide to Key Techniques for User-Centered Design*, Morgan Kaufmann Publishers, San Francisco.

Holtzblatt, K., & Beyer, H. R. (2014). Contextual design. In M. Soegaard, & R. F. Dam (Eds.), *The encyclopedia of human-computer interaction* (2nd ed). Aarhus, Denmark: The Interaction Design Foundation. Retrieved July 18, 2016, from https://www.interaction-design.org/encyclopedia/contextual_design.html.

IEC. (2007). IEC 62264–3 Enterprise-control system integration. Part 3: Activity models of manufacturing operations management.

Kagermann, H., Wahlster, W., & Helbig, J. (2013). *Recommendations for implementing the strategic initiative INDUSTRIE 4.0.* Final Report of the Industrie 4.0 Working Group. Retrieved July 18, 2016, from http://www.acatech.de/de/publikationen/stellungnahmen/kooperationen/detail/artikel/recommendations-for-implementing-the-strategic-initiative-industrie-40-final-report-of-the-industr.html.

Kannengiesser, U. (2015). Agents implementing subject behaviour: A manufacturing scenario. In A. Fleischmann, W. Schmidt, & C. Stary (Eds.), *S-BPM in the wild: Practical value creation* (pp. 201–216). Springer.

Kannengiesser, U., Neubauer, M., & Heininger, R. (2016). Integrating business processes and manufacturing operations based on S-BPM and B2MML. In J. L. Sanz (Ed.), *S-BPM ONE 2016*. New York: ACM Digital Library. Article 12.

Kannengiesser, U., Totter, A., & Bonaldi, D. (2014). An interactional view of context in business processes. In C. v (Ed.), *S-BPM ONE—Application Studies and Work in Progress, CCIS 422* (pp. 42–54). Springer.

Keddis, N., Burdalo, J., Kainz, G., & Zoitl, A. (2014). Increasing the adaptability of manufacturing systems by using data-centric communication. In *IEEE International Conference on Emerging Technologies and Factory Automation, Barcelona, Spain* (pp. 1–8).

Kim, D. (1993). *A framework and methodology for linking individual and organizational learning: Applications in TQM and product development*. Ph.D. Thesis, Sloan School of Management, Massachusetts Institute of Technology.

Kim, G., & Suh, Y. (2012). Building semantic business process space for agile and efficient business processes management: Ontology-based approach. In *Business enterprise, process, and technology management: Models and applications* (Vol. 51).

Kirchmer, M. (2011). What has Jazz to do with MPE? In *High performance through process excellence*, Chap. 11 (pp. 159–169). Berlin: Springer.

Konjack, G. (2010). Case study: AST order control processing. In H. Buchwald, et al. (Eds.), *S-BPM ONE—Setting the Stage for Subject-Oriented Business Process Management, CCIS 85* (pp. 115–120). Heidelberg: Springer.

Korpelainen, E., & Kira, M. (2013). Systems approach for analysing problems in IT system adoption at work. *Behaviour & Information Technology, 32*(3), 247–262.

Lorenz, M., Rüßmann, M., Strack, R., Lueth, K.L., & Bolle, M. (2015). Man and machine in Industry 4.0. *How will technology transform the industrial workforce through 2025?* The Boston Consulting Group, Boston, MA.

Matthiesen, P., Watson, J. A., Bandara, W., & Rosemann, M. (2011). Applying social technology to business process lifecycle management. In R. Schmidt, & S. Nurcan (Eds.), *Proceedings BPMS2'11, 4th Workshop on Business Process Management and Social Software*. Retrieved July 15, 2016, from http://eprints.qut.edu.au/43384/.

McClellan, M. (1997). *Applying manufacturing execution systems.* CRC Press.

McGregor, D. (2006). *The human side of enterprise.* New York: McGraw-Hill.

Mendes, J. M., Leitão, P., Colombo, A. W., & Restivo, F. (2012). High-level petri nets for the process description and control in service-oriented manufacturing systems. *International Journal of Production Research, 50*(6), 1650–1665.

Mendling, J., Reijers, H. A., & Recker, J. (2010). Activity labeling in process modeling: Empirical insights and recommendations. *Information Systems, 35*(4), 467–482.

MESA. (2013). *Business to manufacturing markup language (B2MML), Version 6.* Chandler: Manufacturing Enterprise Solutions Association.

Meyer, N., Feiner, T., Radmayr, M., Blei, D., & Fleischmann, A. (2011). *Dynamic catenation and execution of cross organisational business processes—the jCPEX! approach.* In *S-BPM ONE 2010, CCIS 138* (pp. 84–105). Berlin: Springer.

Meyrowitz, J. (1985). *No sense of place: The impact of electronic media on social behavior.* New York: Oxford University Press.

Montague, G. P. (2012). *Who am I? Who is she? A naturalistic, holistic, somatic approach to personal identity.* Frankfurt: Ontos.

Müller, H. (2012). Using S-BPM for PLC code generation and extension of subject-oriented methodology to all layers of modern control systems. In C. Stary (Ed.), *S-BPM One—Scientific Research, LNBIP 104* (pp. 182–204). Berlin: Springer.

Nakamura, S., et al. (2011). CGAA/EES at NEC Corporation, powered by S-BPM: The subject-oriented BPM development technique using top-down approach. In W. Schmidt (Ed.), *S-BPM ONE—Learning by Doing—Doing by Learning, CCIS 213* (pp. 215–231). Heidelberg: Springer.

Niggemann, O., Henning, S., Schriegel, S., Otto, J., & Anis, A. (2015). *Models for adaptable automation software: An overview of plug-and-produce in industrial automation* (pp. 73–82). Dagstuhl Work-shop MBEES: Modellbasierte Entwicklung eingebetteter Systeme XI, fortiss GmbH, München, Germany.

Nonaka, I., & Von Krogh, G. (2009). Perspective—Tacit knowledge and knowledge conversion: Controversy and advancement in organizational knowledge creation theory. *Organization Science, 20*(3), 635–652.

Ngai, E. W., Chau, D. C., & Chan, T. L. A. (2011). Information technology, operational, and management competencies for supply chain agility: Findings from case studies. *The Journal of Strategic Information Systems, 20*(3), 232–249.

Overby, E., Bharadwaj, A., & Sambamurthy, V. (2006). Enterprise agility and the enabling role of information technology. *European Journal of Information Systems, 15*(2), 120–131.

Pipero, C., & Manjunath, K. (2006). ISA 95 implementation best practices: Workflow descriptions using B2MML. In *WBF North American Conference, Atlanta, GA.*

Prilla, M., Schermann, M., Herrmann, I. T., & Krcmar, H. (2012). Process modeling with SeeMe: A modeling method for service processes. In T. Böhmann, W. Burr, Th. Herrmann, & H. Krcmar (Eds.), *Implementing international services. A tailorable method for market assessment, modularization, and process transfer* (pp. 67–81). Wiesbaden: Gabler.

Pütz, G., & Lüger, R. (2003). Flucht in die Technik oder neue Qualität des betrieblichen Lernens?. In P. Mambrey, V. Pipek, & M. Rohde (Eds.), *Wissen und Lernen in virtuellen Organisationen. Konzepte, Praxisbeispiele, Perspektiven* (pp. 199–215). Heidelberg: Physica.

Resnick, M., Bruckman, A., & Martin, F. (1996). Pianos, not stereos. Creating computer construction kits. *Interactions, 3*(8), 41–50.

Rieckmann, H. (1997). *Managen und Führen am Rande des 3.* Jahrtausends: Theoretisches, Bedenkliches. Peter Lang, Frankfurt/Main.

Rinderle, S., Reichert, M., & Dadam, P. (2004). Correctness criteria for dynamic changes in workflow systems—a survey. *Data & Knowledge Engineering, 50*(1), 9–34.

Rosemann, M., Recker, J. C., & Flender, C. (2008). Contextualisation of business processes. *International Journal of Business Process Integration and Management, 3*(1), 47–60.

Saidani, O., & Nurcan, S. (2007). Towards context aware business process modelling. In *8th Workshop on Business Process Modeling, Development, and Support (BPMDS'07), CAiSE* (Vol. 7, p. 1).

Salovaara, A., & Tamminen, S. (2009). Acceptance or appropriation? A design-oriented critique of technology acceptance models. In P. Saariluoma & H. Isomaki (Eds.), *Future interaction design II* (pp. 157–173). London: Springer.

Sambamurthy, V., Anandhi, B., & Varun, G. (2003). Shaping agility through digital options: Reconceptualizing the role of information technology in contemporary firms. *MIS Quarterly, 27*(2), 237–263.

Scheer, A. W. (1999). *ARIS-business process modeling* (2nd ed.). Berlin: Springer.

Scholten, B. (2007). *The road to integration: A guide to applying the ISA-95 Standard in manufacturing*. Research Triangle Park, NC: International Society of Automation.

Schreiber, G., Akkermans, R., Anjewierden, A., Hoog, R., Shadbolt, N., DeVelde, W. V., et al. (2002). *Knowledge engineering and management: The common KADS methodology*. Cambridge: MIT Press.

Schwaninger, M. (2000). Intelligente Organisationen: Strukturen für organisationale Intelligenz und Kreativität. In A. Papmehl, & R. Siewers (Eds.), *Wissen im Wandel. Die lernende Organisation im 21. Jahrhundert* (pp. 317–360). Wien: Wirtschaftsverlag Ueberreiter.

Seidl, D. (2005). *Organisational identity and self-transformation: An autopoietic perspective*. Aldershot: Ashgate.

Senge, P. (1990). *The fifth discipline, the art and practice of the learning organization*. New York: Doubleday.

Sennett, R. (2008). *The craftsman*. Yale University Press.

Setiawan, M. A., Sadiq, S., & Kirkman, R. (2011). Facilitating business process improvement through personalized recommendation. In *Business information systems* (Vol. 87, pp. 136–147). Lecture notes in business information processing. Berlin: Springer.

Silva, A. R., & Rosemann, M. (2012). 'Processpedia': An ecological environment for BPM stakeholders' collaboration. *Business Process Management Journal, 18*(1), 20–42.

Sinur, J., Odell, J., & Fingar, P. (2013). *Business process management: The next wave*. Tampa: Meghan-Kiffer Press.

Strambach, S. (2001). Innovation processes and the role of knowledge-intensive business services (KIBS). In K. Koschatzky, M. Kulicke, & A. Zenker (Eds.), *Innovation networks. Concepts and challenges in the european perspective* (pp. 63–68). Heidelberg: Physica.

Ulich, E. (1991). *Arbeitspsychologie*. Stuttgart: Schaeffer/Poeschel.

Vieille, J. (2012). ISA-95/B2MML Tutorial: Integration practice from use cases to xml messages. In *ISA Automation Conference, Doha (Qatar), 9 & 10 December 2012*.

Vilpola, I., Väänänen-Vainio-Mattila, K., & Salmimaa, T. (2006). *Applying contextual design to ERP system implementation, CHI '06 extended abstracts on human factors in computing systems* (pp. 147–152). Montreal: ACM.

Vogel-Heuser, B., & Feiz-Marzoughi, B. (2013). Datenkopplung mittels UML-Modellen: Engineering- und IT-Systeme für Industrie 4.0 vernetzen, Automatisierungstechnische. *Praxis, 55*(12), 26–37.

Vogel-Heuser, B., Kegel, G., Bender, K., & Wucherer, K. (2009). Global information architecture for industrial automation. *Automatisierungstechnische Praxis, 51*(1), 108–115.

Von Bertalanffy, L. (1968). *General system theory: Foundations, development, applications*. New York: George Braziller.

Walke, T., et al. (2013). Case Study @ Swisscom (Schweiz) AG: iPhone 5 Self-Service Order App and Process-Workflows. In H. Fischer & J. Schneeberger (Eds.), *S-BPM ONE—2013, CCIS 360* (pp. 264–273). Heidelberg: Springer.

Weske, M. (2012). *Business process management. Concepts, languages, architectures* (2nd ed.). Heidelberg: Springer.

Worley, C. G., & Lawler, E. E. (2010). Agility and organization design: A diagnostic framework. *Organizational Dynamics, 39*(2), 194–204.

Zhu, J. (2009). Information technology, E-learning and organizational learning. In *Proceedings IEEE International Conference on E-Business and Information System Security*. doi:10.1109/EBISS.2009.5138004.

Open Access This chapter is distributed under the terms of the Creative Commons Attribution-NonCommercial 4.0 International License (http://creativecommons.org/licenses/by-nc/4.0/), which permits any noncommercial use, duplication, adaptation, distribution and reproduction in any medium or format, as long as you give appropriate credit to the original author(s) and the source, provide a link to the Creative Commons license and indicate if changes were made.

The images or other third party material in this chapter are included in the work's Creative Commons license, unless indicated otherwise in the credit line; if such material is not included in the work's Creative Commons license and the respective action is not permitted by statutory regulation, users will need to obtain permission from the license holder to duplicate, adapt or reproduce the material.

Lot-Size One Production

4

Udo Kannengiesser, Richard Heininger, Lubomir Billy,
Pavol Terpak, Matthias Neubauer, Christian Stary, Dennis Majoe,
Alexandra Totter and David Bonaldi

Abstract

This case reports on an SME offering the production of atypical, unique and special-purpose machinery, equipment and technological complex units useful particularly in the automotive and electronic industries. The initial situation reveals challenges like the estimation of production times for one-time prototypes, lack of communication between shop floor workers and technologists, lack of information on upcoming production tasks for workplaces, low involvement of workers in decision processes, and lack of information on current state of production. The proposed subject-oriented solution targets to increase the worker autonomy, the worker involvement and information transparency as well as integration across all organizational control layers. In this respect, subject-orientation is applied to integrate real-time information from the shop floor (e.g. location information of parts, power consumption of machines) and business processes (e.g. customer order). A novel S-BPM modelling approach has been developed in the course of organizational design that seeks to model subjects as fine-grained behaviours of actors rather than functional roles. The

U. Kannengiesser (✉) · R. Heininger
Metsonic GmbH, Pfaffenhofen, Germany
e-mail: udo.kannengiesser@gmail.com

L. Billy · P. Terpak
Centire, Bratislava, Slovakia

M. Neubauer · C. Stary
Department of Business Information Systems – Communications Engineering, Johannes Kepler University Linz, Linz, Austria

D. Majoe
MA Systems and Control Limited, Southampton, UK

A. Totter · D. Bonaldi
ByElement, Schindellegi, Switzerland

© The Author(s) 2017
M. Neubauer and C. Stary (eds.), *S-BPM in the Production Industry*,
DOI 10.1007/978-3-319-48466-2_4

revealed behaviours may be assigned to actors (i.e. humans, machines) depending on their capabilities and skills. This allows for dynamic allocation of tasks to humans and machines, process execution support based on skill levels, reflecting performed behaviours of actors and (de-)constructing organizational behaviours. The evaluation is composed of formative and summative elements. The formative evaluation reports on findings based on developer workshops, focus groups and user tests that were conducted in parallel to the design and implementation to ensure a user-centred approach. The summative evaluation reports on findings related to the outcome of the case implementations at the SME.

4.1 Elicitation and Analysis of the Initial Situation

The case described in this chapter has occurred in a manufacturing SME called "Company A" in Slovakia. This company was established in 1990 and is operating in the field of precise mechanical engineering, ranging from mechanical nodes, operational units and systems to special single-purpose machines and technological complexes, including control systems. Until recently it also performed the development, construction and project planning of such devices. In addition to its extensive modern technological equipment including CNC (Computerized Numerical Control) machines, measuring devices and other tools, the company relies on a broad team of engineers and shop floor workers.

Company A produces atypical, unique and special-purpose machinery, equipment and technological complexes (including electronic control systems). Its regular customers are from the automotive and electrical industries. The company production includes the manufacturing of high-precision components by chip machining as well as using unconventional methods of IT 4 class metalworking, encompassing general 3- to 5-D surfaces.

The case analysis and definition involved a range of activities

- Factory visits of project partners
- Face-to-face workshop with project partners (brainstorming sessions, interviews with management and employees)
- Definition of key terminologies ensuring common understanding of partners
- Remote conference calls to further specify the use case
- Discussions and interviews with workers and engineers
- Definition of goals, objectives and criteria by each partner.

4.1.1 Management Workshop

The definition of possible focus areas of the case started with an initial workshop at Company A. One member of Company A's management team and members of the several SO-PC-Pro partners (Regional IT consultant, HCI consultant, hardware developer, S-BPM system provider, JKU researcher) joined this workshop. The goal was to

- Identify and analyze areas of improvement or production problems
- Create ideas to address possible solutions
- Depict possible use case scenarios, and
- Prioritize the results at the end of the workshop in order to focus work and align work packages

The workshop's participants started with a brainstorming session to identify possible areas of improvement. The discussion among the partners led to the definition of the following six use case candidates:

1. *Decentralized coordination of workers in the production process*

In the initial situation, workers operate on the shop floor and do not usually gain insight into production planning. This leads to centralized coordination of tasks by the management, which on the other hand may lead to inefficiencies and unnecessary idle times. Decentralized coordination of work tasks and involvement of workers in operative planning of tasks at the shop floor is envisioned as solution to this problem.

2. *Task assignment by workers*

Workers gain autonomy in choosing their work task at the shop floor. This could increase self-efficacy and is believed to shorten idle times of machines and workers.

3. *Proactive maintenance of the machines*

If machines on the shop floor need to be maintained, these machines cannot be used for production. Therefore, a proactive maintenance of the machines during idle times would increase productivity—machines would be out of order to a lesser extent.

4. *Material tracking*

Another issue at Company A is the predictability of delivery dates of finished work pieces. Due to the prototype-based production setting nearly every piece has a different production plan. Therefore, it is not easy to track material and unfinished work pieces on their way through the shop floor, because pieces have different routes. Location sensing could ensure traceability and tracking capabilities for produced work pieces.

5. *Machining task complexity versus worker skill level prediction and management complexity of the new parts*

The production planning of new work pieces always takes place in the technological preparation office. It is primarily based on the experience of technologists. The introduction of indicators for task complexity and required worker skill level could help technologists to estimate needed work time. As a result, a better estimation regarding the needed production time for new work pieces could be calculated.

6. *Making use of the idle time*

When workers are waiting for a machining task, they usually have to wait until this task is finished. Workers could prepare their next steps during this idle time (e.g. get tools for the next operation), if they could get insight into the production plan. On the other hand, the machining task has to be observed by sensors to ensure that workers get notified in case a manual intervention is necessary.

The identified use case candidates were then evaluated according to five dimensions as the next step. These dimensions were derived with respect to the overall goals and the specified work packages of the SO-PC-Pro project. The five dimensions are

- Aspects regarding process automation
- Human-centeredness aspects
- Impact on Company A's management and effectiveness of production
- Potential usage of S-BPM for supporting communication and execution
- Degree of involvement of the project partners.

The first use case candidate was prioritized highest after the discussion along these dimensions. It was additionally possible to extend this use case with elements of the other candidates. However, proactive maintenance of machines was dropped after this discussion.

4.1.2 Interviewing the Employees

The next step in identifying areas of improvement was to conduct semi-structured interviews with various employees of the company. The result of the initial workshop was taken into account for structuring the interview, however, employees were able to address their problems without reservations. The in-depth interviews revealed the following four use case candidates from the employees' perspective.

1. *Monitoring tools on the shop floor to decrease production postponing*

Employees reported during the interviews that tools cannot be found on the shop floor occasionally. The finding process involves production manager as well as employees. Therefore, it would help workers to track the location of tools, and it would increase productivity as it decreases preparation time.

2. *Communication improvement between workers on the shop floor, technologists and production management*

Shop floor workers commented on unrealistic and improvable time estimations of technologists. They mentioned fostering communication of all involved parties in the production process as significant potential for improvement.

3. *Proactive machine maintenance*

The periodic maintenance of machines can be postponed by shop floor workers. Thus, machines are not maintained in time, rather too late, namely in the event of an error. Proactive maintenance could help to reduce machine breakdowns.

4. *Cooperation on production time estimation*

Shop floor workers want to participate in estimating production time to avoid unnecessary time pressure, because time estimations were perceived rather optimistic at that time. This issue was addressed in the interviews in the context of improving communication among employees.

The following paragraphs highlight selected statements from the conducted interviews. The citations have been translated and edited for readability

> It's a constant struggle to satisfy our customers, to ensure quality, and also quantity. It is about finding a balance between these dimensions. Hopefully this project helps to make things easier and provides an improved management system taking a different perspective on the production operation of the company. The current system is outdated and not the right one. New IT systems are more flexible, and help the management of the company to operate more efficiently and flexibly. (An employee on the everyday work at Company A)

> The human represents a major influencing factor, I think that simply providing a new system is not a good solution…Work procedures should be more standardized. However, this is challenging due to the fact that our company offers single-piece production and more or less prototyping. We do not do serial production, and repeatability is rather low… I would estimate 20 % of the orders. The introduction of a new system for reducing the waste of time in production will be challenging. The new system should provide information on the current distribution of tools among dedicated locations (e.g. workplaces or the tool warehouse). Workers often require a tool which is currently used by someone else or even not available on the shop floor at all. In the latter case, the work task needs to be interrupted and the shop floor leader needs to procure the necessary tool. Such cases lead to my opinion to severe delays and waste of time. (An employee on the possibility of introducing a new system solving the waste of time in production)

Every worker receives the work to be done on the shelf related to his workplace in terms of the blueprint and the material/part required to perform a given operation. A worker is supposed to deal with orders on the shelf according to the deadlines on the blueprint. Of course there are situations, when the management tells a worker: This order is now more important, work on this. However, people are diverse – sometimes they choose what they want, and change planned sequences. That is how people actually perform work today. (An employee on the lack of autonomy regarding task selection)

Work became much harder, in former times it was easier. We have had small serial production and also single-piece production. However, in both cases the estimation of the actual production time is hard to estimate. Someone (a technologist or production manager) estimates a time for a certain manufacturing operation, and even that time is five times smaller than the actual time, workers need to deal with it. It dishonours our work. I have no clue why they always decrease the time in order to increase our work speed, I really don't know. (An employee on the difficulty of accurate time estimations)

The communication between involved people – technologist, shop floor leader, worker – is important. Typically, workers are the last one in the design of the manufacturing operations for a certain order. However, workers know how to perform manufacturing operations best… Therefore, direct communication between the technologists and shop floor workers is important.

Technologists should definitely visit the shop floor more frequently. There is a lack in communication with respect to the times for manufacturing operations technologist indicate on the blueprints. A technologist should be more interested, he should inform about production opportunities. We (technologist, worker) should communicate more, since more heads are better than one.

(Two employees on the importance of communication between different departments)

The current tool tracking works as follows. There is a database storing the tools and tasks assigned to a workplace. This database is manually updated by the shop floor leader when someone e.g. finishes a task, or takes a tool from the tool warehouse. However, sometimes the data in the database are not updated, or the tool is left at a workplace even though the database is updated. Then, the shop floor leader or the worker need to search the tool and valuable time is wasted. (An employee on the issue of misplaced tools)

Machine maintenance has not been working very well lately. Only when a machine breaks down, an error is handled. Regarding the regular maintenance, each machine defines maintenance intervals. My machine displays a required maintenance. However, one may easily reset the maintenance interval and proceed working without any maintenance. This results in the fact that workers ignore maintenance until the machine breaks down. (An employee on the machines maintenance)

4.1.3 Analysis and Goal Definition

Based on joint discussions of the project team, the list of problems at Company A has been defined. On this basis, the problems have been addressed by different use cases. The common agreement singled out the first use case candidate of the initial workshop as the most appropriate and most important use case. Its importance was confirmed by the in-depth interviews with the shop floor workers.

The results of the workshop and the interviews were summarized subsequently. When doing so, the following hindering factors have been identified:

- The one-time production of prototypes (batch size = 1) challenges time estimation
- Lost material/parts and tools
- Lack of communication between workers on the shop floor, technologists and production management (e.g. on-time estimations, possible process optimizations)
- Workers lack of information considering upcoming manufacturing tasks which could be beneficial to prepare in advance and make use of the idle time
- Production manager is a single point of failure. He needs to distribute parts across different workplaces manually and, therefore, lacks time for planning and monitoring
- Machined parts are often forgotten on the shelf, which affect the production fluency. There is also missing information about when a task started or ended (this information is inserted in the internal production software by the production manager after certain period of time)
- The current production control system cannot measure the time taken for each manufacturing step at a workstation. The system is not capable of automatically monitoring the current production status of a given part. It depends on manual data input by the production manager. Furthermore, it cannot trace the location and therefore provide tracking information in case parts are lost
- Prioritizing of task/orders/production steps is not documented in the system and easily accessible
- There is a lack of worker-to-worker and worker-to-management communication. This often causes interruption of production fluency by, e.g. forgetting to machine a part or to deliver a machined part to another workplace. Communication is then triggered only in case of a problem

The goals and objectives considering this use case have been defined collaboratively with the project partners. In a further step, each project partner contributing to this case defined goals and objectives relevant from its point of view. The following consolidated list comprises goals and objectives which are addressed in this use case (also see Table 4.1). It is the result of an iterative process aiming for aligning the partners' viewpoints.

Optimized production processes through automation support are the umbrella goal for the three main goals identified for the case implementation. The first main goal is the decentralization of task assignments. This goal is composed of the following two objectives:

- Support employees' work-autonomy by self-determined task selection in alignment with the overall production plan
- Involve workers in the decentralized distribution of work pieces in line with the production plan.

The decentralized assignment of tasks follows the idea to decrease operational effort of the production manager and **increase the autonomy of the worker**. To do so, workers should be enabled to select manufacturing tasks individually on the basis of the current production plan. Support information could be a prioritized list of upcoming manufacturing tasks as well as already estimated manufacturing times. This information would also allow workers to plan ahead within the context of their workplace and for example, make use of the idle time by preparing for upcoming work tasks. Beyond that, the first goal comprises the involvement of workers in the distribution of parts, e.g. workers bring proactive parts to the next station within the idle time or they get parts to be manufactured from other workers.

Facilitation of real-time production state tracking is the second main goal in this use case. This goal will be achieved by reaching two objectives. These objectives mainly address the issue regarding lost parts and tools.

The *increase of the transparency of material/part location by real-time tracking* on the shop floor focuses on providing information about the actual production state. Having this real-time information allows on the one hand for a better over-view of the production from the production manager's view point (e.g. production planning, estimation) and on the other hand gives the workers information about upcoming tasks, and thus, improves task preparation (e.g. preparation of programs).

The reduction of time needed to search for lost tools and parts/materials does not focus on providing status, but rather on actual location information. It could reduce the time needed to search for certain part/tools. Moreover, the availability of this data supports the workers in the decentralized distribution of work pieces as described above.

The third main goal covers the **improvement of mutual information exchange between subjects**. Subjects are actors within processes and can be represented by either humans or machines involved in the manufacturing process. This goal is detailed by the following four objectives:

- Improving human 2 human communication
- Improving human 2 machine communication
- Improving machine 2 human communication
- Improving machine 2 machine communication

The *improvement of human 2 human communication* comprises, e.g. the improvement of communication between worker and technical planner on time estimations in terms of the alignment and negotiation of estimated and actual manufacturing times. The *improvement of human 2 machine communication* addresses an easy and non-obstructive support for workers to capture information on ongoing manufacturing tasks. This also relates to the second goal in terms of capturing production states in real time. The *improvement of machine 2 human communication* focuses on providing workers with comprehensive, relevant con-textual information such as upcoming tasks and the ongoing production status. The forth objective addresses seamless information exchange between production machines and the production planning systems, e.g. integration of production

Table 4.1 Consolidated goals and objectives

Overall goal	Goal	Objective
Optimized production processes through automation support	Decentralization of task assignment	Support employees work-autonomy by self-determined task selection in alignment with overall production plan
		Involve workers in the decentralized distribution of work pieces in line with the production plan
	Facilitation of real-time production state tracking	Increase transparency of material/part location by real-time tracking on the shop floor
		Reduction of time needed to search for lost tools and parts/materials
	Improvement of mutual information exchange between subjects	Improve H2H communication (e.g. communication between worker and technical planner on time estimations)
		Improve H2M communication (e.g. easy and non-obstructive support for workers to capture information on ongoing manufacturing tasks)
		Improve M2H communication (e.g. comprehensive information of workers on upcoming tasks and ongoing production status, relevant contextual information)
		Improve M2M communication (integration of production control and planning system with information provided by machines about current state)

control and planning system with information provided by machines about current state. For each objective, measurement criteria and methods were defined. Generally, the measurement of objectives comprised qualitative as well as quantitative data.

Overall, the current situation, goals and objectives, the scope and an initial solution idea were defined within the initial use case definition activities. Furthermore, the implementation strategy, testing and evaluation as well as potential risks related to the uses case were defined. Based upon the initial use case definition, additional workshops have been conducted to elicit and narrow down organizational, functional and technical requirements. These requirements are described in terms of S-BPM processes and user stories in the subsequent sections.

4.1.4 Defining Requirements

4.1.4.1 Organizational Requirements

To improve the quality of the production process at Company A, it is essential to collect production data in real time, particularly information about the current status of individual production operations and the current location of work pieces. Currently this information is captured manually by the production manager, leading to

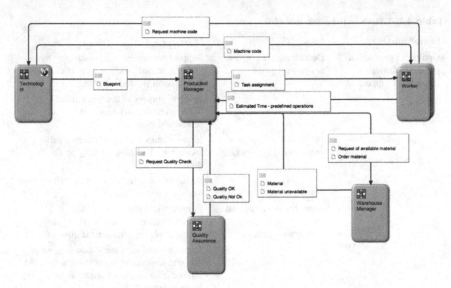

Fig. 4.1 The as-is production process at Company A

time delays and potential errors. The proposed solution will automate the production process, and move the collection of data closer to the production process, by enabling employees and machines to directly access the data in a decentralized way. The solution will be based on an extension of the subject-oriented methodology, consisting of executable models of interacting entities (called the "subjects") representing human operators and machines. Interactions include conveying different types of data, namely, about the status of operations, operators and work pieces/material. They all be described as messages between subjects that can be interpreted by a subject-oriented workflow execution engine. This allows for the integrated execution, monitoring and analysis of production data, and real-time visibility of production operations. As a result, production orders can be prioritized, providing better guidance for workers when selecting tasks and coordinating their work steps.

Figure 4.1 shows how production is organized at Company A today, using a Subject Interaction Diagram. In the process model, the following subjects (i.e. process-centric roles) are included

- Technologist
- Production Manager
- Worker (shop floor)
- Quality Assurance
- Warehouse Manager

The initial task of the process is the preparation of a technical specification by the *Technologist*. After receiving a customer order, the *Technologist* prepares a technical specification, which comprises the list of required material, the defined technological steps, time estimations for each step, and the required manufacturing precision. These specifications are documented in written form and stored in a production management system, from which a printout, called "blueprint", is produced and given to the *Production Manager*.

Upon receiving the blueprint, the *Production Manager* firstly checks with the *Warehouse Manager* for the availability of required material. If the material is in stock, the *Warehouse Manager* will provide it directly to the *Production Manager*; otherwise it will first need to be ordered. The *Production Manager* assigns to each task defined in the blueprint a particular *Worker* and *Machine*, writing this data directly into the production management system. A printout of the production plan is then produced and associated with technical documentation and the corresponding raw material. Subsequently, the *Production Manager* brings this set of information and material to a small storage shelf near the workplace (i.e. machine and worker) where the first production step is to be executed.

After receiving the task, the *Worker* checks for the tools required (e.g. milling tool, drilling tool, etc.). If a CNC machine code is needed, the *Worker* requests it from the *Technologist*, either directly or via the *Production Manager*. The *Technologist* prepares the code and uploads it to a central file server with a unique identifier consisting of *order id*, *machine id* and *operation id*. While waiting for the CNC code, the *Worker* prepares the workplace and puts the raw material into the machine. Each machine is connected to central file server via Ethernet, so the *Worker* can find the code, upload it to the machine, validate it and start machining. When the machining operation is finished, the *Worker* takes out the machined part and puts it on a storage shelf for machined parts. On the production plan, he writes down the time he needed to machine the part. Then, the *Production Manager* takes the machined part from the shelf and moves it to next workplace. This process is repeated until the last production step is reached.

The last step of the production process is the quality check performed by the *Quality Manager*. The Quality Manager is responsible for measuring the actual dimensions of the parts produced and checking them against required precision criteria and technical standards. The output is a quality report that includes information on whether the part fulfils desired quality criteria. If the quality has been found insufficient, the *Production Manager*, in cooperation with the *Technologist*, devises possible solutions to fix the defects of the part or decides to discard the part and restart the production process.

The current production management system is highly heterogeneous and not sufficient for the needs of Company A. It consists of three independent modules: planning, accounting and warehouse management. It does not support communication via Web services. The database side is not documented well. Consequently, it is almost impossible to ensure correct data exchange between systems, which is crucial for production purposes.

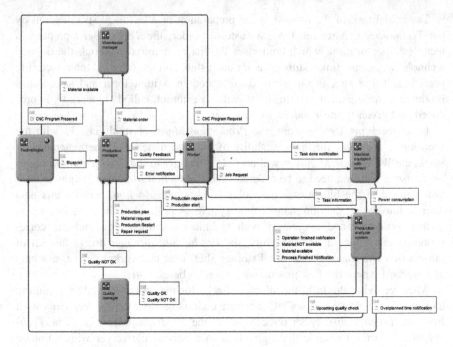

Fig. 4.2 To-be production process at Company A

An initial solution idea for the to-be model of the production process is shown in
Fig. 4.2, representing an improved production process with two additional subjects:
Machine equipped with sensor and *Production Analyzer System*.

The production process begins with the *Technologist* defining the required
production information (technical documentation): material, technological steps and
estimated time for preparation and production, and required manufacturing precision. Once he has completed this step, he sends this information electronically (via
a production planning system) to the *Production Manager*.

The *Production Manager* first checks for the availability of the required material
with assistance from the *Production Analyzer System*. If not in stock, the *Production Manager* sends a request to the *Warehouse Manager* to order the desired
material. Then, he evaluates the technical documentation and assigns each task for
particular *Workers* and *Machines* using the *Production Analyzer System*. Each task
is associated with a plastic tray with sensor and the material or part to be machined.

After accepting a task, the *Worker* checks for availability of all required
resources (e.g. material, tools) and CNC codes, and prepares the machine. The
moment when he begins to prepare the workplace, the *Worker* should communicate
this state to the *Production Analyzer System* for time measurement purposes
(preparation time). When the *Worker* clamps the part into the machine, optionally
loads the CNC code, he should communicate the state "production start" to the
Production Analyzer System.

Each machine (in the scope of this project) will be equipped with a power consumption sensor attached to machine's power cord. This sensor is crucial to get information whether there is a part being processed on the machine by measuring the amount of power consumption. When power consumption converges to zero, it indicates that the machining operation is almost finished. The system then sends a notification to the *Worker*.

After taking the processed part out of the machine, the *Worker* should do a quick quality check. If the *Worker* finds a defect, he should immediately notify the *Production Manager* about this situation. The *Production Manager* then decides whether the part is repairable or restarts production from scratch. The *Worker* should notify the *Production Analyzer System* of the time needed for preparation and processing. After confirming the completion of a part, by writing a production report, the *Production Analyzer System* determines the next operation and notifies the relevant *Worker*. Then, he takes the processed part with the plastic tray and moves it to next workplace. On the shop floor, the plastic tray equipped with a sensor in combination with wireless access points could provide real-time information where the desired part is located on the shop floor.

The *Production Analyzer System* monitors the entire production process, gathers signals from sensors via beacon devices as well as location data of parts and tools. The *Production Analyzer System* also accepts data inputs from the *Worker*, the *Production Manager*, the *Quality Manager* and the *Warehouse Manager*.

In the very last step of the process, the quality control should take place. The *Production Analyzer System* notifies the *Quality Manager* when the quality check is needed. After the *Quality Manager* has finished the quality check, he produces a quality check report. If the part fails the quality check, the *Quality Manager* notifies the *Production Manager* to take further decisions on how to resolve the issue.

4.1.4.2 Functional Requirements

In individual workshops with the management and the workers, *user stories* have been applied to elicit (functional) requirements. A user story describes a usage scenario using simple natural language. This ensures that all stakeholders, particularly the users of the system to be developed, can understand and contribute to the specification of required system features. Every user story is concerned with exactly one system feature to be implemented, including a description of who will use the feature and for what kind of goal. The following list of user stories contains selected user stories from a management workshop conducted at Company A (Table 4.2).

4.1.4.3 Technical Requirements

In addition to organizational and functional requirements, basic technical requirements have been defined as part of the requirements definition activities. These requirements were classified into requirements related to (1) Company A, (2) the S-BPM processing system and (3) potential sensors to be applied within the use case.

Requirements related to Company A mainly address the availability of devices to access the S-BPM processing system, network configuration, interface

Table 4.2 User stories

Story narrative	As a	I want	So that	Priority	Relation to goal
Increased task autonomy	Machinist	to define in which order to perform "on the shelf" tasks based on a list of high and low prioritized tasks	I can have a level of freedom and variety of complexity	2	1
Availability of CNC program	Machinist	info on next 3 tasks specifically CNC program	I can upload it or inform technologist I don't have it	5	3
Feedback on quality	Machinist	to have a detailed and timely feedback on the quality of a task	I can fully understand what was the failing	6	3
Quality check planning	Quality Manager	to know how many work pieces are in the last processing stop before quality check	I can plan my working time	7	1,3,2
Planned time exceeded	Technologist	to get informed if my planned time is exceeded by more than 30 %	I can clarify the reasons and improve my estimation of problems during production	8	–
Actual energy consumption for machine	Production Manager	to see the energy consumption for a specific machine at specific time	I can check if a machine is operated by the worker	9	3
Which workpieces are at a specific machine	Production Manager	to see the list of orders at a workplace	I can optimize the production plan	10	2
Error notification by worker	Production Manager	the worker notifying me if he makes an operation error	I can manage the issue	14	3

Note The numbers in the last column ("Relation to Goal") relate to the use case goals specified in Sect. 4.1.3: 1—Decentralization of task assignment; 2—Facilitation of real-time production state tracking; 3—Improvement of mutual information exchange between subjects

definitions to existing production support systems involved in the use case and a server set-up for the S-BPM processing system. Requirements related to the S-BPM processing system Metasonic Suite comprise the operating system and database configuration. Requirements related to the sensor application are on the one hand generic in terms of "not-invasive" (e.g. power metering of a machine) and on the other hand include the compliance with OPC UA (IEC 62541) since a vendor-independent implementation of interfaces between S-BPM processes and sensors has been the target of Metasonic.

4.2 Process and Solution Design

The solution design and development followed a user-centred design approach. Based on the people-centred workplace analysis and requirements specification, first user interface prototypes and S-BPM process specifications were generated by the regional IT consultant and the S-BPM platform provider Metasonic. Subsequently, the results of the initial solution design for the user interfaces are presented.

4.2.1 Prototyping User Interfaces

Dedicated user interfaces for workers in the shop floor and the management (production manager, quality manager) have been designed. The user interfaces for workers on the shop floor comprise the following functionalities:

- Provision of upcoming tasks and production information for individual workplaces
- Propose change in task list to optimize workplace-related task sequence (Fig. 4.4)
- Request CNC code (Fig. 4.5)
- Report error (Fig. 4.6)

Figure 4.3 displays the current ordered task list at a certain workplace on the left-hand side. When selecting a certain task, the details appear in the main area. In Fig. 4.3 a "cutting" task related to the order 14285 for Bosch is selected. For the operation the order details, material details, technical operations and the technical documentation may be checked by the worker. Two buttons on top allow to "start production" (green button) or to "propose a change in the task sequence" (grey button). When requesting a change in the proposed task sequence, a worker may reorder the list and provide his rationale for the reordering request before sending it to the production management (cf. Fig. 4.4). After requesting a change in the task sequence, the changed tasks are displayed in grey on the left-hand side (cf. Fig. 4.5). After starting a certain operation (cf. Fig. 4.5), a worker may report an error (red button), request a CNC code, or finish the task without any CNC code request. Reporting error (Fig. 4.6) is supported in the mock-up via a text field for describing the error and a radio group for selecting the type of error. Thus, context-sensitive error reporting is facilitated.

Additionally, interfaces dedicated to the production management have been designed. Inspired by the Kanban approach, the UI designers proposed a Kanban board-like visualization of the current state of production. Thus, the production management may take a look at which tasks are for example currently assigned to "Technological Planning", "Plan Validation", "Work Task Delegation" (cf. Fig. 4.7). One may also filter the distribution, e.g. according to "Only Active Tasks", "Only Inactive Tasks", or "Only my Tasks".

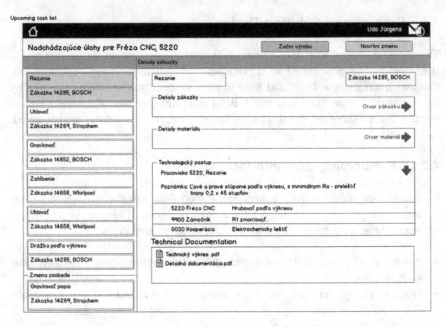

Fig. 4.3 Provision of upcoming tasks and production information for individual workplaces

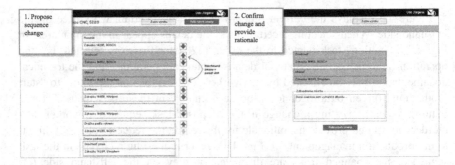

Fig. 4.4 Propose change in task list to optimize workplace-related task sequence

The Kanban View also allows checking details for certain views. For instance, Fig. 4.8 displays the details for "Technological Planning". Here, the technical operations need to be defined for two orders, for one order the required material needs to be defined, and for three orders the technical documentation needs to be created. When selecting a certain operation (see Fig. 4.8), details are displayed on the right-hand side (e.g. KPIs like average time for task, frequency of tasks, start time).

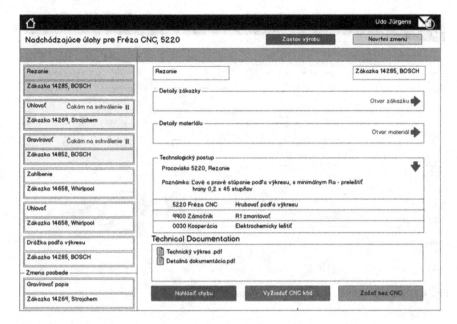

Fig. 4.5 Request CNC code

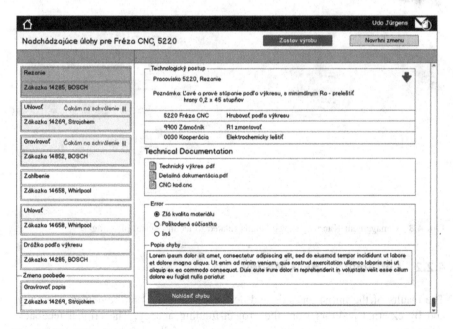

Fig. 4.6 Report error

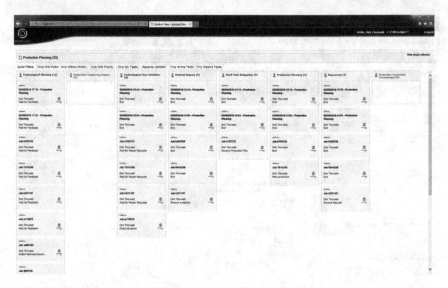

Fig. 4.7 Management Kanban View—overview

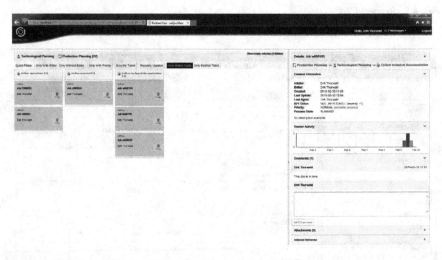

Fig. 4.8 Management Kanban View—details related to technological planning

4.2.2 Reframing S-BPM Models

The results of the initial analysis and design phase have been reviewed internally
and by external auditors from the project-funding agency. The critical feedback
related to the initial solution design comprised the following two aspects:

- The additional value of the S-BPM solution compared to existing standard technologies was not immediately understood
- The potential change and improvement due to the S-BPM solution could not be identified with respect to people-centred workplace (re)design

Additionally, Company A started in parallel a new project for implementing a state-of-the-art production management system. The feedback and parallel developments required to highlight the benefit and additional value of the S-BPM project developments and a clear separation of concerns. This triggered a change in perspective. Starting from the S-BPM solution, the researchers from the University partner proposed an alternative, innovative approach to S-BPM modelling. Instead of modelling subject in terms of coarse grain organizational roles (cf. Fig. 4.1 "Production Manager", "Technologist"), the researchers proposed a more fine-grained approach focusing on behaviours like "Plan Validation", "Material Inquiry", or "Error reporting". This behaviour-oriented approach to S-BPM modelling structures organizational patterns in a more fine-grained way and depicts the required communication for alignment between behaviours. A part of the alternative approach is depicted in Fig. 4.9 which shows the "Production Planning Process" and its interfaces to "Manufacturing Preparation", "Manufacturing", and "Quality Control".

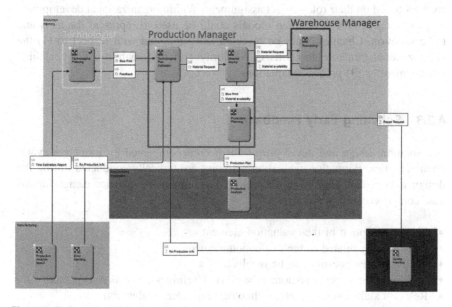

Fig. 4.9 Reframed—production planning process

The original (role-centred) process design and the behaviour-centred process design are different with respect to the following aspects:

- The original production process is divided into four separate processes
- The amount of subjects increases in the behaviour-oriented approach due to the fine-grained modelling of functional behaviours as subjects. Overall, the amount of subjects increased from 7 to 17 subjects
- Internal behaviours are simplified and the amount of modelling elements for each subject is reduced. This is due to the decomposition of behaviours into functional entities ($\rightarrow$ similar to encapsulation, modularization in software engineering).

In S-BPM roles are used to aggregate subject behaviours. Taking the original role-based approach, the role and the subject are potentially the same. Within the new behaviour-oriented approach subjects represent "responsibilities", or "functional behaviours" that are aggregated by certain roles. The fine-grained modelling approach supports the flexible assignment of responsibilities to certain roles and organizational actors. Thus, rights and duties related to an employee may be flexibly defined and dynamically changed based on, e.g. varying competences and qualifications. For example, experienced workers may handle errors themselves, whereas novices need to communicate with the production manager.

Furthermore, the approach allows generating competence profiles for certain workers based on their role-subject assignment. Within organizational development projects such behaviour-oriented models could be used to represent the as-is and to-be situation. Changes could be revealed and supported with respect to (1) the organizational structure in terms of authority and responsibility, (2) personnel development or (3) process adaptations.

4.2.3 Soliciting Early Feedback

The solution design and development has been accompanied by formative evaluation activities. Formative evaluation activities are typically conducted during the design and development phase of a project. The formative evaluation design for this case comprised several elements

- Short description of the evaluation element
- Functionality related to the evaluation element
- Technical key questions to be resolved
- User interaction key questions (Usability, Usefulness, Social Acceptance)
- Relevant stakeholders (users, technology provider, evaluators)
- Evaluation methods to be applied

Technical key questions have been discussed and resolved in dedicated developer workshops. (Social) Acceptance questions have been discussed with workers and the management in specific focus groups. In a third step, user tests addressing usability, usefulness and acceptance have been conducted with a prototype.

4.2.3.1 Feedback Through Focus Groups

The worker-specific focus group involved overall seven workers representing different types of workplaces involved in the solution design ($3\times$ Milling Machine, $1\times$ CNC Developer, $1\times$ Technologist, $1\times$ Quality Assurance and $1\times$ Assembly). In this focus group, the regional IT Consultant presented the mock-up prototypes of the user interfaces dedicated to support the daily operations of workers, internal communication on errors and task changes, as well as power metering and location tracking support (cf. Sect. 4.2.1).

In general, the workers declared interest in the *prototype supporting their daily work*. They appreciated that the prototype enables summarizing their daily work plan, and thus they will have an opportunity to prepare better for upcoming tasks, especially with respect to work tools and required material.

Regarding the *CNC request support* functionality, the workers agreed that it will be very beneficial to see in advance whether the CNC program exists for the upcoming tasks. Furthermore, they appreciate the opportunity to request this program in advance. However, the workers mentioned that, at the moment they need to decide whether a CNC program is required when a production task is assigned to their workplace. One worker suggested that the technologist should already assess whether a CNC program is required and ensure its in-time availability at the shop floor workplace.

With respect to the provided *error report* functionality the workers provided the following feedback: Errors related to individual components are approximately 30–40 %. Less serious errors are fixed by experienced workers while more serious errors need to be consulted with the production head who proposes a solution. They appreciated the recording of errors and would also like to be able to reuse this knowledge in future production situations. As common errors the workers identified the following categories:

- Incorrect technical documentation causing errors in the production
- Material error (5 %)
- Error from the previous operation (previous production step)
- Error in the operations order

In addition to the error handling, workers may provide a *production report* to the planning department. This enables reviewing differences between planned time and real production time. The workers agreed that this opportunity may improve planning and increase the efficiency handling of an entire order. However, they noted that

> (Time estimation) is a matter of understanding. When he (technologist) doesn't want to understand it...he can come, he can observe and notice what actually is required to conduct a manufacturing operation...

I have disputes with technologists…they never come to me asking: Why do you scold me? They do not want to hear an answer. However, I would tell them.

Time estimation works as follows – a technologist writes down 2 h, a worker works 4 h. The technologist gets back the manufacturing protocol and he corrects 4–3 h…but the worker doesn't know. Then they make some statistics claiming that workers miss 10 h. The technologist is not forced to change the time estimations. They are not reflected in the final product price. The pressure for the technologists is missing…

The technologist is limited by the sales price. Based on the actual production time the future price should be negotiated.

Concerning the *location tracking of parts and the real-time production state tracking*, the workers provided positive feedback, especially the assembly department. This is reflected in the following statements:

This kind of information is useful for the assembly or for cooperation, i.e. departments where tools and parts are collected. The current state is crucial for the assembly to plan ahead. When 80 % is already produced, it is goof to know where the remaining 20 % reside. Furthermore, it is useful for reporting urgent matters (e.g. delays). However, related to tool tracking, it is not always possible to determine according to technological blueprint whether a dedicated tool is needed for the assembly. Therefore, I could need information on the location of certain tools.

It is always good to know what I can expect and plan…

The workers declared concerns regarding *power consumption monitoring* of machines. They had concerns on the usage and interpretation of the measured data. Especially, the workers were afraid that the management could use the numbers to better measure the individual productivity of workers at a certain workplace. They recommended to carefully interpret the data, since different tasks require different effort in time for preparing task accomplishment. Hence, the operation time of the machine should not be the only indicator of worker productivity. A worker stated to that respect

It depends how the management will evaluate this kind of data…if it is measured or not, we will work in the same way…given…the management will not take the power consumption as the final number. Out of 8 h the spindle might only spin 1 and half hour…. the remaining time might be required for preparation….

In the management focus group, the regional IT consultant presented both, the mock-up prototypes for workers on the shop floor and the intertwined interactive management view, so called Kanban View (cf. Sect. 4.2.1). The focus group with the management comprised three managers, the sales manager, the production manager and the manager of technological department.

With respect to the provision of *feedback and reports* related to *time estimations* the management indicated the following: Feedback on the estimations has to be justified. A common challenge is that the actual production time will always differ depending on workers' experience and work practice. Some workers note shorter production times than real, others overstate the time actually needed for a certain production task. However, the actual time should be measured and taken into account within future planning cases to ensure profitability of production offers.

Regarding the *proposal of changes related to upcoming task list* at a certain workplace, the management noted that such a mechanism is already implemented, but not supported by an IT system. Change proposals are basically noted on the paper-based blueprints, either with stroking/deletion or some notes. The change in the order of operations or tasks is also possible, but usually occur based on the initiative of a supervisor. Furthermore, the management confirmed that the communication does not work properly (e.g. between technologist and workers). The management appreciates a solution to *support transparent communication* between the different workplaces involved in production orders.

The designed *Kanban View* for the management allows tracking the current state of production, e.g. checking what is in preparation, currently operated at a certain machine, or in quality control. According to the perception of the management, the Kanban tool may help to monitor the current state of production. Furthermore, the management recognized that the system might also help to better support less skilful workers in task planning and during task operation.

4.2.3.2   Feedback from User Tests

User tests were conducted involving three workers on the shop floor, in order to assess the tablet interface already presented within the focus group. The tested interface was developed by Metasonic and comprises the functionalities encoded in the initial mock-up prototypes. However, the look and feel differed slightly from the prototype, and only a reduced set of functionalities was available. In the user tests, actual data from production were used to simulate a realistic work situation. Furthermore, the tests were conducted at the actual workplaces of the users using a portable tablet device.

During the test users were requested to *"Select an upcoming task"* from the *"In Preparation"* list and subsequently *(a) check the details, (b) check the required materials, (c) check the operation description as well as (d) the documentation.* Furthermore, users were asked to *"Request the CNC Code", "Check part location", "Start production", "Prepare a machine for predefined technological operations"* and to *"Stop the production of a current task".*

The observation of the users during task accomplishment revealed the following: The younger users (age 35 and 40) were able to accomplish the tasks within a few seconds. However, an older user (60) struggled to navigate through the application, since he was not used to tablets at all, and the basic user interaction concepts were not familiar for him. Furthermore, the older user insisted from the very beginning on the existing "paper based work style" he was used to work with—although he agreed that all the information required to fulfil a certain work task is provided within the application. Related to the interaction with the system, the observations showed that two users were unable to determine the location of a part on the shop floor, because they did not find the related user interface element. Moreover, within the preparation of work task, workers required a program path not provided in the user interface.

In summary, user 1 declared that the user interface was easy to use and to navigate through, although he thought that information should be structured in a better way, and put in a single view, so e.g. he does not need to click to see the detail of technological operation. In addition, user 1 appreciated the part-location tracking support, and thought that this system would help better to communicate with managers. User 2 noted that he would appreciate to see the list of predefined tools in the operation detail screen as well as their availability and location.

Aside from interaction issues, significant performance issues in terms of long response times could be observed during the user tests. This performance issues are related to deploying the application on an old test server with limited capacity. Furthermore, in two user tests the part location was not correctly retrieved. Hence, system failures occurred and the system crashed.

4.2.3.3 Feedback from User Interaction Questionnaire

After each user had accomplished the tasks, they were asked to fill in a questionnaire. Using the questionnaire participants reported the perceived usefulness and the perceived ease of use of the system as well as aspects concerning social acceptance. Additionally, they have been asked to list most negative as well as positive aspects. In total, three people filled in the questionnaire.

Listed **negative aspects**:

I think the iPad is not suitable to be used in the manufacturing environment. It could be easily damaged or crashed. As well I think, that most of my colleagues won't be able to easily use the device, but for younger it won't be problem.

I think that this system is more suitable for bigger productions than TC Contact.

For the work we are doing it sufficient to use the old system we're used to work with.

One person also listed the following **positive aspect**:

Using this system I would definitely have better overview of my tasks, where the part is located on the shop floor, when production begins and who is working on it.

The users were asked to indicate how unlikely or likely several statements were on a scale from 1 (unlikely) to 7 (likely) or "Not applicable". The statements were clustered along the following dimensions:

1. Perceived usefulness
2. Perceived ease of use, and
3. Social acceptance of "Process Automation Support" prototype

1. Perceived usefulness: The younger users (age 35 and 40) indicated to some extend at least that the "Process Automation Support" prototype is useful and would increase their productivity. The older user (age 60) did not perceive the system to be useful at all. All users rated the prototype more or less unlikely to improve their productivity.

2. Perceived ease of use: Answers related to the ease of use indicated a positive trend. The users seemed confident to find it easy to learn to operate the prototype successfully. The older user did not find it very likely that the device could be easy to use for him or that the system would be flexible when interacting with it.

3. Social acceptance: In addition to usefulness and ease of use, the questionnaire included items related to social acceptance. All three users indicated a positive trend to having the knowledge, but not necessarily the resources to use the system. Concerning emotions when using the "Process Automation Support" prototype, all the users stated that the system was somewhat intimidating to them. They also would hesitate a little bit to use the system, since they fear to make mistakes they cannot correct.

The results of the user tests with workers need to be interpreted carefully, since only three users interacted with the system. Nevertheless, the users seemed confident to be able to learn how to operate the system successfully. With respect to the usefulness and the social acceptance of the prototype, improvements need to be implemented in the final system. In particular, older users seemed reluctant to use such a system. As consequences and measures, the following topics were derived to be carefully considered within the case study implementation:

- Performance optimization of worker-related user interface
- Provision of path to CNC code within work task preparation view
- Increased visibility of user interface element for part location
- Facilitation of part location retrieval
- Provision of protective cover for tablet in order to decrease workers' fear to crash the tablet
- Clear and transparent communication of the usage of measured power metering data to workers in order decrease resistance and fear
- Addressing adequate workplaces and workers with tablet solutions—it seems older users are likely to be resistant to change

4.3 Case Implementation

In the case implementation the process models, the interfaces to existing systems, the set-up of required hardware and the organizational implementation were fine-tuned at Company A. In this section, especially the organizational and technical implementation will be described.

4.3.1 Organizational Implementation

4.3.1.1 Selected Workplaces

Overall, five workplaces (machines) on the shop floor were selected. The aim of the selection was to choose a set of the principal workplaces most frequently involved in the company's production operations. At each workplace, one worker is operating the machine within a shift. The selected workplaces are listed below (Fig. 4.10):

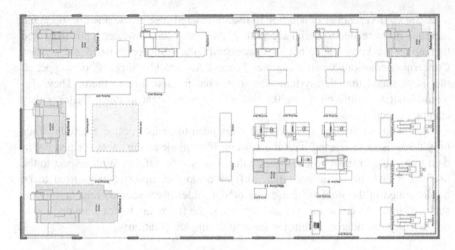

Fig. 4.10 Selected workplaces for the case implementation at Company A

- Turning Machine Mazák
- Milling Machine MCFV1060
- Milling Machine G. Master
- Milling Machine Huron
- Milling Machine DMG DMF260

In the case implementation, the selected workplaces have been equipped with iPod touch devices to detect the location of active trackers related to parts (cf. Sect. 4.3.2). Furthermore, iPads were installed at these workplaces as interface to the provided work support system. The production management accessed the system via its office PCs.

4.3.1.2 Implemented S-BPM Process Support

The implemented S-BPM solution comprises overall seven process as depicted in Fig. 4.11. Subsequently, these processes are described in more detail. In general, Production Planning initiates Manufacturing Preparation. Manufacturing Preparation triggers the Manufacturing process that may result in Feedback on work sequences, work durations, work plans, errors and quality, and necessary steps to repair parts. Furthermore, a "location tracking" process is running continuously to infer the location of parts relevant for "Manufacturing Preparation" and "Manufacturing". Aside from the six core processes, the Master Data Management process supports the configuration of available workplaces and devices.

Production Planning is the partial process that initiates a certain production process. Thereby, the production manager assigns the tasks to certain workplaces and releases the work order for manufacturing. The basic planning and definition of operations and material related to an order is done within the ERP system (Dialog 3000) of Company A. The "Production Planning" subject interfaces the ERP system and automatically retrieves relevant process data based on the order ID. The "Production Planning" subject furthermore encodes the configuration of the

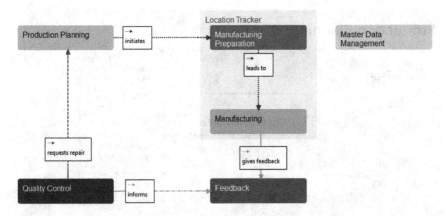

Fig. 4.11 S-BPM process overview

corresponding location tracker for an order. The "Work Task Delegation" automatically distributes work tasks to the defined workplaces. Thus, workers will see the assigned tasks in their list of upcoming work tasks (cf. "Worklist Checking" Fig. 4.12) on their workplace-related tablet.

The tablet interface displays a list of upcoming tasks, tasks in preparation and tasks already in production (subject "Worklist Checking"). In case a worker has more than one upcoming task he can proceed with the following actions:

- Display task details
- Propose a change to task order
- Accept the task

If a worker proposes a change to the sequence of the worklist, the "Worklist Change Approving" subject assigned to the production management is notified. Upon the reception of a change proposal, the production management may evaluate it, and either accept or deny it. Afterwards, the worker will immediately receive the manager's decision.

In case a worker does not propose any change, he may continue with preparing the operation of the work task (subject *Work Task Preparation*—cf. Fig. 4.13). In the preparation step, a detailed task description is shown, containing the following information:

- Name of the order/task
- Pieces to be manufactured
- Material
- Predefined technological operations
- CNC code path
- Technical drawing (part blueprint)
- Part location

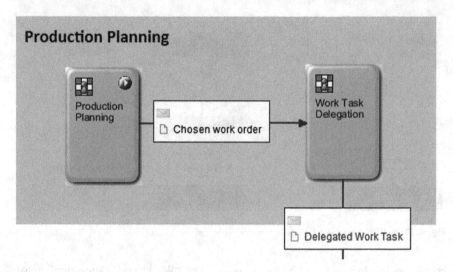

Fig. 4.12 Production planning process

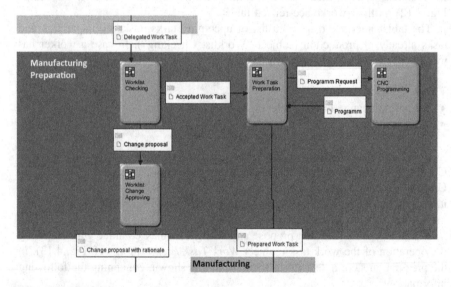

Fig. 4.13 Manufacturing preparation

If the required CNC code does not exist, the worker can decide either to request CNC code from the technologist or to write it on his own, before starting the machining operations (Fig. 4.13—subject "Work Task Processing").

When a worker starts a production task (subject "Work Task Processing"—cf. Fig. 4.14), the processes of measuring power consumption of the workplace-related machine is initiated. Every minute the amount of the current power consumption is

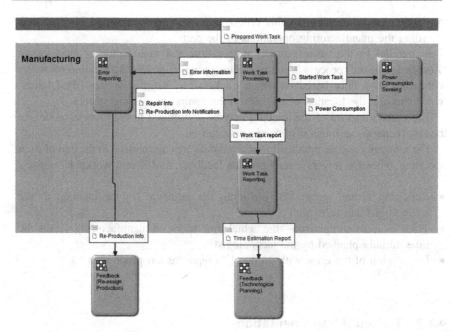

Fig. 4.14 Manufacturing process

retrieved via an OPC UA-enabled power consumption metre (subject *Power Consumption Sensing*). This data is stored in a dedicated business object of the workflow system and allows the management checking the current status of a machine (Standby, Rotating, Changing tool, Full load). Furthermore, the collected data could be used to analyze actual times of machine operations related to pre- and post-processing times. This information could be used for further improving time estimations of operations.

After a machining operation is started, the worker is able to proceed with one of the following actions:

- Report error (Subject Error Reporting)
- Report completion of manufacturing task (Subject Work Task Reporting)

When a worker discovers that a manufactured part is defective, he is able to report that situation with his tablet. After clicking *Report Error* he can send detailed information to the manager about the defect. In addition, he may propose steps for fixing the defect, or request discarding the part and restarting the manufacturing process.

When a machining operation is finished, the worker indicates this status by pressing the *Stop Production* button on his tablet application. Subsequently, the measurement of the power and the general work task reporting form is shown with the work report summary. In this report form, a worker may add his feedback regarding the manufacturing operations of the part.

In parallel to the manufacturing preparation and manufacturing processes a "Location Tracker" process is running. This process updates the location of orders within the shop floor based on active trackers and beacon devices (iPod touch) which transmit the location of trackers to the central processing system.

The update interval of the tracking may be configured in the process model. In the test scenario, an interval of 5 min was chosen.

The manually and automatically gathered data are summarized in the end of each operation. Thereby, a worker may provide feedback to different workplace aspects

- Reporting change proposals (including the rationale for the change) to the technologist and sales staff
- Time estimate comparison—the actual time spent on manufacturing versus the time initially planned by the technologist
- Description of the error with proposal to repair/restart production

4.3.2   Technical Implementation

The technical case implementation considered the development and set-up of the required hardware and software components at Company A. Figure 4.15 sketches the system architecture in term of hardware and software components and the mutual communication on a general level. Basically, each selected machining workplace is enriched with a beacon device, a tablet for digitized work support and a power consumption metre.

Custom trackers have been developed by the hardware developer of the project. The trackers promote their presence via Bluetooth 4.0 to beacon devices nearby. They integrate a Bluetooth 4.0 RF frontend, enabling the micro-controller to

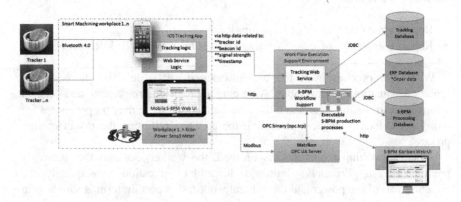

Fig. 4.15 Company A—system architecture

communicate wirelessly with a range of approximately 5 m with other Bluetooth devices. Each tracker is equipped with four LEDs to indicate whether the unit is powered, whether it is functioning correctly or not, and whether it is in proximity range of a beacon. Location trackers broadcast every minute a signal that encodes their identification number, to be detected by beacon devices.

As beacons Apple iPod Touch devices equipped with iOS version 9.2 are used. An iPod app for gathering and transmitting data was built using the Objective-C and iOS Framework. The beacon device represents the workplace it is attached to for location tracking purposes. When the beacon receives the signal from a paired tracker, it passes the tracker ID (encoded in the signal) via a Web service to the backend, together with the signal strength in dBm. The lower the value of signal strength, the greater the distance of the tracker from the beacon device (workplace) and vice versa. This information is used by the Web service to derive the location of the workpiece in terms of the beacon ID that has the highest signal strength for a given tracker. The configuration of the beacon—workplace mapping and the tracker ID and order ID mapping is supported via dedicated S-BPM process logic.

Additionally, workplaces were equipped with non-invasive power measurement sensors. Specifically, Econ Sens3 Power metres were selected since they enable non-invasive power measurement and the accessibility via the Matrikon OPC UA Server. Thus, S-BPM process steps may retrieve data from the sensors via OPC UA refinements (cf. Sect. 3.1.2). The measurement is carried out by applying the Hall effect, without requiring any intervention in electric circuits of the device. The metre is installed on the device feed phases, and its measurement loops are wrapped around each of the three phases on the machine. Parameters such as voltage, frequency and machine capacity can be measured using this device. The measuring device is connected to the network via a standard RJ-45 connector and communicates based on standard Modbus TCP with the OPC UA Server.

The measurement of the current power consumption was intended to infer the machine status and support the automatic determination of preparation-, machine operation- and post-processing times. For inferring the machine status, heuristics for reference values were required. Thus, for each type of machine, measurements were performed to infer the status. For instance, Fig. 4.16 shows measurement heuristics and machine states for the workplace DMG DMF260.

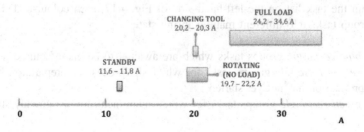

Fig. 4.16 Relationship between machine status and power consumption

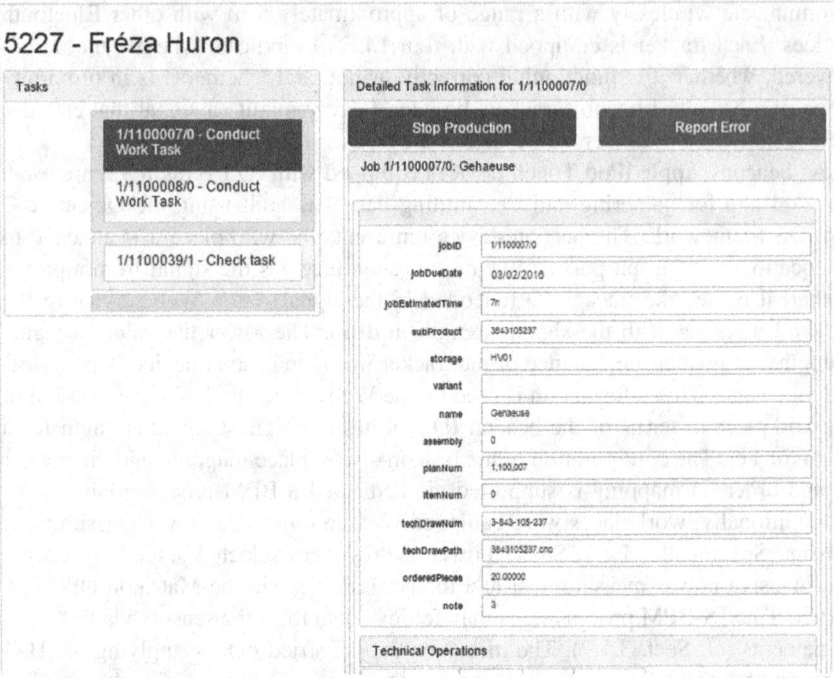

5227 - Fréza Huron

Fig. 4.17 Tablet view for producing a part

A third enrichment of the workplace represented the digitized work support via a tablet and a responsive Web-based workflow user interface. The development of the responsive Web-based user interface applied the presented approach by Kannengiesser et al. (2016). Therefore, in addition to the core production process logic, the user interface logic was modelled within S-BPM UI processes. These S-BPM UI processes serve as basis for the Metasonic Suite to generate dynamic Web pages using the bootstrap framework (http://getbootstrap.com) for responsive design.

Although the look and feel of the developed tablet application differs from the initially developed mock-up prototypes (cf. Sect. 4.2.1), it encodes the main functionalities defined. An example view display when producing a part is given in Fig. 4.17.

Within the task list on the left-hand side of Fig. 4.17, each colour-coded rectangle group tasks into different manufacturing states

- *The blue rectangle* groups tasks which are awaited to be manufactured
- *The yellow rectangle* groups tasks for which the process of preparation began but production has not yet started
- *The green rectangle* groups tasks for which manufacturing has already started

In comparison with the workers, the management accesses the S-BPM processing support via its office PC and the installed Web browser. The developed Kanban UI (cf. Figs. 4.7 and 4.8) represents a Web application accessible via any Web browser. Again, this is a custom interface developed for the case, since the generic Metasonic UI was deemed too rigid and complex.

The "Workflow Execution Support Environment", the "Matrikon OPC UA Server", the "S-BPM Processing" and "Tracking" database were set up and configured on a central server. Moreover, a separate network was installed for the communication among the beacon devices, power metres, tablets and the server components.

The interface to the ERP system introduced in parallel was provided via dedicated database views, which were queried within the S-BPM processes using so-called "DBReader refinements" in Metasonic Suite. The S-BPM processes interface the tracking logic via a Web service call within a dedicated function state.

4.4 Case Evaluation

In addition to formative evaluation activities (see Sect. 4.2.3) informing design and implementation, a summative evaluation framework to evaluate the goal achievement in this industrial case was developed and applied (Fig. 4.18).

This framework defines core case evaluation elements with respect to the case goals, evaluation methods to be applied, and evaluation dimensions. Each case evaluation element comprises (1) a short description, (2) relevant stakeholders, (3) a mapping between goals and IT functionalities related to the case evaluation element, (4) evaluation questions related to the goal achievement, (5) evaluation

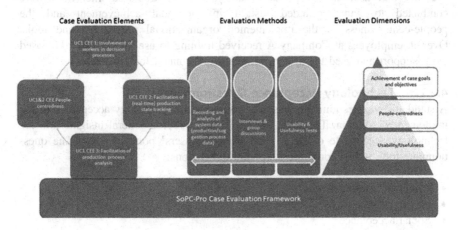

Fig. 4.18 Case evaluation framework for Company A

questions related to usability and usefulness, and (6) data collection methods to be applied. The following four case evaluation elements were defined:

- CEE 1: Involvement of workers in decision processes
- CEE 2: Facilitation of (real-time) production state tracking
- CEE 3: Facilitation of production process analysis
- CEE 4: People-Centeredness

CEE 1–3 mainly address the evaluation dimension "Achievement of case goals and objectives". The evaluation dimensions "People-centeredness" and "Usability/Usefulness" are orthogonal to CEE 1–3. People-centeredness includes developing conditions for higher employee involvement in the production decision-making process. The implemented features were designed to enhance the worker engagement and thus contribute to their self-fulfilment. People-centeredness can be characterized by (1) the People-centeredness of the implemented solution, and (2) the People-centeredness of the project implementation process itself. The dimensions of usability and usefulness combine assessing the solution's practical aspects and its contribution to perceptible changes. In terms of usability, a user is supposed to assess the ease of system operation. For the usefulness dimension, the tool or solution's contribution to the user's performance, productivity and effectiveness is addressed.

4.4.1 Evaluation Steps and Procedure

Qualitative and quantitative data collection and analysis methods were selected to evaluate the case. Subsequently, the evaluation instruments are described. A technology acceptance questionnaire was applied. This questionnaire considers usability and usefulness aspects. In addition, semi-structured interviews were conducted to gain grounded insight in the goal achievement and the people-centeredness of the implemented organizational procedures and tools. Overall, employees at Company A received training to use the provided IT-based work support and used the system in their work context for 2 weeks.

4.4.1.1 Technology Acceptance Questionnaire

A standardized questionnaire was used to assess the technology acceptance of the implemented solution. The results of the survey provide general insights into the technology acceptance of the system from the users' point of view. The questionnaire took into account the following dimensions:

- Perceived usefulness
- Perceived ease of use
- Social acceptance
- Behavioural intention to use the system

Each dimension was operationalized through several statements (items). Users were asked to read each statement and indicate to which extend he or she agrees on a five-point answering scale (absolutely agree to absolutely disagree). Since data from only nine people have been collected, the results of the statistical/quantitative data have to be interpreted carefully. More important, it has to be checked whether these results are consistent with the results of the in-depth qualitative data collection and analysis methods.

Printed questionnaires were distributed among nine employees, including managing director, production manager, technologist and six shop floor workers. The respondents were one woman and eight men. According to the age, the respondents could be divided into three age categories: 20–30 years old (one shop floor worker and executive director), 30–50 years old (four shop floor workers and production manager) and 50+ (technologist and one shop floor worker).

4.4.1.2 Semi-structured Interviews

The qualitative evaluation was operationalized via semi-structured interviews. A list of questions was set up according to the main aspects to be researched. The researchers followed two approaches—a high-level approach and a technical approach. The aim of the high-level approach was to gain insight into respondents' perception of and views on the particular case evaluation elements. The questions were therefore designed as open-ended, focusing on their understanding of and opinion on the feature's impact on performance and the opportunity to use it. The open-ended questions beginning with "how" allowed respondents to express a full, meaningful answer using their own knowledge or feelings.

The technical approach involved more particular, focused questions aiming at getting feedback on the practical use of the implemented features. Consequently, the questions were formed mostly as "have you ever", "what problems have you experienced", "how often have you", etc. They were supposed to provide information on the frequency, problems and (dis)advantages of implemented features.

4.4.2 Summative Evaluation Results

4.4.2.1 Technology Acceptance

Regarding **perceived usefulness**, the responses revealed the following: Three quarter of the respondents indicated a tendency for a disagreement regarding the perceived usefulness. About one quarter of the respondents stated an indifferent attitude regarding the perceived usefulness of the process support.

The **perceived ease of use** was judged as follows: Overall, one-third agreed that the provided system is easy to use. Another third was undecided. The remaining third disagreed with the ease of use. Taking a more detailed look on the items of perceived ease of use, especially learnability and understandability indicated agreement, while especially flexibility and controllability of the support revealed disagreement.

The **social acceptance** was assessed by the respondents quite diverse: Overall, around one-third indicated a positive tendency, one-third was undecided and another third indicated a negative attitude towards social acceptance. Furthermore, the statements towards the **behavioural intention to use the system** indicated that employees do not plan to use the system in the near future (six out of nine respondents).

In summary, the technology acceptance of the implemented work support was assessed as rather average and low, respectively. Although a user-centred design approach was applied within the project at Company A, organizational factors seemed to have a negative impact on the outcome. These factors will be discussed in Sect. 4.4.3.

4.4.2.2 Case Evaluation Elements

The case evaluation elements were investigated by applying qualitative semi-structured interviews. The qualitative analysis complements the quantitative analysis carried out with employees at Company A. The qualitative analysis provides deeper insight into the experience with the implemented solutions, and how the stakeholders perceived the developed features. Subsequently, the results for each case evaluation element are described.

CEE 1: Involvement of workers in decision processes

This element comprises the aspects depicted in Table 4.3. The aspects are detailed in terms of name of the feature, the role using the feature and a general description. Evaluation results with respect to the individual features are stated subsequently.

Proposal of Changes to individual work schedule

In general, respondents consider the option to propose changes to individual work schedules as useful. However, regarding the practical utilization and their experience within the testing phase the answers seem oppositional. Within the testing phase, the six shop floor workers reported no need to request any changes to their daily work schedule. Furthermore, the predominant organizational culture does not encourage workers to propose changes. Workers reported that they face a severe time pressure, try to meet deadlines, and follow what is proposed by the production manager and the technologist. The influence of the established long-term working system on the reluctance to propose changes was also stated by a technologist.

Authorization of change proposals

From the high-level point of view, the production manager assessed the feature as useful, since it digitally records all requests, and a loss of change proposals could be reduced. However, during the live testing phase, the shop floor workers did not request any particular changes of their work flow.

Autonomous decision to request CNC code

The ability to request a CNC program was possible in the formerly established work process at Company A. Now digitized, the shop floor workers tested and used the system in practice. The workers reported concerns on the immediacy of the

Table 4.3 CEE1 aspects

Feature	Role	Description
Proposal of changes to individual work schedule	Shop floor worker	This feature allows shop floor workers changing their work schedules (tasks). Using this feature, a shop floor worker is able to propose a change in the planned production schedule for a particular workplace. The proposed change must be approved by the production manager, before entering the production state
Authorization of change proposals	Production Manager	When a shop floor worker proposes task reordering, the production manager is notified with the change request submitted by the worker. This feature allows him to see the new task order proposal, compare it to the original production plan, and decide to accept/reject the change. After the decision, the shop floor worker is notified
Autonomous decision to request CNC code	Shop floor worker	Using this feature, a shop floor worker can decide whether he needs to be supported with a CNC code from the technologist, or he will write CNC code on his own
Context-sensitive error reporting	Shop floor worker	Shop floor workers are able to report an error occurring during the manufacturing process. When reporting the error, the worker is encouraged to describe the reason why it occurred and propose a solution for fixing the problem if a fix is possible
Work task reporting	Shop floor worker	This feature enables the shop floor workers to report the overall progress of production. The main focus is on gathering real production times so production managers are able to compare the actual time consumed with the time planned by the technologist

response from the technologist. Since technologists are not permanently at their PC, workers fear to lose time when waiting for responses. Finally, especially younger shop floor workers reported their willingness to use the new system.

Context-sensitive error reporting

In general, shop floor workers perceived this feature supportive. Even if they consider it to be of greater benefit for bigger production facilities, workers stated that the feature could also be helpful in their context. However, also related to this feature the immediacy of the response was reported as a potential issue. The implemented process was configured to require the approval of the production manager for fixing an error. Thus, the workers reported that they lose time when waiting for an answer and that they prefer immediate (oral) feedback. Even though, five out of six workers considered digital recording of all reported errors as useful for further order improvements and analyses.

Work task reporting

The technologist and younger staff, including the executive director and one shop floor worker perceived the digitized work task reporting positively. Workers stated that the reporting should be considered for further planning and future price

Table 4.4 CEE 2 aspects

Feature	Role	Description
Display and autonomous selection of work tasks	Shop floor worker	The feature presents a prioritized list of work and allows workers to prepare and conduct certain work tasks
Kanban Board	Production Manager	The management may monitor the current state of operations launched on particular machines on a Kanban Board (cf. Sect. 4.2.1)
Sensor-based location tracking	Shop floor worker, management	Location sensing is concerned with identifying the location of manufactured parts on the shop floor. Each shop floor worker is able to see, as part of the user interface of their tablet, the part's location on the shop floor. The location is visualized in a table with the highlighted workplace the part is closest to

calculations. Older workers seemed to be reluctant due to their preference of paper and pencil.

CEE 2: Facilitation of (real-time) production state tracking

CEE2 comprises the aspects depicted in Table 4.4. In the following, the evaluation results with respect to the individual features are described.\

Display and autonomous selection of work tasks

This feature was already discussed to a great extent in the context of CEE 1. The respondents' answers were mainly linked to statements on the work task reporting and change proposals. An addition was the problem of the simultaneously running system in the company that led to the perception of additional, duplicate work while using the feature.

Kanban Board

The management appreciated the feature's ease of use; the only objection in this matter was manually entering tasks into the system. This is due to the simultaneously implemented and running ERP system. Again, the comment of duplicate work arose, as the system provides similar information as displayed in the ERP system. The opportunity to manage production via digitized work support was considered an advantage. However, the system limitations became apparent in Company A, as the production manager is not permanently present at the computer to follow the tasks. This would require the use of a mobile device by management to immediately receive requests and be able to react.

Sensor-based location tracking

The introduction of a new ERP system in parallel to the case design, implementation and evaluation decreased the initially identified problem of lost parts on the shop floor by manual scanning of items. However, the location sensing has been tested. The respondents stated that it is a good idea but not necessarily required by small companies such as Company A. Furthermore, the duplication of tracking within two systems (new ERP system) and the processing system developed within this case were perceived to increase duplicate work. Related to the technical maturity of the sensors, the respondents noticed that the location updates take too long (sometimes up to 10 min), and the precision of the part location is too coarse grain. Furthermore, they reported for practical application the limited battery lifetime of the active trackers hampering utilization, and trackers getting damaged easily when positioned especially on big parts.

CEE 3: Facilitation of production process analysis

This case evaluation element comprises mainly analysis support features. By gathering context-sensitive process data (power consumption data, location tracking, production time submitted by workers), the system enables analyzing data that could be used in the future production planning process, e.g. for more precise time estimations. This is vital for technologists and the management.

According to a technologist, recognizing the impact of this feature is not possible on short notice, given the short evaluation period in the factory. The data collected on the time spent on particular tasks or orders should be used for further price calculations. The shop floor workers entered the time, but the technologist will only be able to evaluate the usefulness over a longer period. Both, the technologist and manager see the feature's potential not only in further price estimations resulting in more precise price calculations, but also in terms of remunerating employees accordingly.

This feature was also commented on by the executive director and production manager. Both perceive the potential of the feature and its contribution to better price calculations, but need to analyze these features for a longer time period.

CEE 4: People-Centeredness

The shop floor worker perspective

The features presented in CEE 1–2 aimed to increase autonomy and involvement of shop floor workers via digitized work support. However, the interview responses indicate that workers prefer immediate face-to-face communication and fear that digitized communication takes too long and requires too many resources. Especially for their small shop floor with around 35 workers, they consider direct communication to be more effective and efficient than digital support. They are in doubt about the immediacy and added value of digital communication in their company.

Furthermore, the predominant work culture follows a hierarchical organization. Thus, workers do not really question production plans and work schedules, but rather try to implement the targets in the best possible way according to the given specifications. In addition, the time pressure could hinder active participation and involvement of workers.

The management perspective

The shop floor supervisors appreciated the opportunities for employees to be involved in the decision-making and production processes. However, the feedback from shop floor workers questions the willingness of workers to participate in decision-making, proposing and requesting changes. The feature testing showed a kind of reluctance and incredulity of employees towards implemented features and devices. In the case evaluation, the management was able to gain evidence that not only technological changes, such as the developed IT support, need to be carefully implemented, but also organizational changes related to the decision power and encouragement of workers to make them actively contributing to workplace improvement.

4.4.3 Discussion of Evaluation Results

The analysis, design and implementation activities described above were strongly people-centred and aimed to receive early feedback on solutions to direct development accordingly. Hence, one would have expected very positive feedback from the case evaluation. However, (work) reality at Company A has proven to be different. What happened? Why did the project not meet the actual expectations? This section tries to identify factors leading to the given evaluation results.

4.4.3.1 Organizational Changes

Company A experienced several organization changes within the project duration (October 2013–September 2016). Seeking for solutions to stabilize company performance, different managers were hired and alternated predominantly in 2014. The company culture was being adjusted according to the new management's directives affecting employees' positions and personal relations. Especially 2015 brought significant changes to the company's operation. The company management decided to decrease the staff (from 46 to 35), in order to reduce costs and provide higher salaries for the remaining employees. These changes also affected the position of the previous sales manager, Mr. Supportive, who was the main driver of the project implementation in Company A. Mr. Supportive was substantially involved in the implementation and helped to motivate workers to specify the case and propose solutions valuable for them and the project.

The layoff also pertained to three employees who participated in the case formation at the very beginning. Their valuable contributions and motivation within focus groups or internal meetings helped to frame the case implementation that finally led to opposing results in the evaluation.

Simultaneously to the significant organizational changes, the company also faced financial problems, resulting in a potential company closure. This pressure might also have led to the reluctance towards implemented project solutions. Struggling for company survival, the workers rather focused on the daily operation than on comprehensive project implementation.

4.4.3.2 Technical Changes

Aside from the addressed organizational changes, technical changes challenged the project implementation. During the implementation phase, a new ERP system was introduced in Company A. Interfacing this system caused delays in the project progress. Furthermore, the new ERP system covered some functionalities similar to the process support developed within this project. Thus, features have been perceived as duplicated and redundant work effort.

4.4.3.3 Management Commitment

The company changes also affected the management level. In the first two project years, three different managers were in charge with different attitudes towards the project and its implementation. In certain periods, the project was overshadowed by the company's business issues, and its objectives were put to the background. While the company owner together with Mr. Supportive drove the project, some managers perceived the project rather being vague than closely related to the concrete business model of the company. This resulted in some discrepancies in management.

The management installed during the evaluation decided to foster the project implementation, but simultaneously to focus on factory operation, as it pursued cost cutting and similar measures as part of its crisis management. Furthermore, the owner moved to the background, as his daughter became part of the new management team.

4.4.3.4 Takeaways from the Case

Company A and the regional IT consultancy project partner analyzed the project implementation and identified a list of experiences and events that have had impact on the project results. Undoubtedly, the project has created the unique opportunity for both partners to develop innovative solutions, and the project implementation will be definitely useful for different types of production companies. Selected lessons learnt are presented subsequently.

Continuously discuss the project progress with relevant stakeholders

In the course of project implementation, Company A has experienced significant changes on the management and worker level. For instance, due to the required increase of production efficiency, a crisis manager was hired. New managers seemed not always to be committed to the project objectives. Therefore, they did not support the project implementation adequately. It is advisable to discuss continuously the project course with the management and more precisely present the project impact on the current as well as on future production. The same applies to workers. In the case where the workers who were actively involved in the solution design leave the company and the workers who were not part of the design process evaluate the solution, incoherent results are very likely.

Adequately involve workers

The main project objective has been the people-centeredness. The Slovak partners have made a maximum effort to involve all relevant workers, especially shop floor workers. Although shop floor workers have been involved in the project implementation as envisioned in the project proposal, project progress was not adequately presented and discussed with the shop floor workers. The focus of communication was between project managers and higher management representatives at Company A and the regional IT Consultant. This may have circumvented the shop floor workers.

Carefully introduce features related to aspects of "employee monitoring"

Some of the implemented features could be considered to target "employee monitoring" (e.g. power consumption, time monitoring, etc.), although the implemented features were proposed, developed and implemented with regard to people-centeredness. The feedback related to the fear of continuous work monitoring could have had an impact on the worker resistance towards the developed solutions. The employees should to be assured continuously on implementing the solution's benefits for them. Accordingly, monitoring results should be used for triggering people-centred improvements rather than penalties (like salary cuts or negative impact on the position within the company).

Reserve sufficient time for on-site testing

Although the project set out sufficient time for testing, some of the features could not be evaluated to a representative extent—enabling to draw conclusions. Moreover, some of the features show their impact and benefits on a long-term basis. More time should have been reserved for comprehensive tests and deficiency corrections even during initial testing.

Cooperate closely with providers of existing IT systems to be interfaced

During the project implementation, Company A implemented a new information ERP system. Some system features collided with the proposed solutions and, to a certain extent, affected some of the project activities. It would have been more practical for the regional IT consultant to take part in the analytical sessions between Company A and the ERP provider enabling the alignment of redundancies and interfaces.

Changing environments requires agile case specification support

As defined in the original project plan, the use cases were defined in the first project phase at the very beginning. The total project implementation covered the period of 3 years and faced changes on different levels of the company. The changes on the management level, staff layoffs and other implemented changes, had an impact on the relevance of the originally defined case. Changing company conditions led to new requirements that have not immediately been incorporated into the solution. Therefore, an agile approach to specifying requirements and features is considered beneficial to meet industrial demands.

4.5 Conclusion

This case captures the initial situation of Company A, an SME offering the production of atypical, unique and special-purpose machinery, equipment and technological complex units, particularly useful in the automotive and electronic industries. Based on the initial analysis and requirements definition results, the case represents a human-centred design approach accompanied by formative valuation activities. Within the solution development, a novel approach towards modelling S-BPM has been developed and implemented at Company A. The resulting process model also encompasses the integration with sensor technology, in order to support location tracking and power metering of machining operations.

Even though the formative evaluation informed design and implementation to provide adequate solutions for workers, significant organizational changes at Company A during the implementation question the acceptance and benefit of the developed solution as well as the goal achievement with respect to the initial situation.

However, the novel S-BPM approach to modelling the core process as well as the UI process represent major technical innovations. They have been applied for the first time within this project. Furthermore, the enrichment of S-BPM with techniques from human-centred design techniques, such as mock-up prototyping has been experienced as beneficial for aligning different solution ideas among the diverse project stakeholders (i.e. six partners from five different nations).

Reference

Kannengiesser, U., Heininger, R., Gründer T., & Schedl, S. (2016). Modelling the process of process execution: A process model-driven approach to customising user interfaces for business process support systems. In *International Workshop on Business Process Modeling, Development and Support* (pp. 34–48). Springer International Publishing. doi:10.1007/978-3-319-39429-9_3.

Open Access This chapter is distributed under the terms of the Creative Commons Attribution-NonCommercial 4.0 International License (http://creativecommons.org/licenses/by-nc/4.0/), which permits any noncommercial use, duplication, adaptation, distribution and reproduction in any medium or format, as long as you give appropriate credit to the original author(s) and the source, provide a link to the Creative Commons license and indicate if changes were made.

The images or other third party material in this chapter are included in the work's Creative Commons license, unless indicated otherwise in the credit line; if such material is not included in the work's Creative Commons license and the respective action is not permitted by statutory regulation, users will need to obtain permission from the license holder to duplicate, adapt or reproduce the material.

People-Centred Production Design

5

Chiara Di Francescomarino, Mauro Dragoni, Chiara Ghidini,
Nicola Flores, Franco Cesaro, Udo Kannengiesser,
Richard Heininger, Alexandra Totter, David Bonaldi,
Matthias Neubauer and Christian Stary

Abstract

This case reports on a worldwide operating SME producing floor cleaning machines. The SME distinguishes itself from its competitors by providing highly customizable high-quality products. Employees are one of the "most-valuable resources" to the management. However, the initial situation reveals significant improvement opportunities related to the employee involvement and empowerment concerning workplace re-design. The proposed subject-oriented solution aims to involve shop floor workers in workplace (re-)design by providing them structural empowerment means such as social media for suggestion proposals, discussions and negotiations. Furthermore, the newly introduced features are designed to allow for context-sensitive reporting of suggestions and errors. Context-sensitive elicitation provides the basis for analysing impacts of changes (e.g. the affected location or worker) and visualizing potential improvement areas within the shop floor. The generic suggestion and error handling process can be tailored to different organizations. The S-BPM process handling has been

C. Di Francescomarino (✉) · M. Dragoni · C. Ghidini
Fondazione Bruno Kessler, Trento, Italy
e-mail: dfmchiara@fbk.eu

N. Flores · F. Cesaro
Cesaro&Associati, Fumane, Italy

U. Kannengiesser · R. Heininger
Metasonic GmbH, Pfaffenhofen, Germany

A. Totter · D. Bonaldi
ByElement, Schindellegi, Switzerland

M. Neubauer · C. Stary
Department of Business Information Systems – Communications Engineering,
Johannes Kepler University, Linz, Austria

© The Author(s) 2017   113
M. Neubauer and C. Stary (eds.), *S-BPM in the Production Industry*,
DOI 10.1007/978-3-319-48466-2_5

integrated with a semantic wiki allowing for context-sensitive workplace improvement elicitation and change propagation analysis. The evaluation reports on findings in developer workshops, focus groups and user tests conducted in parallel to the design and implementation to ensure a user-centred approach (formative part), and on findings related to the outcome of the case implementations at the given SME (summative part).

5.1 Elicitation and Analysis of the Initial Situation

The case described in this chapter captures an SME operating in the professional cleaning market with the focus on the production of floor cleaning machines on a worldwide level. The company, herein after called "Company B", has about 95 employees and a turnover of about 25 million Euros. It is a family-owned business, as many of the Italian SMEs.

The internationalized system of selling and purchasing enables the company to buy pieces all around the world, assemble cleaning machines, and sell them in more than 70 countries, while competing with large internationally structured companies. The majority of the company's customers are retailers in many different countries all around the globe.

5.1.1 Use Case Definition

The first step towards the elicitation of the requirements was the use case definition according to Leffingwell and Widrig (2003). A number of activities were carried out to define the use case, for instance factory visits and face-to-face workshops, characterized by brainstorming sessions and use case prioritization, definition of key terminologies, development of procedures, virtual and face-to-face workshops, discussions and interviews. Special emphasis was given to the involvement of all stakeholders, in order to capture the different perspectives—ranging from the workers' to researchers' and developers'—following the premises of a participatory people-centred case definition. Specifically, the use case definition was driven by brainstorming and discussion rounds including members of the middle and upper management to develop practices and tools for empowering workers, who were involved in later stages of the project.

In the following, the outcomes of these activities towards the definition of the use case are reported. Especially, the scope of the analysis, with a focus on the initial situation as perceived by the SME, as well as the first steps towards the to-be situation, i.e. purpose, goals and objectives of the use case, are reported. Finally, an initial sketch of the solution is presented in Sect. 5.1.1.

5.1.1.1 Initial Situation

Company B is very sensitive to the quality of its products and achieving high quality standards. These attempts are physically reflected in the factory layout itself. Company B implements a road to quality throughout the whole factory covering areas as the "quality checking—incoming goods area" and the "final check area". Due to the importance of product quality, the quality checking area is one of the most sensitive areas for the company. In this area, incoming goods are identified and the delivered products are quantitatively checked with respect to the due quantity. Quantity control is followed by a conformity check of the received goods with respect to the ones already in the warehouse. Finally, the goods are checked with respect to their quality.

The SME pays a lot of attention to quality issues and tries to foresee problems by carrying out rigorous checks in the receiving and quality checking area. Overseen errors at this stage can lead to problems in the assembly line at a later stage of production. If some pieces are damaged or do not meet the quality standards, they may impact the production process. However, it is time-consuming to check each component. To address this challenge, Company B aims at employees' participation in the suggestion and improvement process. They should make suggestions when reflecting on their actual task accomplishment, and come with proposals for improving their workplace design and the company's performance.

Currently, workers suggest workplace improvements in a completely unstructured way. Suggestions for improvement occur in two different ways:

- **Quality Circles**. Quality circles take place at Company B every week with the production manager and the quality manager. Workers are not directly included in the quality circle. Their suggestions and opinions are only recognized indirectly through one of the managers. These meetings result at least in five suggestions of technical nature at the end of every meeting
- **Face-to-Face Suggestions**. Workers pose suggestions directly (face-to-face) to the responsible manager (e.g.: Quality Manager). These suggestions are discussed by the managers during the quality circle meetings but are not documented or persisted in any form

Workers suggest improvements to the management face-to-face. Sometimes workers immediately receive feedback. Most of the times, however, workers do not know whether their suggestions are taken into account at all. In addition, suggestions could be lost, since they are not documented. The same happens with the process of feedback and rewarding: there is no transparency for workers whether their suggestions are taken into consideration, or why they are rejected.

With respect to the suggestion and improvement process in Company B, the current situation can be described as having no structured procedure processing suggestions, neither for the communication among production workers nor between departments.

5.1.1.2 Goal Definition

Focusing on functionality and efficiency often leads to neglecting a critical factor for sustainable organizational success, the human being. Company B considers humans as one of the most important assets of its operation by putting the worker at the centre of the workplace design. Management aims to engage workers in the (re) design of their work environment and processes. However, the participation of the employees in the workplace re-design is hindered by problems in communication and suggestion making.

Starting with these findings, the goals and the objectives of the use case have been defined in an iterative process involving different stakeholders. The refined and consolidated list of these goals and objectives is summarized in Table 5.1. The development team has identified the global goal as "subject-oriented re-design of production workplaces to empower workers and stimulate teamwork". The empowerment of workers to actively participate in the re-design of their workplace is the umbrella for three sub-goals addressed through the use case implementation at Company B. The first sub-goal is to improve the internal communication and collaboration considering the re-design of workplaces. To achieve this goal, four objectives addressing different aspects have been identified for the use case:

Table 5.1 Consolidated goals and objectives

Overall goal	Goal	Objective
Empower employees to actively participate in workplace re-design	Improve the internal communication and collaboration	Increasing traceability of information flow
		Increasing transparency of communication
		Facilitating meaningful information exchange on workplace improvements
		Application of methods and tools to support collaborative re-design and information exchange
	Increase understanding of relevant work context	Identification of relevant work context by workers
		Enabling workers to create and access context-relevant workplace information supporting context awareness in terms of potential improvements considering processes, communication, collaboration, and workplace designs
		Facilitating the analysis of the impact of changes
	Increase the traceability of suggestions considering error detection	Providing means to supporting access to and creation of context-relevant information for current work task/environment/place

- Increase traceability of information flow. In terms of empowerment this objective could be beneficial for the psychological empowerment dimensions (1) importance and (2) impact
- Increase transparency of communication. Transparency comprises the awareness of employees considering who made a suggestion, who evaluated a suggestion, why it has been implemented or not
- Facilitate meaningful information exchange on workplace improvements. Content needs to be meaningful for its stakeholders
- Application of methods and tools to support collaborative re-design and information exchange. Workplace re-design and proposed suggestions usually affect or could be of value for several employees and/or organizational units. Therefore, a collaborative approach to suggestion making and workplace improvement is necessary

The second sub-goal aims at an increased understanding of the relevant work context. Thereby, work context includes all aspects considering the workplace itself (e.g. temperature, time, conditions of illumination, etc.), as well as all facets regarding the situation of a specific work task (e.g. a worker interacts with others; a worker requires special skills/knowledge to accomplish a certain task, etc.). Accordingly, three objectives should be met:

- Identification of relevant work context by workers
- Enabling workers to identify, create and access context-relevant workplace information, supporting context awareness in terms of potential improvements considering processes, communication, collaboration and workplace designs
- Facilitating the analysis of the impact of changes

5.1.1.3   Sketching the Envisioned Solution

The solution proposed to achieve the objectives of the use case is based on extensions of the following base technologies:

- **Metasonic Suite**—a process management suite for subject-oriented (S-BPM) processes. The Metasonic Suite (https://www.metasonic.de/en) is used for modelling, validating and executing work processes applying the subject-oriented methodology (Fleischmann et al. 2012)
- **MoKi**—a wiki-based collaborative tool for the enterprise modelling. MoKi (Rospocher et al. 2008; Christl et al. 2008; Rospocher et al. 2009; Ghidini et al. 2012) has already been applied to a number of collaborative settings (Casagni et al. 2011; Dragoni et al. 2013), also in multilingual scenarios (Bosca et al. 2014; Dragoni et al. 2014a), and for the analysis of business processes (Dragoni et al. 2014b; Di Francescomarino et al. 2014). MoKi is used for analysing the propagation of workplace changes (including changes related to processes and non-procedural aspects), as well as for supporting discussions, notifications and approvals related to potential workplace improvements

Specifically, these technologies should empower workers in Company B's goods-receiving and quality-checking department by allowing them to:

- Provide access to shared knowledge, thus easing their understanding of procedures
- Improve their workplaces by autonomously suggesting changes, thus increasing their empowerment capabilities
- Exploit semantic knowledge of non-procedural aspects (i.e. "static" concepts or constraints) to analyse, e.g. the impact of changes on other stakeholders
- Provide suggestions, and feedback related to workplace changes, thus improving the internal communication of Company B workers
- Keep track of the provenance and rationale of workplace changes

A possible scenario of how this set of technologies and functionalities can be used in the goods-receiving and quality-check department is shown below (see Fig. 5.1). The "Quality Control" worker becomes aware of potential improvements and would like to propose them to the management. Examples of improvements include changing the temperature in the goods acceptance area, and changing the work procedure. In some cases, the change can be related to non-procedural aspects (technical and workplace modification); in other cases, the change is directly related to a process change (process modification). Moreover, a change analysis could be

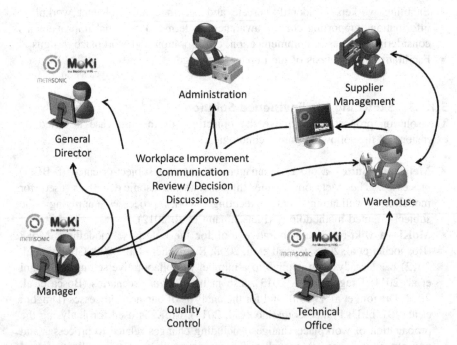

Fig. 5.1 Interactions among goods-receiving and quality-department workers

triggered which would lead to a propagation of the change. The co-workers can be notified and involved in discussions related to already suggested improvements. These discussions, as well as the authorization processes are carried out using the MoKi collaboration features, capturing a network of different stakeholders as shown in Fig. 5.1.

5.1.2 Requirements Elicitation and Analysis

Once the use case had been defined, the requirements elicitation and analysis was started. Based on the activities conducted at Company B to understand stakeholder needs and to define the scope of the use case, additional workshops were carried out to elicit and narrow down requirements within the defined use case. Beyond the functional requirements, a set of technical and organizational requirements have been defined in the requirements engineering process. The requirements engineering approach has been accompanied with setting up a technology acceptance framework.

5.1.2.1 Organizational Requirements

The organizational requirements for this use case are understood as a transition from the current situation ("as-is") to a desired situation ("to-be") at Company B.

The as-is process of making suggestions for workplace improvement at Company B is completely unstructured (see Sect. 5.1.1.1). Suggestions are made by workers directly to their supervisor in a face-to-face interaction, even though the supervisor is not the person in charge of that specific type of issue. In Company B, indeed, it is often the case that the same person is in charge of more than one responsibility (e.g. the person holding the role of Quality Manager also holds the one of Security Manager; the Administrative Manager also holds the role of Human Resource Manager), thus becoming the reference person to whom workers communicate every kind of problem, request and suggestion.

The consequence of this single point of reference is, on the one hand, workers' frustration, lack of self-awareness and trust in the management; on the other hand, it has effects at the production level. For example, in the receiving and quality checking process, in case of goods damages, the Quality Manager has to make decisions on how to proceed. In case of serious damages on goods triggered by a contingent event, or of systematic problems on the same type of items, the Quality Manager is asked to involve other managers, e.g. the Supplier Manager, in the decision-making process. The lack of transparency and traceability of communication makes this process easily subject to delays and unattended requests, thus also potentially causing errors at the production level. No technological means are used for the internal communication at Company B, while an internal network and an ERP server are used for connecting all the partner companies and for managing the administrative and the warehouse department, respectively.

Initial To-Be Process

Figure 5.2 shows the envisioned suggestion making process at the SME. The
displayed Subject Interaction Diagram depicts the interaction of the involved actors,
namely Worker, QM Area manager, Warehouse manager, Purchase manager and
Logistics manager. Additionally, for communication with external process participants, the external subject Supplier is included in this model.

The suggestion making process starts with a worker raising a suggestion and
sending it to the quality area manager. The quality area manager first analyses the
suggestion and provides promptly a first feedback on whether the suggestion will be
further processed or not. In the latter case, the reason for not further following a

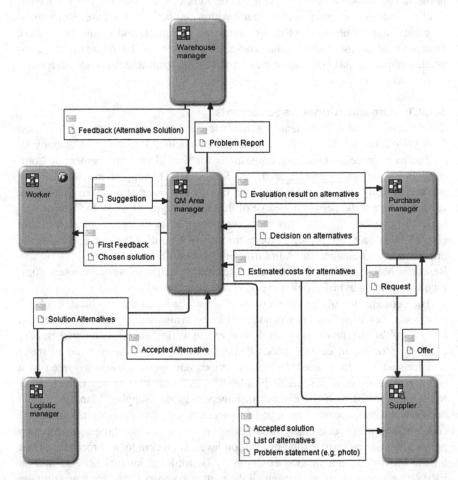

Fig. 5.2 To-be suggestion making process at Company B

suggestion has to be fed back. In case the suggestion is handled further, the quality area manager creates a problem report and sends it to the warehouse manager, who sends back feedback that may contain an alternative solution. The quality area manager also collects solution ideas from other shop floor areas and compiles them into a list of possible solutions. These are called solution alternatives and are subsequently sent to the logistics manager, who decides upon the alternatives. The accepted alternative is sent back to quality area manager. The process is split up in several branches at this stage, according to the concerned decision-makers. Finally, all decision branches are merged into one last action: the worker gets informed about the chosen solution.

5.1.2.2 Functional Requirements

For the elicitation of (functional) requirements user stories have been applied. A user story describes a usage scenario via simple natural language. User stories were defined in a "people-centred" two-stage process involving not only managers but also workers in specifying user stories. In an initial stage, workshops were conducted with the management of Company B, in which a first set of user stories were identified. In a second stage, these user stories were validated by the workers, through workshops in which workers were given the possibility to add, modify or remove (given) user stories. In addition to the user stories, prototypes of as-is and to-be process models were elicited by applying a paper card-based S-BPM modelling approach. These efforts were intended to elicit and validate system requirements engaging the actual stakeholders.

At the end of this process, a final list of consolidated (functional) requirements has been drafted. The requirements related to communication and collaboration can be summarized (from a workers' perspective) as follows:

Req. 1. Easy way to report context-sensitive issues/suggestions, and errors
Req. 2. Control over my suggestions (creation, update, deletion)
Req. 3. Feedback to my suggestion
Req. 4. Getting informed about suggestions that relate to me/my workplace
Req. 5. Receiving comments on suggestions or vote for them
Req. 6. Discussion of suggestions
Req. 7. Status checking of suggestion (approved, implemented, pending, etc.)

Moreover, few requirements related to the non-conformities report and change propagation were also identified. They can be summarized as follows:

Req. 8. Support of the analysis of what and who is how affected by a certain (process) change
Req. 9. Definition and application of rules and policies that can be triggered by a certain change
Req. 10. Reporting, analysis and visualization of non-conformities (e.g. errors for certain types of products).

5.1.2.3   Technical Requirements

A set of technical requirements was identified based on the specific IT environment at Company B and the defined usage of the base technologies (i.e. Metasonic Suite, and MoKi). Company B imposed the following requirements:

- For safety and privacy reasons all data recorded in the technologies to be developed needs to be stored on Company B servers
- A reuse of Company B's existing desktop computers on the shop floor is preferred for any IT solution to be developed

Requirements stemming from the Metasonic Suite relate to its multiple interlinked components. Depending on the desired usage, these components can be installed either on a single system or in a distributed environment. The individual components for the Web applications are available as packed applications (WAR files) to support straightforward deployment on different servlet containers (for example, Apache Tomcat). Typically, the Metasonic Suite requires a JDK (Java Development Kit), a MySQL database and an Apache Tomcat servlet container.

MoKi is developed on top of the MediaWiki[1] package that is based on a standard PHP/MySQL framework. MoKi requires a Web server environment supporting PHP and MySQL. Since MoKi is a Web-based application, it requires the availability of an internal network allowing the connection from a local workstation placed in the production line to the central server on which MoKi is installed. Furthermore, a Web browser needs to be available at the client workstation.

5.2   Process and Solution Design

An iterative approach has been taken in the design phase. The main milestones of this iterative approach can be summarized by the following two steps: (i) the design of a first prototype satisfying the users' requirements; (ii) the iterative refinement of such a prototype. Besides the goals and requirements collected in the requirement and elicitation analysis (Sect. 5.1.2), both steps have been accompanied by so-called formative evaluation activities.

In this section, we sketch the actions and the methodologies that were taken for formative evaluation (Sect. 5.2.1). We also detail the first prototype release (Sect. 5.2.2). Finally, we report on the refinements that have been applied to the prototype as a consequence of the feedback obtained from the formative evaluation, in order to develop a second prototype (Sects. 5.2.3 and 5.2.4).

---

[1]http://www.mediawiki.org.

5.2.1   Formative Evaluation Framework Guiding the Design

The formative evaluation framework has been designed and implemented according to the steps of Stufflebeam and Shinkfield (2011) for the Company B use case. Overall, multiple Skype meetings for aligning activities as well as a face-to-face meeting were conducted. In doing so, the evaluation team:

- Agreed on the formative evaluation framework along the six steps of Stufflebeam and Shinkfield (2011)
- Identified relevant stakeholders based on the use case
- Identified the key elements to be investigated
- Identified three overall (high level) evaluation dimensions (i.e. Usability, Usefulness, Social Acceptance)
- Identified an overall data collection approach (i.e. developer workshops, focus groups, user, prototype tests)

In the following, we detail the instantiation of the six steps of Stufflebeam and Shinkfield (2011) for the Company B use case. The **stakeholders** involved in the formative evaluation are:

- *Technology providers.* This group comprises technology developers as well as solution designers and providers
- *Users.* This stakeholder group includes end-users, i.e. the workers and the management at Company B
- *Evaluators.* Evaluators conduct the formative evaluations. They are responsible for planning, designing and analysing the surveys. Evaluation experts support the evaluators
- *Others.* The formative evaluation could also consider and incorporate other stakeholders if required, e.g. worker union, policy makers (e.g. regarding occupational safety, occupational health and safety practitioners for the involved factories)

The following three **key evaluation elements (KE)** have been identified to be evaluated in the formative evaluation activities at Company B:

- KE1: Change Analysis and Propagation Prototype
- KE2: Prototype for Supporting Re-Design with Collaborative Functionalities
- KE3: Contextual Work Models for S-BPM

The selection and definition of the **key evaluation questions** correspond to the issues raised in the requirements defined in Sect. 5.1.2.3. Thereby, the three dimensions—(1) Technical aspects, (2) Usefulness and Usability and (3) Social Acceptance—guided the definition of the key evaluation questions.

Different **data collection methods** were selected, prepared and used for the evaluation of the use case: the evaluation started with a developer workshop, followed by one or more focus groups with the potential users. The results of these activities were then used to specify, plan and develop the user tests. Observations (e.g. task accomplishments, performance tests) and surveys (e.g. standardized and open questionnaires, interviews, discussions) were conducted and analysed in a qualitative and quantitative way.

5.2.2 The First Prototype Design

The goals and requirements collected in the requirements elicitation and analysis (Sect. 5.1.2) and the ones collected through the formative evaluation (see Sect. 5.2.1) were used to drive the development of the first release of the prototype developed for Company B, named the *Collaboration and change propagation prototype*.

The aim of the prototype was to support the achievement of the main goal of the use case: The empowerment and involvement of workers in the (re-)design of production workplaces. To do so, communication and collaboration among stakeholders (including workers and managers) need to be supported to foster sharing, discussing and negotiating ideas, suggestions or issues related to certain workplaces. The resulting communication and collaboration artefacts typically address specific dimensions of workplaces, such as tasks, tools for task accomplishment, social factors or environmental factors relevant for (re-)design. These dimensions characterize the context of the various statements provided by stakeholders (suggestion, error report, idea, etc.).

A prerequisite for change propagation analysis is the collaborative, (semi-) structured collection of workplace-related data as well as its semantic representation. Having a semantic representation of workplace-related data at hand, allows developing mechanisms to reason upon the collected data, e.g. localizing the impact of changes, performing statistical analyses of workplace-related data, and checking for the violation of rules and policies.

5.2.2.1 Prototype Description

The prototype described in this section applies the enabling technologies introduced in Sect. 5.1.1.3 to provide a means for supporting people-centred workplace re-design and for meeting the requirements identified at Company B. Thereby, it integrates different design-relevant workplace aspects, e.g. organizational procedures in terms of process models, errors within daily operations (process execution level), and relevant contextual dimensions (e.g. environmental, social, tool dimension).

The prototype is composed of two main modules: a module dedicated to the collaborative acquisition of knowledge and data (*Collaboration Module*) and a module devoted to assist users in the management of the acquired data (*Change Propagation and Analysis Module*). The *Collaboration Module* is composed of two submodules:

- A submodule that workers can use for reporting problems related to their workplace and suggestions for the workplace improvement, and
- A special instance of the suggestion module, i.e. a submodule to be used by workers to report errors/non-conformances related to the processes they carry out in their daily work (e.g. errors related to the incoming goods)

The *Change Propagation and Analysis Module* focuses on providing means for analysis as well as supporting the propagation of changes that are suggested by the workers or of changes, imposed by the actual behaviours of the system.

Figure 5.3 shows the conceptual architecture of the *Collaboration* submodules and the *Change Analysis and Propagation* module described above. The figure shows how the two *Collaboration* submodules, together with the *Re-design module*, provide the input for the *Change Analysis and Propagation Module*. Specifically, both, the S-BPM models used for describing the operational procedure, and the context information, are used for building the contextual domain knowledge. In turn, users' suggestions, change suggestions and other analysis output of the *Change Analysis and Propagation Module* act as input for the *Re-design module*.

The different modules and functionalities are accessible through simple interfaces, thus allowing workers with no IT background for quick and easy use of the prototype. In the following, each (sub-)module in terms of its functionality is be described in more detail.

Suggestion Management Submodule

The *Suggestion Management* submodule is in charge of collecting and managing issues and suggestions by workers, according to a generic suggestion handling process. This process (involving the workers, the management and their communication) can be refined and instantiated according to the specific organization in

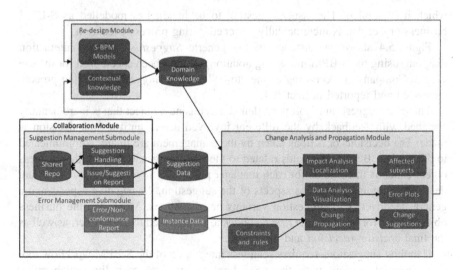

Fig. 5.3 Conceptual architecture of the prototype

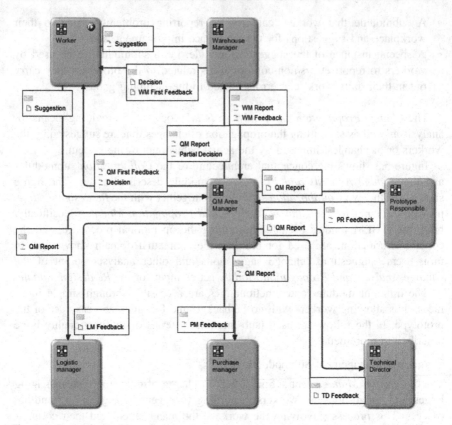

Fig. 5.4 Suggestion making process

which it is applied. The issue/suggestion to be handled is modelled as S-BPM business object that is incrementally enriched during process execution.

Figure 5.4 shows an instance of the generic *Suggestion Making* interaction diagram (using the S-BPM modelling notation) that has been specialized for the use case in Company B, according to the "to-be" S-BPM *Suggestion Making* process envisaged and reported in Sect. 5.1.

The issue/suggestion report is modelled as a business object that is incrementally enriched with feedback by the different involved actors until a final decision is made. The decisions or actions taken by the management are finally communicated to the worker. Besides the fields related to the issue/suggestion report, the business object contains three fields for each manager potentially involved. These fields are devoted to report the positive aspects of the suggestion, the negative aspects and a general feedback, e.g. suggestion variants or adaptations. Moreover, the business object allows for handling the *first feedback* to be provided to the worker, as well as the final decision (*decision* and *rationale*).

Handling suggestions requires seamless integration of the S-BPM workflow tool (in charge of dealing with the procedural knowledge) with the collaborative instrument devoted to acquire context-sensitive issues and suggestions by workers (MoKi). The solution envisaged for achieving such an integration consists of a shared repository and a set of services built on top of the workflow tool enabling the communication between the two components. Both, the *Issue/Suggestion Report* component (MoKi-based interfaces), and the *S-BPM Workflow* component (Metasonic Flow), read and write information from/to the shared repository.

The *Suggestion* submodule provides users with two features: (i) the issue/suggestion management and (ii) the discussion management, which allows workers to discuss and share opinions, not only about proposed suggestions but also about other topics of interest. Specifically, concerning the issue/suggestion management, three main functionalities are provided: the suggestion creation, visualization and update. Workers can report their suggestions using the form reported in Fig. 5.5. Specifically, they can introduce a description of the issue/problem they

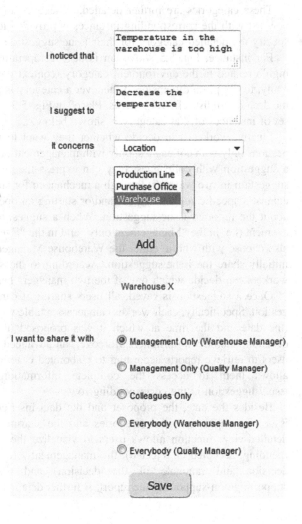

Fig. 5.5 New suggestion form

have observed or/and the suggestion proposed to solve the problem. Furthermore, workers can specify the category an issue or a suggestion refers to via a multi-selection list. The top context categories in the list correspond to the dimensions captured in the "work models" defined in the Contextual Design approach showing (cf. Beyer and Holtzblatt 1998; Holtzblatt and Beyer 2014). We took into account the following context dimensions and corresponding models:

1. Communication/information dimension of workplace context captured in the Flow model
2. Activity dimension of workplace context captured in the Sequence model
3. The environment dimension of workplace context captured in the Physical model
4. Tool/document dimension of workplace context captured in the Artefact model
5. Social/cultural dimension of workplace context captured in the Cultural model

These categories are further detailed. Whenever a (sub-)category is selected, a new list with the corresponding instances is provided to the users so that they can specify the detailed category for their issue/suggestion.

For instance, Fig. 5.5 shows an issue ("Temperature in the warehouse is too high") related to the environment category (context dimension) and, more specifically, to the place dimension. Whenever a category is selected among the ones in the drop-down list (cf. "It concerns: Place" in Fig. 5.5), an updated list containing a set of instances of that category is shown below.

Finally, workers can decide whether they want to share their issues and suggestions only with colleagues, only with management or both. Whenever they share a suggestion with colleagues, they can express their opinion about the proposed suggestion in two ways: (i) through a mechanism for supporting or taking position against a specific suggestion; (ii) and/or starting an open (i.e. free-text) discussion about the reported issue/suggestion. When a suggestion is shared with the management (i.e. in the "Management only" and in the "Everybody" case), workers can also choose with whom, either the Warehouse Manager or the Quality Manger, to initially share the issue/suggestion. According to the suggestion making process, workers can decide which one of the two managers has to be involved first.

Once a suggestion is saved, all users sharing it can read and discuss the suggestion. Specifically, each worker can access a table with the latest ten suggestions (the date and the time at which it was proposed, the proposer as well as the decision) shared with him/her. Moreover, an advanced search functionality allows users to retrieve reports according to elaborated criteria. A detailed-view function allows them to access the complete information related to the specific issue/suggestion in the corresponding row.

Besides the date, the proposer and the data inserted by the proposer (i.e. the issue, the suggestion, the categories and the sharing policy), the popup of the detailed-view function allows users to visualize the current status of the report (pending, accepted or rejected), the management's feedback (first feedback, final decision and rationale of the decision) and the number of colleagues supporting/non-supporting the report. A further detailed view about the status of the

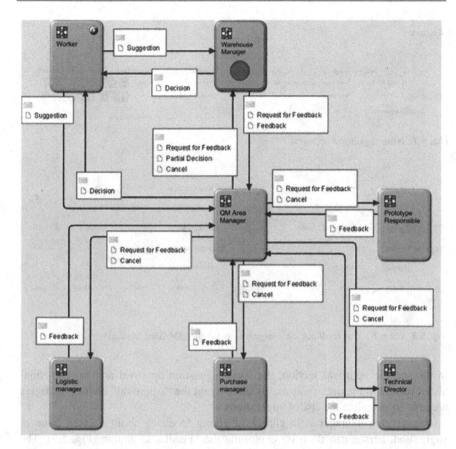

Fig. 5.6 Detailed view of the current status of the process

current suggestion is available when clicking on the "View Status" button (see Fig. 5.6): a red circle indicates the subject currently in an active state (in the Suggestion Management process it is the manager who is currently handling the suggestion). Finally, the popup provides the colleagues of the proposer with the possibility to rate the report through the "I like/I don't like" buttons, as well as to discuss about it ("Discussion" button). The rating buttons increase the counters of the supporters and the opponents for a specific issue, while the discussion button opens a new popup enabling to start or continue a discussion on a certain topic.

In case an issue/suggestion is not shared with the management, it can be updated by the proposer by clicking on the "Update" button in the suggestion menu. Subsequently, users may edit and update all the data related to the selected issue/suggestion or remove it.

When, instead the issue/suggestion is shared with the management, the *Suggestion Making* process (reported above) is triggered and proposers cannot update it anymore. Regarding suggestion management, managers can access reports

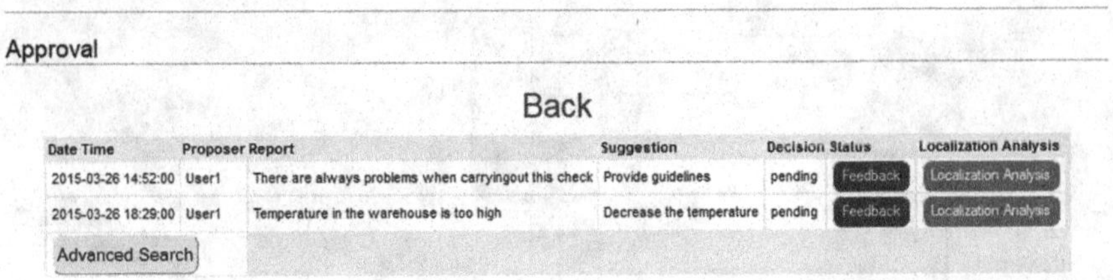

Approval

Fig. 5.7 Issue/suggestion approval

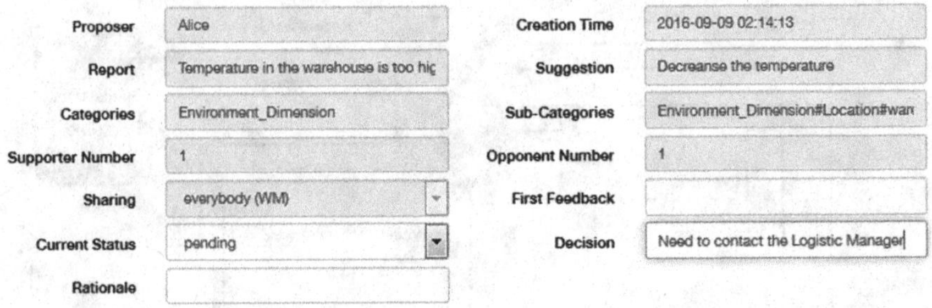

Fig. 5.8 Form for first feedback on a suggestions for the QM Area Manager

in the specific approval section, the issue/suggestion approval and two functionalities related to the data analysis. By clicking on the "Approval" button, managers are able to visualize the list of suggestions.

Whenever a manager is in charge of giving feedback about a given issue or suggestion, he/she can do it by exploiting the "Feedback" button (Fig. 5.7). The "Feedback" button will provide him/her an input form. For instance, Fig. 5.8 shows the input form for the quality manager when providing initial feedback to a suggestion. In this form the quality manager is able report his/her quick feedback about the suggestion, e.g. how long it could take to further process it, and why, or who needs to be involved.

The discussion-management feature, can be accessed both by starting a discussion associated to a specific report, and through a dedicated menu. The discussion menu offers the possibility to start a new discussion by providing a topic and related content, to visualize existing discussions, and to participate in a discussion already started. In addition, for discussions, the advanced search feature can be exploited to retrieve desired discussions.

Error Management Submodule

The error management submodule takes care of collecting the non-conformance reports by workers in their everyday work. Non-conformances can be discovered at different stages of the inspection process, and can be classified according to different criteria. The error management submodule enables workers

- To autonomously report these problems in the system in a simple and efficient way, thus giving them a more active role in the work, while decreasing the load of a single responsible of the error reporting
- To share problems and non-conformances with colleagues, thus making everybody aware of the problems and the issues already reported, and
- To track the non-conformances in a systematic way, thus providing useful data for further analysis

This submodule provides users, similarly to the suggestion management submodule, with three main functionalities: creation of a new error, error visualization and error update.

Workers can report observed errors using the form in Fig. 5.9. Specifically, a multi-selection drop-down list allows them to select the error reporter(s), and the type of error. During the inspection process, for instance, the incoming goods are subject to different checks (DDT^2 Check, package integrity check, quantity check, sample check and quality check). The radio buttons in the form allow workers to select in which of these checks (i.e. at which step of the inspection process) the non-conformance has been detected. Moreover, the interface allows for reporting the codes of the product and product supplier. This information can be read with a barcode reader in order to speed up the process and reduce errors occurring in manual data insertion. Filling in the other fields of the form depends on the type of check selected by the user. According to the type of check, the most common categories of non-conformances for that check are shown to the worker, thus enabling him/her to select the most appropriate. For instance, in the package integrity check case, the worker can provide a textual description and, if necessary, upload a picture proving the problem noticed in the packages (see Fig. 5.9).

Finally, the tool offers functionality allowing users to import special types of non-conformances from a csv file. The user can choose whether to manually insert a single error, or to load a number of new errors from a csv file.

The error visualization functionality makes it possible to visualize the last ten reported errors, by showing at a first glance, the date, the reporter, the error check type and the category(ies). Finally, the advanced search button allows users to search for a particular error by specifying advanced search criteria, as in the case of suggestions, and a view button for each error, allows workers to access the detailed content of the error report.

A popup enables workers to visualize the information reported at the creation of the error (reporter, error check type, description and categories, product, supplier and DDT barcodes, as well as a link to the picture associated to document the event), the date and a link to visualize the specific check phase in the corresponding S-BPM process diagram. Furthermore, the popup visualizing the details of each non-conformance provides an "Update" button allowing workers to immediately update a non-conformance report. In such a form, the worker can change each of

---

^{2}DDT is an acronym for the Italian expression "documento di transporto" (English: transportation document).

Fig. 5.9 New error—
package integrity error

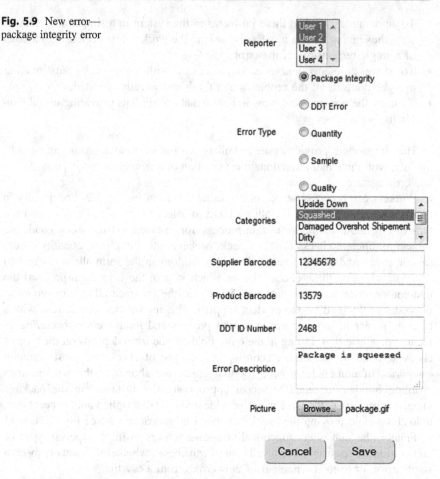

the fields she/he has inserted (including uploaded pictures for errors). Moreover, the form offers the possibility to completely remove the reported error. Such an update form is accessible not only through the "Update" button from the error visualization popup, but also through the "Update" button in the error menu. Such a button provides users with the classical table with the latest ten reported errors for the error update. If the non-conformance is not among those errors, the advanced search can be carried out by clicking on the corresponding button.

Change Analysis and Propagation Module

This section describes ways to analyse the impact and the propagation of changes based on the collection of workplace knowledge. *Impact analysis and change propagation* are concerned with identifying the potential consequences (side effects) of a potential local change for other areas of a system as well as for the system as a whole (Bohner and Arnold 1996). The *change analysis and propagation module* provides three main sets of analysis functions: data analysis visualization, impact analysis visualization and change propagation.

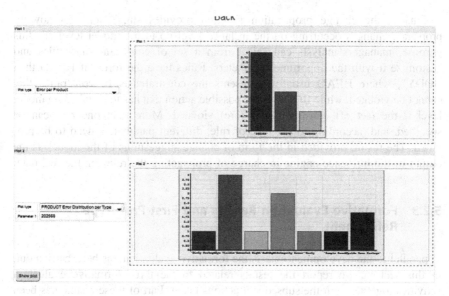

Fig. 5.10 Plot visualization

The purpose of data analysis visualization is to provide a visual representation of the instance data, e.g. related to non-conformances. Specifically, the functionality allows for the parallel visualization of two plots, each showing the trend of the instance data. The manager or the analyst can select, for each of the two plot areas, a specific type of plot, and configure the corresponding parameters. At this point, managers and analysts can visualize the desired trend in the plots. For instance, Fig. 5.10 shows the first plot reporting the number of errors per type of product, and a second one reporting the errors across the different error categories for the product with a specific code.

The impact analysis localization function aims at providing insights into the suggestions proposed by workers by showing which workers are potentially affected by the report. This function can be utilized by managers and analysts by clicking on the "Localization Analysis" button nearby each issue/suggestion in the approval form in Fig. 5.7, in order to understand which workers could be affected by the specific issue and/or suggestion. The *Localization Analysis* functionality relies on the categories defined by the workers and on the domain knowledge encoded in the system in order to understand which subject could be affected by the report. For instance, let us consider the suggestion related to the temperature decrease and the domain knowledge about the subjects that *work_in* the *warehouse* (e.g. the *warehouse_manager*, the *ddt_checker*, the *quantity_checker*, the *quantity_rechecker* and the *quality_checker*). The subjects affected by the suggestion will be the subjects that are related via a *work_in* relation to the warehouse. The concrete people affected by the suggestion report will be those who are assigned to perform the subject behaviour.

Finally, the change propagation function provides suggestions on how to propagate changes occurring on the instance level up to the model level. To this purpose, managers/analysts can select from a set of constraints and rules and customize it with the opportune parameters. Rules have the form "if HEAD then BODY", where HEAD usually represents the constraint/set of constraints that cannot be violated, while BODY is the possible action that has to be taken on model level if the (set of) constraint(s) is (are) violated. More than one rule can be specified, and, according to the type of rule, different parameters need to be provided. The result, provided in the form of change suggestions of the model, is the output of the inference engine in charge of propagating the rules on the real data.

5.2.3 Formative Evaluation Results and First Prototype Refinement

In parallel to the development phase, the formative evaluation has been carried out. In this section, we report the results related to the three formative evaluation activities together with the subsequent actions taken. Part of these results has been used for the definition of the first prototype and part for its refinements.

5.2.3.1 Developer Workshops
During the developer workshops some Critical Technical Issues (**TI**) related to KE1/2/3 have been discussed between developers and evaluators. They are reported in the following, and grouped according to the main prototype functionalities they refer to.

- Suggestion and Feedback Management (SFM)

    - TI_SFM1. User-friendly interfaces for the report and suggestion involvement of workers
    - TI_SFM2. MoKi/MC-Flow integration

- Error Management (EM)

    - TI_EM1. Quick and easy-to-use interface for the everyday use by workers.

- Change Analysis and Propagation (CAP)

    - TI_CAP1. Data acquisition from a proprietary ERP software. In Company B a proprietary ERP IT solution is used for collecting data related to everyday errors. Since these data represent the input for the Change Analysis and Propagation module, possible solutions have been discussed for the acquisition of the data

- Workplace Re-design (WR)

  - TI_WR1. MoKi/MC-Build integration

5.2.3.2   Focus Groups

Two focus groups—Focus Group I and Focus Group II—were conducted at Company B in order to investigate and collect feedback about KE1, KE2 and KE3:

1. *Suggestion and Feedback Management* mainly investigated during Focus Group I
2. *Error Management* mainly investigated during Focus Group I
3. *Workplace Re-design* mainly investigated during Focus Group II

Focus Group I has been conducted with 8 users, including both warehouse workers and managers. Focus Group II has been conducted one month later and involved the same 8 employees. In both cases, goals and purposes of the focus group were introduced to the users.

In Focus Group I, a prototype based on dynamic mock-ups was shown to the users in order to allow them to get an idea of the dynamics required for the collaborative reporting of *issue and suggestions* as well as of *errors*. Focus Group II was conducted at Company B to collect and gather information and feedback to the context dimensions. The focus group was split into 2 sessions, one together with the workers and one with their superiors. The questions for the workers addressed the understanding of work context dimensions (see Sect. 5.2.2.1) and motivational aspects. The workers were asked to provide samples related to the defined work context dimensions "Tools", "Communication and Information", "Task and processes", "Environment" and "Cultural/Personal". We explored identical issues involving the management. Additionally some questions regarding re-design topics, e.g. the evaluation of work issues and related business analytics were discussed with the management. Based on their experience all workers were able to report several work issues for all the work context dimensions. The focus group showed that the general concept of the proposed workplace context dimensions is well understood, and thus applicable for the workers.

In the following the feedback gathered from the focus group participants is reported. Results are organized per prototype functionality according to Acceptance Issues (**AI**), Usefulness Issues (**UI**) and Design Issues (**DI**).

Suggestion and Feedback Management (SFM)

Acceptance of Suggestion and Feedback Management (AI_SFM)
Workers at Company B provided positive feedback with respect to means for communication and suggestion support through electronic instruments (rather than by means of face-to-face communication). Workers perceived this kind of tools as helpful to allow them to keep track of the reported issues and suggestions. However, they did not have a shared opinion about the possibility to report their issues directly to the

upper management [AI_SFM1]. Some of them would like, when it is the case, to directly communicate with the owner, while others do not feel that to be necessary.

The main concern workers have with respect to using the presented solution for reporting problems and suggestions is related to the possibility that their input is **neglected** by the management [AI_SFM2]. Management, on the other hand, is mainly afraid that workers could not **actively participate** in the project and that could limit their suggestions in the system to few instances. They are not convinced that receiving feedback would for sure motivate workers to make their proposals, also because not all the proposals can be implemented. A second concern is related to the **anonymity** issue. Few workers would prefer to have the possibility to make anonymous suggestions, while the others do not see the need to keep their suggestions and reports anonymous [AI_SFM3]. Last but not least, managers do not believe that the proposed technology-based solution can be fast and they do not want it to interfere with the workers' work [AI_SFM4].

Perceived Usefulness of Suggestion and Feedback Management (UI_SFM)

The main expectation workers have with respect to the use of electronic support for communication is getting feedback from the management [UI_SFM1]. They hope this feature could allow them to work better and to find actual solutions for their problems. Moreover, both workers and managers believe that introducing electronic means for reporting issues and suggestions would be useful for traceability purposes. Managers hope that workers can be actually active in providing solutions and that the system could help in improving the company process and climate, fostering the workers' understanding.

Design of Suggestion and Feedback Management (DI_SFM)

Workers would like to have the possibility to provide feedback to colleagues' suggestions [DI_SFM1]. Managers, on their side, would like to support the electronic answer also with the verbal communication in order not to neglect the human dimension. Moreover, for security and external access reasons, managers do not like the idea of using electronic devices outside of the workplace [DI_SFM2].

Workplace Re-design (WR)

Acceptance of Workplace Re-design (AI_WR)

Workers do not have particular concerns about collecting issues and suggestions together with the contextual dimension(s) they belong to (see Sect. 5.2.2.1). On the other hand, management believes that being aware of the work context and acquiring information is in general important to better organize the work.

Design of Workplace Re-design (DI_WR)

Workers believe the most important aspects for (the improvement of) their workplace relate to the communication/relationship dimension and to the procedural one. The view is only partially shared by some of the managers, who believe that company's procedures have already been optimized at the best and that special care has already been given by the company to the communication. Moreover, workers and managers also identified concrete examples of workplace issues/suggestions referring to the tool, environment, as well as the cultural social environment category [DI_WR1].

5.2.3.3 User Tests

Two user tests—User Test I and User Test II—were conducted at Company B in order to investigate and collect feedback about the following main components of KE1/2/3:

1. Suggestion and Feedback Management during User test II
2. *Error Management* during User test I
3. Change Analysis and Propagation during User test II

User test I was conducted with 7 users, while User Test II was conducted few months later and involved 5 warehouse workers and 1 manager. In both cases an introduction about the purpose and the goal of the user tests were provided to the participants. Later on, a demo about the prototype functionalities to be investigated in the specific user test was shown to the users.

Specifically, in User test I, the functionalities of the *Error Management* component were shown to the users. In User test II, first the *Suggestion and Feedback Management* component was demonstrated to workers, and in the second phase, it was presented to the managers by showing them how to provide feedback to the workers. Finally, in the third phase, the *Change Analysis and Propagation* module was presented to the manager, who is responsible for this type of analysis. After each presentation session, users have been observed by at least an observer while accomplishing simple tasks exercising the different functionalities to be evaluated. For instance, workers were asked to simulate a situation in which they need to report an issue, using the functionality for the creation of a new issue of the *Suggestion and Feedback Management* component.

Finally, after users had experienced the components, they were asked to fill in a questionnaire (inspired by the ISONORM 9241/10), in order to capture their perception about ease of use, efficiency, ease of understanding, usefulness, and overall impressions and suggestions about the system. The items were mostly questions on a 5-point Likert scale (where 1 = *I strongly agree* and 5 = *I strongly disagree*).

Suggestion and Feedback Management

The following Functionalities (**F**) have been investigated for the *Suggestion and Feedback Management* (**SFM**) during the user tests:

F1_SFM. Creation of a new issue and suggestion report
F2_SFM. Retrieval and visualization of a suggestion report
F3_SFM. Suggestion discussion reply
F4_SFM. Suggestion voting
F5_SFM. Suggestion status
F6_SFM. Retrieval and update of a suggestion report
F7_SFM. Advanced search of a suggestion report

F8_SFM. Discussion creation
F9_SFM. Suggestion feedback by managers

The findings related to the functionalities are described in the following. Findings are reported as USability Issues (USI) related to the Suggestion and Feedback Management (USI_SFM):

- Issues related to the capability to describe itself:

  – Some labels containing terms not translated from English to Italian (because terms sometimes used in Italian) were not clear for the users [USI_SFM1]
  – Some labels were not clear for users who did not understand the meaning of the corresponding field or button [USI_SFM2]

- The labels of some of the buttons are difficult to read [USI_SFM3]:

  – Sometimes users were a bit confused about which context dimension (among the proposed ones) to associate to the suggestions [USI_SFM4]

- Issues related to the navigability of the system:

  – When the number of items in lists is too high, users found it difficult to use the advanced search in order to be able to visualize older items [USI_SFM5]
  – Sometimes, after a save or an update action, the interface is redirected to the main menu, thus making users confused about the action carried out [USI_SFM6]

- Issues related to its capability to fit the user needs:

  – Managers asked about the possibility to receive e-mail notifications [USI_SFM7]
  – Managers asked about the possibility to refine the designed suggestion process [USI_SFM8]
  – Managers asked about the possibility to export the stored suggestions [USI_SMF9]

- Issues related to its efficiency:

  – The tool was slow [USI_SFM10]

User test questionnaire results—Suggestion and Feedback Management
After each user test, the users filled in a questionnaire. The results related to the main items can be summarized as follows:

- *Perceived Ease of use.* All users (absolutely) agree on the ease of learning to handle the module. Only one out of 6 users declared to be not sure about the overall ease of use of the module. Overall, however, users agreed on the ease of use of the module

- *Perceived Efficiency.* Overall, users do not have a homogeneous perception of the extra time required for using the module. However, in general they disagree about the fact that using the suggestion module would require a huge quantity of extra time. They rather perceive they have enough knowledge and resources
- *Perceived Usefulness.* Concerning the capability of the module to improve the accomplishment of personal tasks, users showed some doubts, though still overall resulting in a positive evaluation. However, overall, users totally agree about the positive effect on introducing the module in their working environment
- *Positive Aspects.* Among the most appreciated benefits the users expect from this specific module, is the improvement of the collaboration between workers and managers, as well as the workers' empowerment

Error Management

The following Functionalities (**F**) of the **Error Management** (**EM**) module have been investigated:

F1_EM. Creation of a new error report and picture upload
F2_EM. Retrieval and visualization of an error report
F3_EM. Retrieval and update of an error report
F4_EM. Advanced search of an error report

The findings related to the functionalities are described in the following as Usability Issues of the **Error Management** (**USI_EM**):

- Issues related to its capability to describe itself:

  - Some labels were not clear for the users, who did not understand how to use the corresponding field or button [USI_EM1]
  - For some inputs it was not clear to users whether the input is compulsory or not [USI_EM2]

- Issues related to the navigation elements of the system:

  - Some of the buttons in the interface are not easy to find [USI_EM3]. For instance, they found it difficult to find the "Back" button in the interface
  - Some functionalities in the system cannot be accomplished in an efficient way [USI_EM4]. For instance, they found it inefficient to update an error when they visualize it. Indeed this would require users to close the current visualization popup (see Fig. 5.15), go back to the error management menu, and press the update button rather than having the possibility to directly update the visualized error

- Interfaces had a resolution not fitting the use of monitors at the shop floor in Company B, thus demanding users a lot of effort with the scrolling bars [USI_EM5]

- Issues related to its capability to fit the user needs:

  - Users asked about the possibility of using different devices [USI_EM6]. For instance, they proposed the use of tablet or smartphones for the creation of suggestion reports

- Issues related to its efficiency:

  - The tool was slow [USI_EM5]

User test questionnaire results—Error Management
After each user test, the users filled in a questionnaire. The results related to the main items can be summarized as follows:

- *Perceived Ease of Use.* Overall users *agree* about the ease of use of the module. Specifically, they all (absolutely) *agree* about the ease of use when learning to use the tool and the ease of using it as they want
- *Perceived Efficiency.* All users (absolutely) *agree* about the fact that they have the needed resources to use the module and only one *has doubts* about having the required knowledge to use the system. They overall *do not know* whether using the module would require extra time. However, overall, users *agree* about the efficiency of the module
- *Perceived Usefulness.* All users (absolutely) *agree* about the usefulness of the module not only for a more efficient accomplishment of the personal tasks, but also for the company. Moreover they all believe that using the module in actual operation is a good idea
- *Negative Aspects.* Among the main drawbacks of the module, the users listed the fact that the module is not integrated with their ERP system
- *Positive Aspects.* Workers reported about several benefits that they perceive the system could provide to them: The possibility to report errors quickly, to track errors, and to make available statistics about errors per supplier, thus improving the relationship with suppliers

Change Analysis and Propagation

The following Functionalities (**F**) of the Change Analysis and Propagation (**CAP**) component have been investigated:

F1_CAP. Impact Localization
F2_CAP. Error Analysis Plot Definition and Visualization
F3_CAP. Change Propagation Rule Definition and Application

The findings related to the functionalities are described in the following. Findings are reported as USability Issues (USI) related to the Change Analysis and Propagation (USI_CAP):

- Issues related to the capability to describe itself:

  - The labels used for specifying the input required in the analysis plot definition are difficult to understand [USI_CAP1]
  - The labels shown in the result visualization are difficult to read [USI_CAP2]

- Issues related to its capability to fit the user needs:

  - Managers asked about the possibility to persistently store the defined rules [USI_CAP3]

User test questionnaire results—Change Analysis and Propagation
The questionnaire related to the *Change Analysis and Propagation* component was filled in by a single user—the Quality Manager. Hence, the results cannot be considered as significant like the other ones. Overall, the user has a neutral position concerning the perceived ease of use and efficiency of the module, and he *agrees* about the usefulness of the *Change Analysis and Propagation* module for improving the performance of the team and about its benefit when introducing it into the work environment.

5.2.3.4 Consequences and Measures
The discussion of the criticalities identified during the developer workshops, focus groups and users tests, led to the adoption of some changes, both on the use case and on the system level. In some cases, the same functionality has been iteratively refined during the three formative evaluation activities. In the following, we report for each of the prototype components the actions taken as a consequence of the formative evaluation.

Suggestion and Feedback Management

The feedback gathered during the developer workshops [TI_SFM1, TI_SFM2] inspired the implementation of the *Suggestion and Feedback Management* component (see Sect. 5.2.2). The focus group confirmed the acceptance and usefulness of the easy-to-use interfaces developed for the system [AI_SFM2]. Furthermore, the focus group influenced design choices specific to the use case (e.g. not allowing the use of the system from alternative devices [DI_SFM2]) and inspired enhancing the existing prototype with certain functionalities, such as the suggestion voting [DI_SFM1]. Finally, user tests supported further refinements of the user interface components. In the following, we exemplify some of the improvements:

- Labels have been translated [USI_SFM1] and reworded [USI_SFM2] (e.g. see screenshot in Italian in Fig. 5.11)

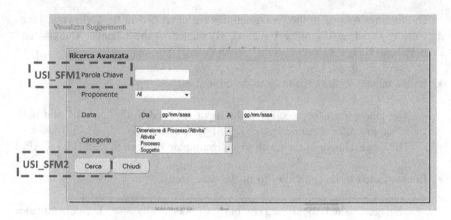

Fig. 5.11 Suggestion advanced search—translated and reworded labels (USI_SFM1 and USI_SFM2)

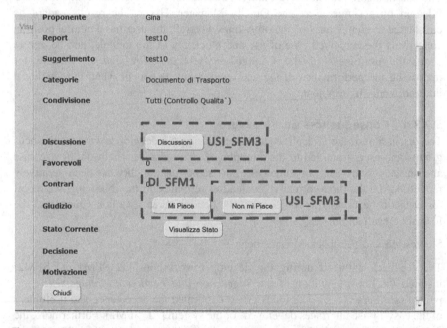

Fig. 5.12 Suggestion view—increased button size and voting functionality (USI_SFM3 and DI_SFM1)

- The size of buttons has been increased in order to make labels readable [USI_SFM3] (see screenshot in Italian in Fig. 5.12)
- Buttons Previous and Next to navigate among suggestions have been added [USI_SFM5] (see screenshot in Italian in Fig. 5.13)

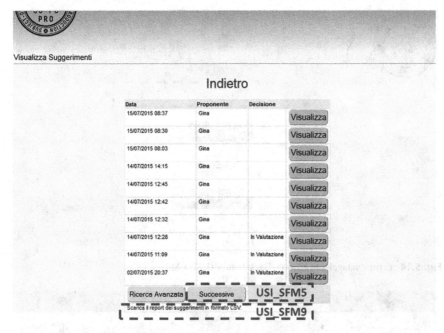

Fig. 5.13 Suggestion visualization—added previous and next buttons (USI_SFM5) and CSV export functionality (USI_SFM9)

- Redirection after approval of a suggestion to the main menu rather than to the pending suggestion list has been introduced [USI_SFM6].
- Export functionality in csv has been introduced [USI_SMF9] (see screenshot in Italian in Fig. 5.13)

Error Management

As a consequence of the developer workshops and of the focus groups [TI_EM1], a first prototype for the *Error Management* has been implemented (see Sect. 5.2.2). User tests allowed for further refinements of the *Error Management* component of the prototype:

- The "Back" button has been moved on top of the page and its size has been increased [USI_EM3] (see Fig. 5.14)
- A functionality for directly moving from the error visualization to the error update has been introduced [USI_EM4] (see Fig. 5.15)
- Problems with scrollbars have been fixed [USI_EM5]

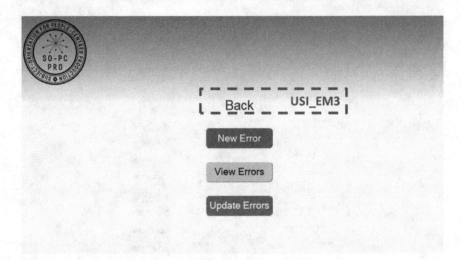

Fig. 5.14 Error management menu—Back button (USI_EM3)

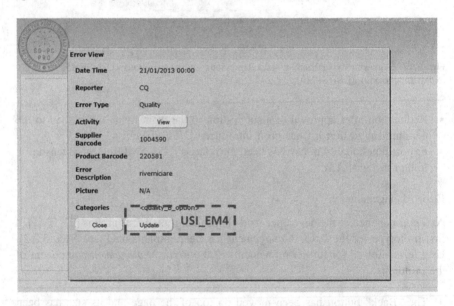

Fig. 5.15 Error view—functionality for the direct navigation from the error view to its update (USI_EM4)

Change Analysis and Propagation

As a consequence of the developer workshops and of the focus group [TI_CAP1], a first prototype for the *Change Analysis and Propagation* has been implemented (see Sect. 5.2.2). User tests allowed for further refinements of the *Change Analysis and Propagation* component of the prototype, such as the space size of the labels in the plot has been increased [USI_CAP2].

Moreover, the feedback provided by users revealed further improvement opportunities for the *Change Analysis and Propagation* module, such as the possibility of introducing the persistent storing of the defined change propagation rules [USI_CAP3].

5.2.4   The Second Prototype Design

This subsection reports the refinements applied to the *Change Propagation and Collaboration* prototype as a consequence of the requirements provided by the users after the formative evaluation.

5.2.4.1   Suggestion and Feedback Management

The following New Functionalities for the *Suggestion and Feedback Management* modules (**NF_SFM**) were introduced concerning to the second prototype:

- NF_SFM10: the suggestion process enactment has been enriched with a mechanism that enables the involved managers not only to visualize the new suggestions in the prototype but also to be notified via e-mail when a new feedback is requested from their side
- NF_SFM11: an exception handling mechanism has been added to the Suggestion Process in order to avoid dead ends of the process. In case involved managers do not respond to a request for feedback, the flow of the process can be recovered

5.2.4.2   Error Management

The following new functionalities for the Error Management module (NF_EM) were introduced concerning the second prototype:

- NF_EM5: a new functionality for uploading data from CSV files exported from other systems has been implemented. For instance, Fig. 5.16 shows screenshots of the two import interfaces for quality errors and for new batches, respectively. Data in the first group are errors (and as such the upload functionality has been added to the error page) already tracked in another system, while data in the second group are incoming batches used in the analysis phase. A new utility functionality controlling the format of the csv files to be imported has also been implemented. For instance, Fig. 5.17 shows the messages printed out when the csv import procedure succeeds or fails, respectively
- NF_EM6: a new functionality carrying out checks on the format of (some of) the data (e.g. product or supplier codes) inserted in the system has been implemented. For instance, Fig. 5.18 shows alert messages (in Italian) popping up in case the product barcode and the supplier barcode are not in the correct format, or the description has not been inserted into the error form

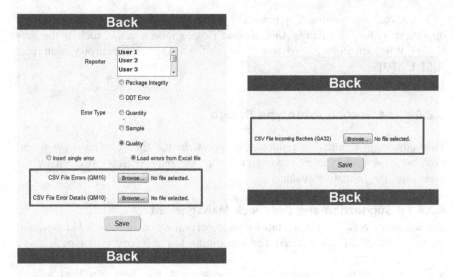

Fig. 5.16 New csv data import functionality (EM5)

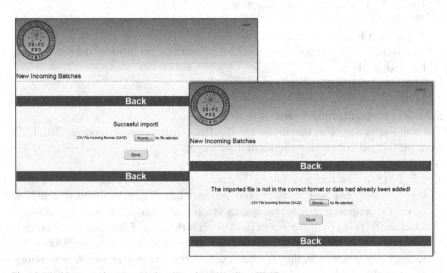

Fig. 5.17 New csv import check utility functionality (EM5)

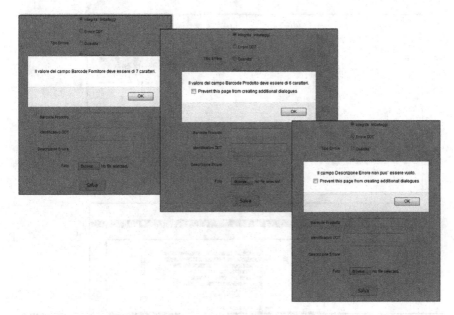

Fig. 5.18 New error data check (EM6)

5.2.4.3 Change Analysis and Propagation

The following new functionalities for the Change Analysis and Propagation module (NF_CAP) were introduced concerning the second prototype:

- NF_CAP3: a new functionality for persistently storing instantiated rule templates has been developed. Specifically, the functionality allows for grouping instantiated rule templates into configurations and for using these off-the-shelf rule configurations when needed. Figure 5.20 shows an example of a rule configuration that can be immediately used for propagating changes (button "Propagate Changes"), or just to store, in order to be used later on for the change propagation (button "Save Configuration"). The Change Propagation and Collaboration prototype offers the possibility not only to create new rule configurations (in order to store or to propagate them), but also to retrieve a specific configuration, as well as to (retrieve and) update existing rule configurations (Fig. 5.19)
- NF_CAP4: a functionality for the automatic check of the active rule set configuration has been implemented. This functionality allows for the execution of change propagations of a single rule set configuration (the only one marked as the active configuration in the system) with regular frequency (e.g. every day), and for the e-mail notification of the results of such an execution

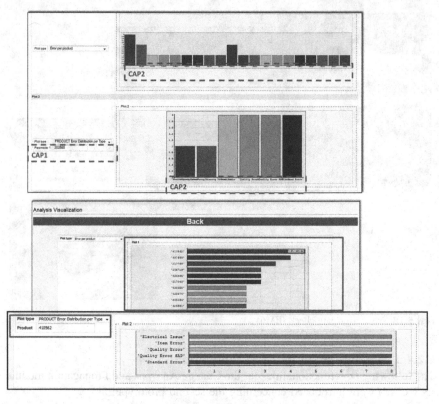

Fig. 5.19 Refined requirements CAP1 and CAP2 (*top screenshot*), and changes performed (*lower part screenshots*)

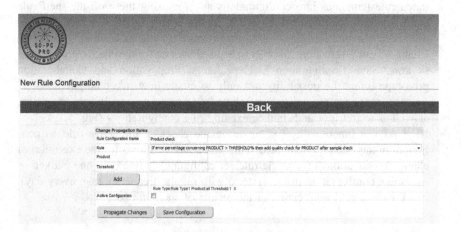

Fig. 5.20 Definition of a new rule set configuration (CAP3)

5.3 Case Implementation

This section describes the implementation steps carried out in Company B, both on the organizational (Sect. 5.3.1) and the technical level (Sect. 5.3.2).

5.3.1 Organizational Implementation

The organizational level is crucial for every type of project in SMEs. Within these companies it is important to value each individual as a professional, capable of autonomously taking his/her own responsibility and, at the same time, as part of a group to which a valuable contribution is made (Cesaro 2016). In order to allow all people involved to feel part of the project and be active on what it is evolving within the company, from the management to the workers, including directors and owners, different steps need to be performed. The Company B case was such a case, since the people-centredness was the core focus of the intervention.

The first step was an analysis of the company's as-is situation concerning both, technology and organization, together with the use case definition (see Sect. 5.1). In order to maximize people's acceptance, Company B's employees have been involved since the initial phases. Specifically, top management (the purchase manager and the logistic manager), middle management (the quality manager and the warehouse manager) and workers from the shop floor of the goods-incoming area (5 workers different for ethnicity, gender and age-class) were involved personally in this process. Thereby, they were asked to contribute according to their perception inputs about the workplace and their specific needs and expectations.

The next step was the definition of the requirements for both workers and managers. To this aim, based on the defined use case, user stories were formulated by workers, management and requirement experts, defining functional requirements (see Sect. 5.1.2.2). A two-phase approach was implemented for the user story collection in the company. First, a set of user stories has been defined by management and, subsequently, the set has been validated and edited by workers. Specifically, workers were encouraged to add, change, prioritize and even remove user stories. Moreover, different focus groups were held in Company B, aiming for feedback and inputs from workers as well as management.

After requirements elicitation, the first software mock-ups were built. These mock-ups have been presented and collaboratively refined in the course of focus groups carried out in the context of the formative evaluation (see Sect. 5.2.1). The focus groups offered also the opportunity to update all the people involved in the company about the different steps carried out, and to collect direct feedback in an open format. Different sessions were put into place with the workers, with the managers and with the whole group (workers + managers). The different sessions supported the analysis of the needs of different subjects in the process, and allowed to merge the results and feedbacks from different point of views.

Based on the results from the focus group sessions, a first software release was created and tested with employees in Company B. In dedicated user tests (see Sect. 5.2.1), employees were able to explore different features and provide immediate feedback on positive/negative aspects and potential improvements. In advance to the actual user tests, two different training sessions were conducted, a session with the management and another one with the workers. During these sessions, the software features were explained and the people involved could directly try them out and ask for clarifications when needed. In each of the two user-test sessions, users have been asked to use the system and have been observed in their interaction with the system, while exercising its different functionalities. Finally, they have filled in a questionnaire (inspired by the ISONORM 9241/10), aiming at capturing their perception about the ease of use, efficiency, ease of understanding, usefulness and overall impressions and suggestions about the system. The outcome of the user tests was considered as input to the successive development steps.

The developments at Company B aimed to empower people to contribute to workplace re-design and improvement. In the literature, two complementary views on empowerment at work and employee involvement have emerged: a socio-structural and psychological perspective (Liden et al. 2000; Spreitzer 2007). The socio-structural perspective focuses on "conditions that enable empowerment in the work-place" whereas the psychological perspective focuses "on the psychological experience of empowerment at work" (Spreitzer 2007, p. 54). In general, socio-structural empowerment can be subsumed as the sharing of decision-making power between superiors and subordinates (Liden et al. 2000; Spreitzer 2007). Empowering employees to take part in innovation and improvement processes requires organizational structures facilitating employee involvement as well as adequate tools supporting employee commitment (Fairbank and Williams 2001). In line with (Fairbank and Williams 2001), the developments at Company B targeted such organizational procedures and adequate tool support for empowering workers and management.

We conducted semi-structured interviews with workers and managers of the two company's departments involved. The main purpose of the semi-structured interviews was looking at the workers' and managers' perception of the objective achievement. Moreover, some of the defined questions were also devoted to investigate the users' perception about the usability and usefulness of the provided instruments. Among the different aspects investigated with the semi-structured interviews (see Sect. 5.4), the empowerment has been thoroughly inspected by taking into account the different dimensions described by Spreitzer (1995). All workers declared to feel deeper involved in the workplace improvement process than before, as well as to be motivated on keeping suggesting new ideas, since they can clearly see the path of their suggestions. They also stated receiving a feedback even if the suggestion was refused was a sufficient driver to keep them motivated to insert new suggestions. At the same time, the opportunity to give a suggestion and receive feedback or report an error, increased their perceived ability of making meaningful actions, in order to improve the workplace. Moreover, the fact of being taken into consideration helped some of them, especially the youngest workers, to ask for more responsibilities and power for actively participating to workplace re-design. Managers shared that perception, although some of them agreed workers could have been further motivated by offering them other forms of incentives.

5.3.2 Technical Implementation

Concerning the technical implementation, the developments carried out had to be adapted for the hardware and software support already existing in the company. Data in Company B are stored in a central database. The server can be accessed through a number of devices located within the factory. Three main company areas are involved in the use case: (i) the incoming goods area; (ii) the office of the acceptance area; (iii) the quality manager's office. Each of these three areas is equipped with a PC for communicating with the server and tracking the arrival of incoming goods, reporting quality errors, deciding on whether to move the incoming goods to the warehouse or to the production line. Specifically, the acceptance area is equipped with a PC shared by the workers in charge of dealing with the incoming goods. The office in the acceptance area is equipped with four PCs and the quality manager's office with another one.

Moreover, in the incoming goods area, workers are provided with barcode scanners to simplify data input. Due to security reasons, a solution based on existing PCs has been preferred. However, the components of the IT solution are built in order to be easily adapted to other devices such as tablets or smartphones. IT components are installed on a server in Company B and can be accessed by workers through the PCs in the incoming goods area, in the office of the incoming goods area and the project manager office.

With respect to software components, the implementation of the software modules installed at Company B required the integration of two main base technologies: The Metasonic Suite and the MoKi-based collaboration environment. Metasonic Suite, by exploiting a proprietary database (*Metasonic Suite DB*) enables the execution of S-BPM process models (e.g. the suggestion handling process model) through simple and portable user interfaces, *FlowNG interfaces*, which are automatically built starting from the business objects of the S-BPM process models. Although these interfaces can in principle be adapted to different devices, Company B preferred to use these interfaces only from company internal. MoKi offers a collaborative environment for issue and suggestion reporting enriched with reasoning capabilities for analysis utilities (e.g. rule-based propagation of data changes). The interaction between Metasonic Flow and MoKi is mediated via a shared repository, which guarantees the communication and the synchronization between the two system components and their corresponding repositories.

5.4   Case Evaluation

This section describes the case study evaluation carried out at Company B in order
to investigate the achievement of the use case goals and objectives as defined in
Sect. 5.1.1. In the following, the evaluation framework (Sect. 5.4.1) and the results
are presented (Sect. 5.4.2).

5.4.1   Summative Evaluation Framework

Figure 5.21 depicts the case evaluation framework adopted for the Company B use
case. The basis of the framework contains three pillars: the case evaluation elements, the evaluation methods and the evaluation dimensions. The case evaluation
elements represent important realized case components (e.g. prototypes, methods)
to be evaluated. The evaluation methods are the methods that are used for the
evaluation. Finally, the evaluation dimensions are the high-level perspectives that
we are interested in to evaluate each case evaluation element. We detail each of
these pillars for the current case subsequently.

The following four case evaluation elements (CEEs) have been defined during
the case evaluation design for the "Empowered Workplace Improvement" case:

- CEE1. Improvement of the internal communication and collaboration
- CEE2. Facilitation of context-sensitive error reporting
- CEE3. Facilitation of change and error analysis
- CEE4. People-Centredness

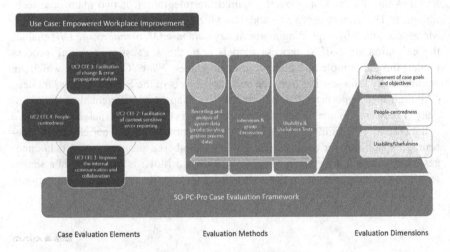

Fig. 5.21 Case evaluation framework instantiated for the Company B case, i.e. the "Empowered
Workplace Improvement" case

Three **evaluation dimensions** have been investigated:

- *Achievement of goals and objectives*: this dimension focuses on the achievement of the use case goals and objectives defined in Sect. 5.1.1. It aims at evaluating the achievement of the use case goals
- *People-centredness*: this dimension focuses on the overall objective to providing adequate instruments supporting the involvement and the participation of factory workers. Empowering people to participate in the improvement of their work-place requires both organizational structures facilitating employee involvement as well as adequate tools supporting employee commitment (Fairbank and Williams 2001)
- *Usability and Usefulness*: this dimension focuses on the IT system provided to support the workers in the achievement of the goals. Specifically, it aims at eval-uating the ease of use of the proposed solutions, their efficiency in the economy of the everyday work, as well as their usefulness to achieve the main objectives

As for the data collection and analysis, both quantitative and qualitative eval-uation methods have been used. Specifically, semi-structured interviews have been designed and conducted, paper-and-pencil questionnaires have been prepared and provided to users, and system data has been collected and analysed.

According to the summative evaluation framework, a number of tasks have been performed when evaluating the case. We report the details about the instantiation of the summative evaluation framework for the Company B case in the following.

The case refers to the material check in the acceptance area and the quality management in Company B. Workers and managers belonging to two departments have been involved in the evaluation: the incoming goods area and the quality check department.

Three main groups of **stakeholders** were involved:

- Technology Providers, i.e. the technology providers involved in the imple-mentation of the IT solutions as well as in the training of the system
- Users. Company B workers and management of the two departments described above. Specifically, 8 persons have been asked to participate in the summative evaluation: 5 of them belong to the category of workers, 2 of them to the category of management and, finally, one of them, who belongs to the middle management, actually holding the role of both, worker and manager. The age of the involved users is well distributed across different ranges, thus allowing us to receive different feedbacks on the basis of the age of the person involved. Specifically, the age of the workers encompasses four different age categories: one worker is under 20-years old, one is in the range 20–30, one worker over 50-years old, and all the others are between 30 and 40 years old. The managers are all in the range 40–50. Finally, concerning the gender distribution, one out of eight persons is female, while the remaining seven are males
- Evaluators. A team of different experts has been appointed to prepare and carry out the evaluation

For each of the four CEEs, a set of detailed objectives has been carefully designed and, in turn, for each of the objectives, a set of questions and methods to investigate their achievement and to evaluate usability and usefulness of the system provided to support the users has also been prepared.

Three different types of data collection methods have been designed and implemented: (i) semi-structured interviews; (ii) paper-and-pencil questionnaires; (iii) system data. Semi-structured interviews have been mainly used to evaluate the dimensions related to the achievement of goals and objectives, and people-centredness. On the other hand, the paper-and-pencil questionnaires provided a means for evaluating mainly the usability and the usefulness of the system supporting the workers. Finally, analysing the data collected from the system facilitated to investigate more than one dimension. They reveal the workers' involvement and engagement (people-centredness dimension), the achievement of goals and objectives, such as the communication improvements (achievement of goals and objectives dimension), as well as, in part, the ease to use the tool. All the three methods involved the same group of users. In the following, each of the data collection methods is detailed, in terms of aim and research design.

5.4.1.1 Semi-structured Interviews

The main aim of the semi-structured interviews is evaluating the users' perceived involvement in the project activities and in the workplace re-design, as well as their perception about the achievement of the case evaluation elements objectives. The interviews have been collaboratively designed by the evaluators. Specifically, a set of objectives has been defined for each case evaluation element. In order to investigate the achievement of each of these case evaluation elements, a set of items has been defined. In the following, the objectives for each of the case evaluation elements are listed:

- CEE1. Improve the internal communication and collaboration

    - Increase traceability of (suggestion and feedback related) information flow
    - Increase transparency of communication (related to workplace improvements)
    - Facilitate meaningful information exchange of workplace improvements
    - Application of methods and tools to support collaborative re-design and information exchange

- CEE2. Facilitate context-sensitive error reporting

    - Error description
    - Error classification
    - Error display and search

- CEE3. Facilitate change and error analysis

  - Facilitate error analysis
  - Facilitate automatic proposal of error-related improvements
  - Facilitate subject impact localization regarding suggestions

- CEE4. Ensure people-centredness

  - Investigation of worker involvement/participation in workplace design
  - Investigation of worker empowerment

5.4.1.2 Paper-and-Pencil Questionnaires

The aim of the paper-and-pencil questionnaires is evaluating the perceived usability and usefulness of the IT system supporting the users in order to achieve the main goal and objectives of the case evaluation elements. Three paper-and-pencil questionnaires have been designed, in order to evaluate the IS support for the case evaluation elements CEE1, CEE2 and CEE3. Specifically, the following main mapping between case evaluation elements and the IT system components for the users' support can be devised:

- CEE1. Improve the internal communication and collaboration → Suggestion and Feedback Management component
- CEE2. Facilitation of context-sensitive error reporting → Error Management component
- CEE3. Facilitation of change and error analysis → Change Analysis and Propagation component
- CEE4. People-Centredness → no direct IS support exists for this case evaluation element, which is orthogonal to the other CEEs

Each questionnaire, inspired by the ISONORM 9241/10, has been designed to investigate the following aspects for each case evaluation element:

- Perceived ease-of-use
- Perceived efficiency
- Perceived usefulness
- Willingness to use the system

5.4.1.3 System Data

Finally, system data has been collected with the aim to get a clear and objective assessment of the usage of the technical solutions provided to the users, and to directly or indirectly evaluate the achievement of some of the objectives. The selection of the system data to be collected has been designed, in order to overall evaluate the actual usage of the technical components as well as to investigate some of the specific objectives defined for each case evaluation element. In detail, the following main metrics have been collected for the different case evaluation elements:

- CEE1. Improve the internal communication and collaboration

  - number of workers' suggestions, number of suggestions per user, number of accepted suggestions, quality of the suggestions, number of involved managers per suggestion, number of suggestions per affected workplace context, number of discussions, number of supporters and opponents per suggestion

- CEE2. Facilitation of context-sensitive error reporting

  - number of errors, number of errors per error category

- CEE3. Facilitation of change and error analysis

  - number of rule configuration instantiation for the change propagation

Quantitative as well as qualitative (content) data analysis methods have been used for analysing the collected data. Specifically, quantitative methods have been used to analyse most of the paper-and-pencil questionnaires and the system data, while qualitative data have been used for the analysis of the semi-structured interviews. Both, Company B workers and managers have been interviewed and asked to fill the paper-and-pencil questionnaires. The interviews have been carried out in a one-day evaluation workshop at Company B. Each respondent has been interviewed for about half an hour, and his/her answers were recorded. After the interview, respondents have also been asked to fill in the questionnaires. After collecting the data, they have been processed, analysed, interpreted and translated to English.

5.4.2   Summative Evaluation Results

In this subsection, the results of the evaluation carried out for each case evaluation element were used. The semi-structured interviews concerned each defined CEE. The paper-and-pencil questionnaires and system data were used to evaluate those CEEs demanding information system support, i.e. CEE1, CEE2 and CEE3.

5.4.2.1   Semi-structured Interview Results

Subsequently, we report the findings per case evaluation element and per objective. Moreover, some of the defined items were also devoted to investigate the users' perception about the usability and usefulness of the provided instruments. Some of the case elements (i.e. CEE1 and CEE4) can be seen both from the workers' and the managers' perspective. Consequently, different sets of items, looking at the same objective from two different perspectives, have been designed for the two categories. The others, instead, are relevant for only one of the two categories.

CEE 1: Improve internal communication and collaboration

This case evaluation element has been evaluated by taking into account both the managers' and the workers' perspective.

Increase traceability of (suggestion and feedback related) information flow
The answers provided to this set of items reveal that all the involved workers participated in the suggestion making process and found it easy and useful to track the status of their suggestion(s), though some of them preferred to use the instrument in collaboration with their colleagues (both, for making suggestions, and for tracking the feedback). Similarly, all the managers participated in the management of at least one suggestion either alone or together with their colleagues. The managers' opinions about the traceability and the formalization of the information flow are discordant. While part of the management perceives the importance and the need to trace the information flow, another part of the top management feels it is not necessary due to the minimal context of the use case.

Facilitate meaningful information exchange on workplace improvements
The results of these items show that categorizing issues and suggestions within predefined categories is not always easy to achieve, especially in a dynamic environment of a factory. Among the possible impediments for some of the workers, the fear of discussing ideas with the management has been mentioned. Moreover, all the workers would really like to extend the usage of the system to other departments.

Application of methods and tools to support collaborative re-design and information exchange
The workers' answers related to this set of items highlight that, although they do not always use the system for voting about colleagues' suggestions, the fact of inserting a suggestion into the system stimulates the discussion in person. Although many of the respondents (both workers and managers) prefer to discuss face-to-face, most of them believe that it is of utmost importance to have the possibility to track a suggestion in the system because this encourages the management to provide an answer. Finally, both workers and (most of the) managers believe that the introduction of the suggestion and discussion management has had an impact on the workplace improvement, either in terms of implementing a suggestion, or improving the discussion.

CEE 2: Facilitate context-sensitive error reporting

This case evaluation element has been evaluated by taking into account only the workers' (authors of the errors) perspective.

Error description
Although not all the workers have directly reported an error in the system, all agree that it is easy to do so. They all agree that the instruments they can use for reporting errors, i.e. the textual description and the possibility to upload pictures, are sufficient for their purposes. Many of them have noticed an overall improvement in the behaviour of some of the suppliers.

Error classification
Overall, all the workers are satisfied with the five error categories the technical support currently provides them to classify the errors. Moreover, all the workers who have reported errors in the system have noticed that some of the error categories are more "important" than others, indicating with this statement that some errors (e.g. quantity errors) affect the daily activities of more than one worker, thus resulting in a loss of time for some of the workers. Before introducing the system, these errors were not recorded, and the management could not see their frequency and the actual impact on workers, neither in terms of taking actions per se nor towards suppliers in order to solve them.

Error visualization and search
All workers highlighted that they only searched errors that have been reported by themselves, and left any type of error analysis to the management.
CEE 3: Facilitate change and error analysis
This element was investigated only from a management point of view.

Facilitate error analysis
As for the workers (see CEE 2) also the managers agreed on the correctness and completeness of the error categories available so far for characterizing the occurring errors. Moreover, the management declared that the plots provided by the error analysis functionality are easy and clear, but they would also like to add further features, in order to be able to create and modify the plot, according to their needs.

Facilitate automatic proposal of error-related improvements
Concerning the change propagation functionality (providing managers with proposals of improvements and changes to apply), all the managers asserted that the rule templates that can be instantiated for the change propagation are well designed, and that they are able to instantiate them for their specific needs. They also assessed that they have never had the need to create new rules or modify existing ones so far. Finally, they also highlighted the usefulness of the e-mail notification mechanism for the change propagation results.

Facilitate subject impact localization regarding suggestions
According to the top management, it could be useful to extend the functionality to the workers, in order to enable them to understand who and which department are involved in a specific suggestion. As top management, being in charge of designing the process they are already aware of the involved people.

CEE 4: Ensure people-centredness

The CEE 4 aims at investigating workers' perceived change, involvement and empowerment. The items have been presented to both, workers and managers and related to workers' experience, expectations and point of view.

Investigation of worker involvement/participation in workplace re-design
All workers declared that a clear improvement has occurred especially with respect to the communication among the different departments. In general, all workers perceived an improvement of the workplace design as a whole: on-line suggestions and discussions have led to face-to-face discussions and vice versa. In addition, sharing ideas before entering a suggestion helped to increase the quality and frequency of communication among people. Moreover, both workers and managers assessed that suggestions and discussions are supported and fostered by the management.

Both workers and management noticed an increase in the workers' involvement. Workers feel involved in participating in workplace re-design, not only by inserting suggestions, but also sharing suggestions on how to improve their environment. For instance, an important issue shared and discussed by everyone was the one related to safety. Overall, workers feel that the value of their suggestions is taken into account by both management and colleagues.

The opinions of the managers, instead, are slightly different. Most of them agree with the workers in assessing that workers feel to be taken into account and empowered, while some of them believe that this is not the case for all the workers, only for those that already have a relationship with the management, i.e. the oldest ones.

Concerning the possible drawbacks and obstacles in the usage of the system, many workers, especially the youngest ones, pointed out the rigidity of the usage of the personal computers. Hence, they suggested to create a specific app in order to be able to make suggestions directly from a smartphone, even when they are not at work. Another suggestion consists of embedding the system functionalities in their current ERP system. According to the workers, among the possible obstacles to the usage of the system, there is the impossibility of making anonymous suggestions. This aspect, that had already been taken into consideration during the user-requirements elicitation, and had been excluded based on a shared decision involving workers as well, popped up again. This could mean that some suggestions, eventually about relationship issues, have not been reported in the system.

Investigation of worker empowerment
All workers declared to feel more involved in the workplace improvement process, as well as to be motivated on keep suggesting new things, since they can clearly see the suggestion path. They also stated that receiving feedback even when the suggestion was refused, was sufficient to keep them motivated to insert new suggestions. At the same time, the opportunity to create a suggestion and receive feedback, or report an error increased the perceived ability of making meaningful actions in order to improve the workplace. Moreover, the fact of being taken into

consideration helps some of them, especially the youngest workers, to ask for more responsibilities and power for actively participating in workplace re-design. The same workers' involvement is also perceived by the managers, although some of them agreed that workers could have been further motivated by offering them other forms of incentives.

5.4.2.2 Paper-and-Pencil Questionnaire Results

Three different paper-and-pencil questionnaires have been proposed to the Company B users. The first questionnaire (CEE1) mainly focuses on the *Suggestion and Feedback Management* component, the second one (CEE2) on the *Error Management* component and the third one (CEE3) on the *Change Analysis and Propagation* component. As for the semi-structured interviews, the paper-and-pencil questionnaire related to the CEE1 component has been provided to both, workers and management, the one for CEE2 has been given only to workers, and the one for CEE3 only to management. The items were mainly close questions on a 5-point Likert scale (where 1 = *I strongly agree* and 5 = *I strongly disagree*).

CEE 1: Improve internal communication and collaboration

On average, users (both managers and workers) agree on the perceived ease of use and ease of learning of the *Suggestion and Feedback Management* component. Different from what expected, the answers provided by the workers are slightly more positive than the ones provided by the management. This result can be in part explained by the different tasks that the two types of users were asked to perform on the component, which could require different efforts. Concerning the perceived efficiency component, while on average, all the respondents believe they have enough knowledge and resources in order to be able to use the component, half of them partially or completely believe that the usage of the system is time consuming. In this case also managers agree on the fact that interacting with the component requires some extra time, while workers disagree. This can in part be due to the difference of complexity of the tasks. In addition, the answers related to the perceived usefulness are overall positive: they all agree that the component speeds up task and team performance, as well as the communication and the re-design. In this case, the opinion of the workers is more positive than the one of the managers. Finally, all users agreed about their willingness to continue using the system. Among the strengths of the approach, managers appreciated the idea of a shared suggestion system, while workers appreciated the possibility to be involved in workplace improvements.

CEE 2: Facilitate context-sensitive error reporting

Concerning the perceived ease of use, the workers, with respect to the *Error Management* component, almost completely agree on the component's ease of learning and its overall ease to of use. With respect to the perceived efficiency, on average, all the respondents believe that they have enough knowledge and resources, many of them partially believe that the usage of the system is time consuming. In the case of the perceived usefulness, the answers of the respondents were overall positive, too: they all agreed that the component speeds up task and team performance, as well as that it is overall useful for the company. Finally, on average, workers expressed a positive willingness towards the component's usage. Among the strengths of the system, some of them mentioned the potential benefits stemming from continuously monitoring supplier errors.

CEE 3: Facilitation of change and error analysis

Concerning the perceived ease of use of the *Change Analysis and Propagation* component, managers, on average, agree about the components' ease of learning and its ease of use, while they are slightly more sceptical about its ease to be understood. Concerning the perceived efficiency, managers are not completely convinced to have sufficient resources to use the system. They are a bit more confident to have enough knowledge to use the component and, in general, tend to agree with the fact that using the system would require more time. A similar trend can also be observed for the perceived usefulness of the component. On average, managers tend to agree about the fact that the support improves team performance, and that it is useful for the warehouse re-design; they have some doubts about speeding up task performance.

5.4.2.3 System Data Results

In this subsection, the data collected in order to evaluate the usage of the provided IT system support are reported.

CEE 1: Improve internal communication and collaboration

Overall, 19 suggestions have been put into the IT system in a period of usage of about one year. They have been directly inserted in the system by 5 different workers, although some of the suggestions have been added by two or more workers together. Out of these 19 suggestions, 4 have already been approved (at the time of writing), 2 have been rejected, while 12 are still pending. Most of the suggestions relate to the improvement of workplace aspects that concern more than one worker or colleague rather than the only proponent. According to the assessment of managers, the quality of the collected suggestions seems to be overall good. By inspecting the rejected suggestions, non-approvals are mainly due to missing capabilities of the company to meet the worker requests (either in terms of financings or management). Only 5 out of the 19 inserted suggestions have been classified according to a predefined contextual category. The lack of a classification for some of the activities can be mainly due to a difficulty the workers experience when selecting a category. By looking at the distribution of the sharing strategies, it turns out that in most of the cases workers have chosen to share their suggestion also with colleagues. Besides the feedback provided by the managers, while processing the suggestions discussions have also been used by the management to provide feedback after a suggestion's approval or rejection. Hence, any communication among workers and managers should be traceable, not only during the suggestion processing, but also when the suggestion has been accepted, and is going to be implemented.

CEE 2: Facilitate context-sensitive error reporting

Overall, 1229 product errors stemming from the incoming good area of the ware-house and from the quality check department have been inserted in the system. About half of these errors have been imported from the company ERP system, while the remaining ones are errors that have been manually inserted by the workers. Most of the errors are quality errors imported from the ERP system, followed by errors related to the transportation document and by errors due to incorrect quantities. Very few errors related to the comparison of the received items with the items already in the warehouse have been detected. No package integrity errors have been reported.

CEE 3: Facilitate change and error analysis

By looking at the plots and analysis offered by the system, managers are able to find the error rate per supplier and take decisive actions against error-prone suppliers. For instance, the data shows that the error rate of one of the suppliers has reached 10 %. With such data at hand, the management could, e.g. push the supplier to be more careful when delivering material.

5.5 Conclusion

The activities carried out throughout the case have been driven by a people-centred methodology based on the assumption that the *force and power of the individual* as a person can be understood according to three meanings (Cesaro 2016):

- The opportunities that the individual recognizes in himself which are the basis of his life plan
- The capabilities and potentialities the individual can exploit
- The possibility in the sense of giving oneself hope (it is possible that ...)

   The starting point of this methodology is the historic philosophic thought about the relationship between human being and machine and people's alienation. This situation especially occurs when there are daily needs that have to meet product-related process automation of economies of scale, and people need to respect timing and methodologies imposed by the machine. The fundamental question has always been whether to maintain the *human/machine/human* relation or rather the most frequent *machine/human/machine* requested by productive needs and by the technology domain over humans.

   This methodology puts at the first place the relationships among people (human/human) taking into consideration that hierarchies, and the need of making decisions must find a balance between power exercise and a positive organizational climate. The second point of attention is related to the workplace life quality, particularly focusing on the actual measurement of those parameters that could be related to safety, stress level, health and rhythm within the company and working time. A good working relationship facilitates problem solving for workers who can perceive and communicate useful changes in the workplace. Making the working environment efficient and effectual is the natural consequence of a way of working in which both communication and a solid trust system could become the key element of a positive organizational strategy. Saving time and positive economic results are the most important objectives in every company. However, these goals have to be shared by all the different levels of the company organization. Starting from these assumptions, the methodology is based on three main pillars:

1. People
2. Company processes (both organizational and industrial processes)
3. Tools (IT tools, ERP systems and the like)

These three pillars can be, respectively, supported by three types of activities that complete and strengthen each other:

• Proper specific training
• Ad hoc consultancy
• IT tool implementation.

These basic activities have to be instantiated based on the actual needs of each company. By applying the methodology, we have learned that these three activities need to be balanced in order to make interventions on the company effective and efficient. Such a balance can be reached only by connecting people, the organizational system and IT solutions, i.e. providing training activities, on-the-field consultancy and adequate solutions in terms of products and services. Training activity alone, indeed, is perceived as lacking of practical implications. On the other side consultancy and support activity alone lack awareness and answers to the many different daily problems oriented to people's autonomy. Using tools and technologies helps reducing activities timing and costs.

By looking at the case as a whole, beyond this general lesson, few concrete lessons can be learnt for each of the three aspects.

[People] Involving users from the beginning of the project increases their willingness to participate. The people-centred approach adopted from the initial phases on and the involvement of the workers in the analysis and design phases supported the project participation in terms of motivation and commitment. Both Company B management and workers declared that such an active involvement allowed creating something actually useful and helpful for their daily working experience.

[People] Formative and case evaluation complement each other. Formative and case evaluations are useful for a twofold purpose: (i) supporting the system development and iterative refinement; (ii) user-centredness. On the one hand, they provide an effective means to support the development process, starting with the design of the system until iterative refinements. Since the perception a developer

has of the to-be system is likely to differ from user expectations, early feedback and iterative development supports the alignment between users, the organization and the development. On the other hand, the involvement of workers in the suggestion and evaluation phases and the importance given to their feedback increases their understanding of the system as well as their motivation to use a system.

Furthermore, the following aspects with respect to formative and case evaluation activities were observed to be beneficial:

- Management commitment
- Discussion of different support aspects for certain groups of users (to develop a common understanding)
- Sufficient time for workshops (thus avoiding that participants have only a limited amount of time and do not really engage in the evaluation activity)

[Company processes] S-BPM modelling is not always intuitive. The S-BPM process modelling language has been easily understood and learned by Company B management. Company B managers, indeed, are used to work with processes—e.g. they designed and certified the company quality process (e.g. quality process through ISO certifications). Shop floor workers, who do not have a process-oriented background, instead, found the S-BPM full-fledged notation, e.g. the behavioural diagrams, too complex to understand, while they found quite intuitive the S-BPM Interaction Diagrams, i.e. subjects exchanging messages. The Subject Interaction Diagram of the suggestion handling process has indeed been added to the users' interfaces of the system as a facilitator of understanding the process orchestration. The workers' background was not based on processes but on tools and mechanical knowledge. In addition, their training at work is more related to daily-job routines. Thus, the addition of a graphic representation of the process turned out as facilitator for workers, and a necessary system feature to be developed.

[IT solutions] The system has to be tested on-site. It happened that some of the components remotely tested did not correctly work in the field, e.g. the scrollbars of the user interfaces on the monitors of the Company B devices or the e-mail server for sending e-mails. Before deploying a system, it is hence of utmost importance to test the system also on-site.

Finally, by looking at the last phase, i.e. the case evaluation, it seems that there is still room for improving the provided solution not only on the implementation level but also on the methodological level. Involving employees from the first phases and throughout all the intermediate steps is essential, since it allows for their actual involvement in the design of the solution they are going to use. Collecting feedback and understanding fears and worries related to people and the organization as a complex system is extremely important throughout all the phases. In real and complex scenarios such as a factory, it is always important to use, as in economics and psychology sciences, a systemic approach, allowing researchers to take into consideration not only the people and the variables in the studied group but also all other circumstances, such as company culture, collective and individual values, as well as other employees not involved in the project and their interactions. The case implementation provided evidence that workers want to continue using the system. This suggests a high motivation for improving their workplace and a strong commitment to the company.

By looking back, it would be probably worth to involve users even more in all the phases. In particular, it would be useful to provide users with a more intensive training phase so as to help them to better understand and get in touch with the new functionalities, as well as to expand the evaluation phase, e.g. by planning intermediate evaluation steps that would allow developers and evaluators to get further interesting feedback after the system has been used for a while.

For the future, it would be interesting to apply the devised approach, enhanced with the lesson learned so far, to other use cases.

References

Beyer, H., & Holtzblatt, K. (1998). *Contextual design: Defining customer-centered systems.* San Francisco: Morgan Kaufmann Publishers.

Bohner, S. A., & Arnold, R. S. (1996). An introduction to software change impact analysis. In S. A. Bohner & R. S. Arnold (Eds.), *Software change impact analysis.* Los Alamitos: IEEE Computer Society.

Bosca, A., Dragoni, M., Di Francescomarino, C., & Ghidini, C. (2014). Collaborative management of multilingual ontologies. In P. Buitelaar & P. Cimiano (Eds.), *Towards the multilingual Semantic Web* (pp. 175–192). Berlin: Springer.

Casagni, C., Di Francescomarino, C., Dragoni, M., Fiorentini, L., Franci, L., Gerosa, M., et al. (2011). Wiki-based conceptual modeling: An experience with the public administration. In L. Aroyo, et al. (Eds.), *The Semantic Web—ISWC 2011* (Vol. 7032, pp. 17–32). Lecture notes in computer science. Heidelberg: Springer.

Cesaro, F. (2016). *I've done it for you. Generational Cohabitation and the Family Business.* Milano: Guerini & Association.

Christl, C., Ghidini, C., Guss, J., Lindstaedt, S. N., Pammer, V., Rospocher, M., et al. (2008). Deploying Semantic Web Technologies for work integrated learning in industry—a comparison: SME vs. large sized company. In A. Sheth, et al. (Eds.), *ISWC 2008* (Vol. 5318, pp. 709–722). Lecture notes in computer science. Berlin: Springer.

Di Francescomarino, C., Corcoglioniti, F., Dragoni, M., Bertoli, P., Tiella, R., Ghidini, C., et al. (2014) Semantic-based process analysis. In P. Mika, et al. (Eds.), *The Semantic Web—ISWC 2014* (Vol. 8797, pp. 228–243). Lecture notes in computer science. Springer International Publishing Switzerland.

Dragoni, M., Di Francescomarino, C., Ghidini, C., Clemente, J., & Sánchez, Alonso S. (2013). Guiding the evolution of a multilingual ontology in a concrete setting. In P. Cimiano, et al. (Eds.), *ESWC 2013* (Vol. 7882, pp. 608–622). Lecture notes in computer science. Berlin: Springer.

Dragoni, M., Bosca, A., Casu, M., & Rexha, A. (2014a). Modeling, managing, exposing, and linking ontologies with a Wiki-based tool. In N. Calzolari, et al. (Eds.), *Proceedings of the Ninth International Conference on Language Resources and Evaluation (LREC'14)* (pp. 1668–1675). European Language Resources Association.

Dragoni, M., Bertoli, P., Di Francescomarino, C., Ghidini, C., Nori, M., Pistore, M., et al. (2014b). Modeling and monitoring processes exploiting semantic reasoning. In M. Horridge, M. Rospocher, & J. Van Ossenbruggen (Eds.), *ISWC-PD'14 Proceedings of the 2014 International Conference on Posters & Demonstrations Track* (Vol. 1272, pp. 121–124). CEUR-WS.org.

Fairbank, J. F., & Williams, S. D. (2001). Motivating creativity and enhancing innovation through employee suggestion system technology. *Creativity and Innovation Management, 10*(2), 68–74.

Ghidini, C., Rospocher, M., & Serafini, L. (2012). Modeling in a wiki with moki: Reference architecture, implementation, and usages. *International Journal on Advances in Life Sciences, 4*(3), 111–124.

Holtzblatt, K., & Beyer, H. R. (2014). Contextual design. In M. Soegaard, & R. F. Dam (Eds.), *The encyclopedia of human-computer interaction* (2nd edn). Aarhus, Denmark: The Interaction Design Foundation. Retrieved July 18, 2016, from https://www.interaction-design.org/encyclopedia/contextual_design.html.

ISO/IEC 9126-1. (2001). *Software engineering-product quality—Part 1: Quality model*. ISO.

ISO 9241-11. (1998). *Ergonomic requirements for office work with visual display terminals (VDTs) Part 11: Guidance on Usability*. ISO.

Krueger, R. A., & Casey, M. (2000). *Focus groups: A practical guide for applied research*. California: Sage Publications.

Leffingwell, D., & Widrig, D. (2003). *Managing software requirements: A use case approach*. Addison-Wesley.

Liden, R. C., Wayne, S. J., & Sparrowe, R. T. (2000). An examination of the mediating role of psycho-logical empowerment on the relations between the job, interpersonal relationships, and work outcomes. *Journal of Applied Psychology, 85*(3), 407–416.

Mate, J. L., & Silva, A. (2005). *Requirements engineering for sociotechnical systems*. Hershey, PA: IGI Global.

Rospocher, M., Ghidini, C., Serafini, L., Kump, B., Pammer, V., Lindstaedt, S. N., et al. (2008). Collaborative enterprise integrated modelling. In *SWAP 2008, CEUR Workshop Proceedings* (Vol. 426).

Rospocher, M., Ghidini, C., Pammer, V., Serafini, L., & Lindstaedt, S. N. (2009). MoKi: The Modelling wiKi. In *4th Semantic Wiki Workshop (SemWiki 2009) at the 6th European Semantic Web Conference (ESWC 2009), CEUR Workshop Proceedings* (Vol. 464).

Spreitzer, G. M. (1995). Psychological empowerment in the workplace: Dimensions, measurement, and validation. *Academy of Management Journal, 38*(5), 1442–1465.

Spreitzer, G. (2007). Toward the integration of two perspectives: A review of social-structural and psychological. *The SAGE handbook of organizational behavior: Volume one: Micro approaches* (Vol. 1, pp. 54–72). London, UK: Sage Publications.

Stufflebeam, D. L., & Shinkfield, A. J. (2011). *Evaluation theory, models, and applications*. San Francisco, CA: Wiley.

Open Access This chapter is distributed under the terms of the Creative Commons Attribution-NonCommercial 4.0 International License (http://creativecommons.org/licenses/by-nc/4.0/), which permits any noncommercial use, duplication, adaptation, distribution and reproduction in any medium or format, as long as you give appropriate credit to the original author(s) and the source, provide a link to the Creative Commons license and indicate if changes were made.

The images or other third party material in this chapter are included in the work's Creative Commons license, unless indicated otherwise in the credit line; if such material is not included in the work's Creative Commons license and the respective action is not permitted by statutory regulation, users will need to obtain permission from the license holder to duplicate, adapt or reproduce the material.

Human-Controlled Production

6

Matthias Neubauer, Florian Krenn, Ioan-Alexandru Schärfl, Christian Stary and Dennis Majoe

Abstract

In factories of the future, the worker and his or her well-being is regarded a crucial part of manufacturing situations. Human factors are recognized as vital to achieve sustainable organizational success. Advances in the area of wearable sensors proclaim that sensing human properties within manufacturing settings is technically feasible. Thereby, sensing human properties, such as the level of comfort or stress, may be used to adapt system behaviour in manufacturing situations. This chapter revisits related work from adaptive systems design addressing triggers for adaptations and impacted dimensions. The related work can be considered as design space for developers of S-BPM-based adaptive processes. In line with the related work, a laboratory setting at the Johannes Kepler University Linz has been designed and utilized for testing sensor-based process behaviour and control. Essential findings are described with respect to system architectures and S-BPM process design. The chapter concludes with relating modelling adaptive to human-aware S-BPM processes on a concept layer, and future work.

M. Neubauer (✉) · F. Krenn · I.-A. Schärfl · C. Stary
Department of Business Information Systems – Communications Engineering,
Johannes Kepler University Linz, Linz, Austria
e-mail: matthias.neubauer@jku.at

D. Majoe
MA Systems and Control Limited, Southampton, UK

© The Author(s) 2017
M. Neubauer and C. Stary (eds.), *S-BPM in the Production Industry*,
DOI 10.1007/978-3-319-48466-2_6

6.1   Related Work

In factories of the future, humans represent a crucial part for increasing flexibility, agility and competitiveness. Today, the achievement of manufacturing objectives relies inter alia on the seamless interaction among humans and machines. The research field of *adaptive systems* investigates how joint human–machine systems may *"change their behaviour to meet the changing needs of their users"* (Feigh et al. 2012). A prerequisite for the selection of adequate changes is the assessment of the user's current situation (cf. Fig. 6.1). The advent of IT and sensor technology has enabled the assessment of human properties in order to align the interactions among humans and machines.

However, yet the design and implementation of adaptive systems remains a challenging task. In this chapter, the applicability of S-BPM for the design and implementation of human-aware adaptive production systems is investigated.

The design space and respective guidelines in the field of adaptive systems are revisited subsequently. Figure 6.1 illustrates the elements of a generic adaptive system according to Feigh et al. (2012). It comprises a "perceive, select, and act" cycle. A "Context Assessment" component is responsible for perceiving certain changes in different types of states, e.g. human state, system state and task/mission state. Based on the perceived state, the "Adaptions Manager" is responsible for selecting appropriate system adaptations, e.g. rescheduling of tasks or new

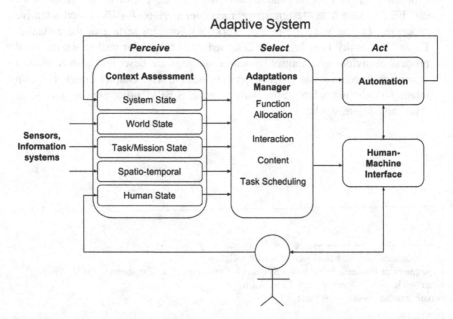

Fig. 6.1 Generic adaptive joint human-machine system (adapted from Feigh et al. 2012, © Human Factors and Ergonomics Society)

allocation of functions. These changes may affect the current system actions in terms of modified automated system behaviour or changes of the human–machine interface.

Feigh et al. (2012) present a twofold framework for adaptive systems containing: (1) triggers for adaptation and (2) types of adaptation. Adaptations may be triggered by operators, the system state or mode, a certain environmental state or event, a task state or mission event or a spatio-temporal event (cf. Fig. 6.2).

Operator-based triggers can be directly initiated by operators; in other words, humans control system adaptations through their input. Furthermore, states of operators can be measured by system components and trigger changes. For instance, a tiredness sensor in a car observes the driver and triggers an audio warning signal when it detects the risk of micro-sleep.

System-based triggers can originate from a change of the system state or mode. Feigh et al. (2012) refer to system state as *"description of the current configuration of the automation"*, e.g. a smart home may trigger different behaviours depending on the state "Cooling | Heating" with respect to the sun-blinds. In case "Cooling" is activated, the temperature in a room is above a certain threshold, and the sun is shining, the sun-blinds will go down. A system mode represents a group *"of several system configurations under one label where typically each mode corresponds to a set of unique system behaviours"* (Feigh et al. 2012 cited in Johnson 1990).

Environmental-based triggers refer to triggers that occur due to environmental changes being external to the operator or system components. Typical examples for such changes are changing light level, temperature, humidity or wind.

Task- and Mission-based triggers occur when a certain task, e.g. "drill part" or a mission "produce high precision lot-size 1 part" is accomplished. The distinction between task and mission is stated by Feigh et al. (2012) as *"A mission is typically organized into phases or subgoals, each of which is subject to constraints such as the time to complete and pre- and postconditions. Adaptation management based on task state uses the initialization, completion or partial completion of tasks (regardless of their impact on mission goals or objectives) to drive changes in automation"*.

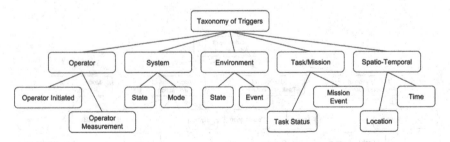

Fig. 6.2 Taxonomy of Triggers for adaptive systems (adapted from Feigh et al. 2012, © Human Factors and Ergonomics Society)

Spatio-temporal triggers represent system changes that are triggered based on certain times or location, e.g. every day at 7 o'clock the sun-blinds go up, after 10 min of full speed a machine stops to ensure long lifetime and when a qualified employee is near a machine that need to be maintained, he/she will be notified.

The triggers given above may result in different types of adaptations as depicted in Fig. 6.3. The adaptation types sketch the system elements that can be adapted when a certain trigger occurs. For example, stress measurement of operators could trigger task reallocation.

In their taxonomy, Feigh et al. (2012) identify four fundamental elements that may be affected: (i) Function Allocation, (ii) Task Scheduling, (iii) Interaction and (iv) Content.

Function Allocation refers to mechanisms that determine who (human or machine) is responsible to perform a certain function or task. In the literature, static and dynamic function allocations are differentiated. In case of static function allocation, the assignments are defined at design time, whereas in the case of dynamic function allocation the assignment may change during runtime. Such assignments need to consider responsibility and authority of system agents. From an operator's point of view, the modification of function allocation gets evident with respect to task sharing and task offloading. According to Feigh et al. (2012), task sharing refers to the division of work between operators and automated systems, and task offloading aims to shift tasks from operators to automated system elements. However, sharing and offloading may also occur among different operators and not solely between operators and machines.

Task Scheduling considers the timing, duration and prioritization of tasks to be executed by a system. Timing refers to the point in time when a certain task is instantiated. The priority of a task can be differentiated by urgency and importance. Urgency depends, e.g. on the time available to respond or the certainty of a given information. Task importance refers to the potential impact of task failure, e.g. arising safety issues. Aside from the timing and the prioritization, tasks take a certain amount of time. The duration of a task may vary depending on tools used, skills of workers or other contextual factors (e.g. temperature at shop floor) (Feigh et al. 2012).

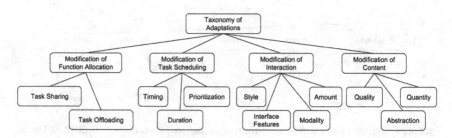

Fig. 6.3 Taxonomy of adaptations for adaptive systems (adapted from Feigh et al. 2012, © Human Factors and Ergonomics Society)

Modification of Interaction focuses on the adaptation of human–machine interaction. According to the taxonomy, such modifications can affect interface features, interaction styles, the frequency of interaction and the modality of communication. The modification of interface features affects the layout or the navigation means provided to humans. When considering the frequency of interaction between humans and machines, one needs to define how much interaction at which point in time is required. Modality of communication refers to the adequate communication channel between humans and machines, e.g. a machine could simply display information or provide the information via text-to-speech means in an auditory way. Interaction styles define "rules of engagement", e.g. pro-active or re-active communication patterns between humans and machines.

Modification of Content considers the modification of content exchanged between machines and humans. Thereby, content may vary with respect to quantity, the level of abstraction or quality. The quantity of content addresses the amount of information displayed. For example, on mobile devices typically less information is displayed compared to larger screens of desktop PCs. Content may also be modified regarding the degree of abstraction. Information may be aggregated to support human operators and reduce processing times. Vice versa, it may be provided in a more detailed form if necessary. Furthermore, Feigh et al. (2012) consider the modification of the quality of content relevant for system adaptation, e.g. videos or pictures may be shipped with different resolutions depending on device and network connection.

The framework of Feigh et al. (2012) aims to provide a guideline for designers, evaluators and researchers when building, evaluating or researching adaptive system behaviour. In addition to Feigh et al. (2012), Steinhauser et al. (2009) propose design guidelines for adaptive automation:

1. Adaptive function allocation should be used intermittently
2. Energetic human qualities should be considered in design
3. Emotional requirements of the human operator need to be considered
4. The system should be calibrated to the individual operating it
5. Task transformation should be used to simplify tasks for operators
6. The environmental context of the system should be used to determine allocation
7. Tasks should be partitioned when both the human and the system can contribute effectively
8. Adaptation should be controlled by the system, but be open to human intervention when the system fails to recognize new conditions or demands

Beyond guidelines, the well-being of humans plays a crucial in design. Findings from occupational psychology reveal *"the number of employees experiencing psychological problems related to occupational stress has increased rapidly in Western countries"* (Van der Klink et al. 2001, p. 270). Basically, stress can be measured by applying (i) psychological questionnaires (ex-post to stressful situations) or (ii) by measuring physiological measures like heart rate variability or blood pressure (cf. Taelman et al. 2009; Lawler 1980; Kelsey 1991). The latter, in combination with wearable sensors, enables live sensing of human stress levels in certain work situations. Such live data provide a basis for analyzing human conditions in work situations, adapting system behaviours at runtime and informing workplace (re-)design activities. For example, tasks could be reallocated based on the current workload and stress level of workers, process steps in which a high stress level occurs could be investigated and redesigned or individuals could monitor and self-assess their own stress level in order to increase their stress-awareness.

A detailed investigation of the efficacy of psychophysiological measures for implementing adaptive technology is presented, e.g. by Screbo et al. (2001). They reviewed physiological measures, such as Eye Blinks, Respiration, Cardiovascular Activity, and beyond that, cortical measures like EEG Bandwidths: Arousal, Attention and Workload; EEG and Biofeedback; EEG Biofeedback and Task Performance; Event Related Potentials; Cerebral Metabolism and Blood Flow.

In the subsequent sections, human-aware S-BPM designs are explored taking into account physiological measures and guidelines for adaptive systems design.

6.2 Stress-Aware Lego Assembly

Today's factories employ people to perform the semi-automatic assembly of a variety of mechanical and electro-mechanical products. Increasingly, the assembly lines are run lean and just in time. When products are built to incoming orders, factories typically perform activities such as: production, packaging and shipping. Production of a single product may be achieved by a single assembly person or a line of them. Once a unit is complete, it needs to be tested, quality checked and then packed. The wrapped parcel then needs to undergo relevant customs and shipping formalities.

The workflow has the conveyor belt and the workers at its centre. Incoming orders need to be shipped as soon as possible. However, enabling workers to perform at an optimum rate (high productivity, high quality, low errors and high job satisfaction) needs to consider a number of critical factors:

- Is there sufficient challenge in the job?
- Is there insufficient challenge leading to long idle times and too much boredom?
- Is the quality of assembly meeting the required standards?
- Is the accuracy (e.g. shipping docs) 100 %?
- Is the workflow under the control of the worker, or is it reverse?
- Stress may arise due to a number of factors; is the level of stress at acceptable limits?
- Is the job challenge/boredom/stress level of one person the same as that of another person?

The work rate on a production line and the error rate (or qualities achieved) are the most important factors for the factory management. Working the line at high rate for long periods will inevitably result in costly errors and worker dissatisfaction.

There are two control points in the workflow: raising a new order and the rate of flow of the conveyor. Using statistical averages, for a given order input rate, theoretically, the conveyor belt should run at a given rate for a given level of quality. However, this statistical rule does not take into account the individuality of the workers who may swap roles on the shop floor and who may achieve higher productivity, as they balance their challenge and boredom levels across several roles at several different times.

When new parts for assembly are introduced, workers may need much more time than statistically allowed for, so that they can become familiar with a particular part. The continuous roll of the conveyor belt can also cause stress for workers simply because (apart from emergency cases) they do not control the conveyor belt per se. Handing over some level of control to the worker slowing down or stopping the belt could empower the worker.

Stress on the production line has been investigated in different research. A study by Lundberga et al. (1989) shows that perceived stress at an assembly line is consistently reflected in cardiovascular and neuroendocrine functions of the workers. Work induced a significant elevation in almost all psychological and physiological measurements. Levels were consistently lower in workers reporting a 'good' workday compared to those reporting a 'normal' or a 'bad' day. Correlations between self-reports and physiological values showed that catecholamine and cortisol responses, respectively, tend to be associated selectively with different psychological conditions, catecholamine values being associated with feelings of time pressure and pressure by demands, cortisol values with irritation, tenseness and tiredness.

Catecholamines are released into the blood when a person is under physical or emotional stress. Catecholamines increase heart rate, blood pressure, breathing rate, muscle strength and mental alertness. They also lower the amount of blood going to the skin and intestines and increase blood going to the major organs, such as the brain, heart and kidneys.

It has been shown by Jacobs et al. (1994) that skin conductance level should be useful in studies assessing the impact of mental stress on cardiovascular function. First, measures of electrodermal activity such as skin conductance level have been found to be highly suitable for monitoring autonomic nervous system activity because such an activity is determined by the sympathetic branch of the autonomic nervous system, which is predominant in stress. Second, as with indexes of cardiac performance such as blood pressure and heart rate, electrodermal response has been found to reliably increase during laboratory mental stress (Boblin 1976; Kelsey 1991; Lawler 1980; O'Gorman and Homeman 1979) and under other threatening, novel or challenging conditions.

Fig. 6.4 LEGO creator building kits

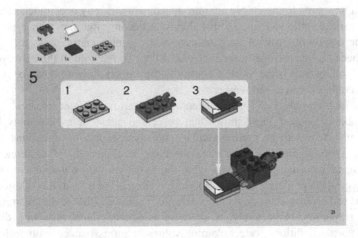

Fig. 6.5 LEGO creator building instructions. *Source* LEGO Group. http://lego.brickinstructions.com/lego_instructions/set/6914/TRex

Jouven et al. (2009) found when working with 5713 subjects that the mean heart rate increased during mild mental stress was 8.9 ± 10.8 b.p.m. (beats per minute) and the cut-off values of the tertiles of heart rate increase during mild mental stress were, 4 b.p.m., between 4 and 12 b.p.m., and above 12 b.p.m. Therefore, in order to assess the stress on a worker over periods of time, we propose that sensors are used to measure heart rate, blood pressure and skin conductance.

By combining data from these sensors and calibrating them for different workers, the work stress may be estimated and indicated. Subsequently, a laboratory study is presented in which test persons assemble different types of LEGO creator models supported by dedicated building instructions (cf. Figs. 6.4 and 6.5). Thereby, their heart rate is measured and the stress level is indicated via a PLC control LED.

6.2.1 Assembly Workplace Setup

The LEGO assembly workplace is sketched in Fig. 6.6. It comprises the following elements:

- Multiple Boxes for assembly orders containing
- LEGO bricks
- Order sheet with QR-Code
- A webcam to identify an order and the related assembly task
- A monitor to display building instructions
- Three LED lights (green, yellow, red) to indicate stress level (low, medium, high)
- The BioRing sensor to measure heart rate, skin conductance, accelerometer data of test persons
- An iPod touch receiving the BioRing data and forwarding them to the S-BPM processing system

The test sessions were structured as follows:

- Introduction of laboratory test and assembly workplace to test person
- Equipping test person with BioRing sensor and initializing of iPod Touch app and S-BPM processing system
- 5 min baseline measurement of test persons in calm state
- 20 min LEGO assembly

Fig. 6.6 Laboratory LEGO assembly workplace

When building certain assembly order, the building instructions were displayed at the screen. In advance to the tests, an experienced LEGO builder assembled the test order and his timing for certain assembly instructions was measured. This reference timing was used as target time for test subjects who were not experienced in building the given types of LEGO models. The target timing and different model variants were intended to challenge test persons and simulate stressful situations.

6.2.2 S-BPM Implementation

Figure 6.7 depicts the implemented system architecture for the LEGO assembly test case. The architecture intertwines the BioRing Sensor, dedicated S-BPM processes implemented in Metasonic Suite and Programmable Logic Controller (PLC) for indicating stress levels. In the given architecture, the Metasonic workflow execution system MFlow comprises the logic for data interpretation and context-sensitive behaviour execution. Thereby, sensor data related to a workplace can be provided by both individual human sensors and the shop floor related low-level controls (cf. PLC in Fig. 6.7). However, in the given scenario the PLC mainly acts as indicator and not as sensor.

The interaction among the system components depicted in Fig. 6.7 can be described as follows. Sensor data are associated with a unique identifier linked to a specific worker. This information is required, in order interpret measured live data with respect to individual baseline and furthermore indicate levels at the workplace where the actual workers remain. A sensor has neither a direct interface to the S-BPM process execution environment nor the low-level controls. The measured data is instead sent to a mobile device using Bluetooth 4.0 and a low-level protocol. This allows for exploiting the connectivity of mobile devices (e.g. WiFi).

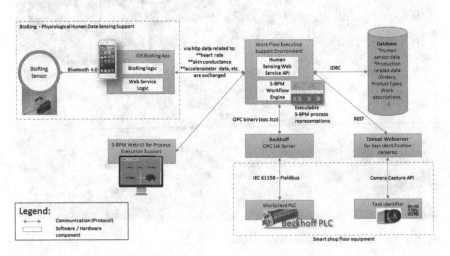

Fig. 6.7 System components for stress measurement and indication when assembling LEGO

Furthermore, a pre-processing (e.g. aggregation, buffering) of the measured data can be done on the mobile device. Additionally, the mobile device may provide worker-related data, e.g. name, location or motion, relevant for context-sensitive process execution.

To forward the pre-processed data to the workflow execution system, a mobile application is used. This mobile application may interface the workflow system via an API (e.g. Web Service API). In the given application, the communication is mediated via a "Human Sensing Web Service API", which encapsulates the data low-level data exchange protocol used by the BioRing and provides means for the S-BPM workflow system to access individual data on a higher degree of abstraction. Based on the sensor data, the workflow system may adapt its process behaviour or trigger changes at PLCs. In the implemented architecture, the communication between Metasonic Flow and the Beckhoff PLC is realized using OPC UA (OLE for Process Control Unified Architecture, cf. https://opcfoundation. org/) to change different stress indication modes.

The implemented S-BPM process design for the LEGO Assembly is described in the following. Thereby, the process logic has been divided into two processes: (i) the LEGO assembly process and the (ii) stress measurement and indication process. The LEGO Assembling subject (cf. Fig. 6.8) represents the start subject and triggers the start and end of an assembly session. When triggering such a session, the Task Identifier subject and the Stress Measurement subject are notified via dedicated messages.

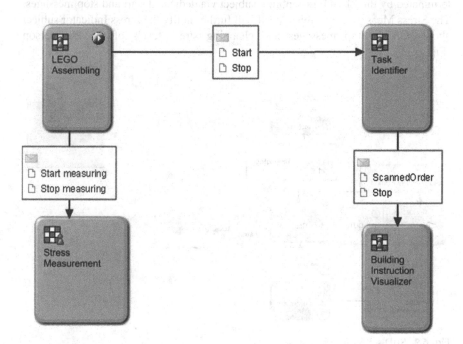

Fig. 6.8 SID—Lego Assembling process

The Task Identifier subject exhibits the behaviour for scanning a QR-code and triggering the Building Instruction Visualizer. Figure 6.9 depicts the subject behaviour of the Task Identifier. Upon receiving the start message from LEGO Assembly, Task Identifier proceeds with scanning QR-codes. Within the function state 'Scan code', a refinement (custom java code) is executed that accesses the camera via a dedicated camera API and reads a QR-code. The QR-code corresponds to orderIds, and thus supports to identify which building instructions shall be displayed and in which state of production a certain assembly order currently remains. In case a QR-Code is successfully read, the scanned orderId is sent to the 'Building Instruction Visualizer'. At any point in time a 'stop' message from LEGO Assembling may be received, which terminates the task identification behaviour. This event is realized via the message event handler 'abort' in Fig. 6.9

The 'Building Instruction Visualizer' subject acts upon the receipt of 'ScannedOrder' messages from the Task Identifier. The message comprises the orderId that allows querying the relevant data from the database in the 'Retrieve order details' function. Based on the queried data, a custom refinement retrieves relevant building instructions for the current order and displays them in a temporal sequence on the screen. When completing the given assembly step, the order is updated and the next scanned order will be displayed (Fig. 6.10).

In parallel to the LEGO Assembling process support, a Stress Measurement and Indication process will be executed for each worker. This process is triggered or terminated by the LEGO Assembling subject via dedicated start and stop messages. The Stress Measurement subject itself will further notify the Stress Indicator subject about start or stop messages and changing stress levels of the test person (Fig. 6.11).

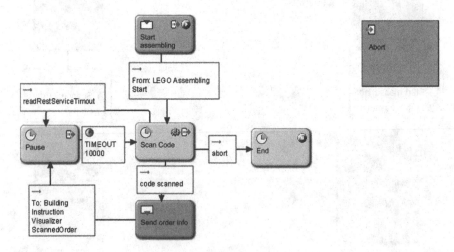

Fig. 6.9 SBD—Task Identifier subject

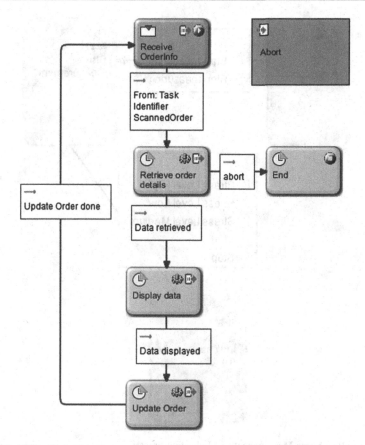

Fig. 6.10 SBD—Task visualizer

The internal behaviour of the Stress Measurement subject is presented in Fig. 6.12. The S-BPM process and the sensor data are intertwined via a database storing human physiological data. Thus, equipping the test person with the sensor and running the App on the iPod touch for communicating the measurements to the human physiological database is a prerequisite for the process execution. Within the process, the 'Stress measurement' subject determines within the initial 5 min the individual baseline of the test person. Subsequently, the stress level of a test person is evaluated on a regular basis (in Fig. 6.12, for example, each and every 8 min) and either 'low', 'medium' or 'high' is sent to the 'Stress Indicator' subject. Again, this process may be terminated at any point in time via receiving a 'Stop measuring' message within the Abort message event handler.

The 'Stress Indication' subject defines the behaviour when changes in stress levels of a test person arise. Thereby, the subject interfaces the PLC via a configured OPC UA server and dedicated OPC UA refinements for different stress levels (cf. Indicate low, medium and high stress function states in Fig. 6.13). An extension

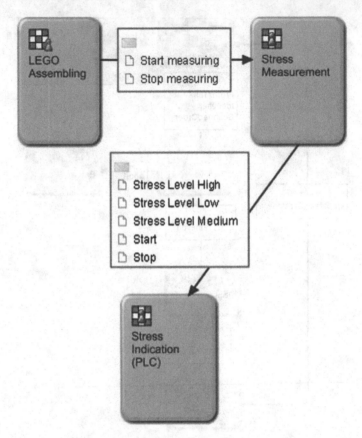

Fig. 6.11 SID—Stress Measurement and Indication process

to Metasonic Suite provides OPC UA refinement templates enabling to get/set values on a PLC based on business object values in the Metasonic Suite. For example, in Metasonic Suite, a business object 'StressIndication' may exist that includes three Boolean values (i) green ON, (ii) yellow ON and (iii) red ON. In case the stress level is low, the values of the business object should be green ON = true, yellow ON = false, red ON = false. These values may then be transferred to the target PLC using the OPC UA template (cf. Fig. 6.14 OPC UA template).

6.2.3 Findings

6.2.3.1 Measuring Human Physiological Data in Work Situations
Within the SO-PC-Pro project, the team aimed to investigate the measurement of human physiological data with the BioRing sensor, a research prototype developed

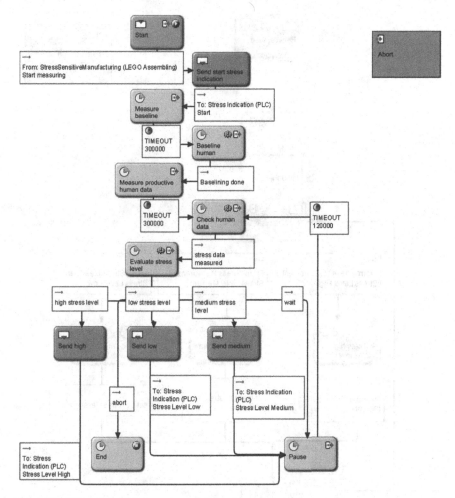

Fig. 6.12 SBD—Stress Measurement subject

by MA Systems. Hence, initial tests investigated the physiological data measured by the BioRing. In order to be able to compare measurements of the BioRing prototype, the users were asked to wear additionally a commercially available Polar H7 chest belt for measuring the heart rate (cf. http://www.polar.com/uk-en/products/accessories/H7_heart_rate_sensor). The Polar H7 measurements were recorded via a customized Android app, in order to support ex-post data analysis and comparison.

Initially, the measurement frequency of the BioRing and the Polar H7 sensor differed. In contrast to the continuous measurement of the Polar H7 sensor, the

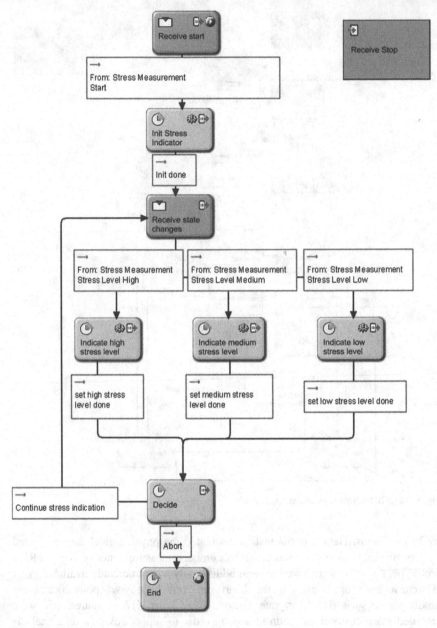

Fig. 6.13 SBD—Stress Indication subject

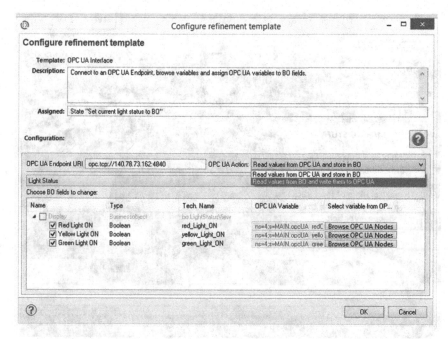

Fig. 6.14 OPC UA template for interfacing OPC UA server variables

tested BioRing prototype measured every 10 s for a duration of 4 s. In order to enable the comparison of the measurements of the two different sensors, the following approach has been taken:

- Definition of measurement periods—1 period lasts 15 s
- Calculation of the average heart rate per measurement period

Within an initial Lego assembly test three male users, aged between 20 and 35, were tested with the BioRing and the Polar H7 chest belt in parallel.

The initial data analysis of the BioRing compared to the commercially available Polar H7 chest belt revealed that there is still room for improvement in order to be able to apply the ring in productive settings. The degradation of the BioRing measurements during the Lego assembly phase is assumed to be due to motion artefacts, since the BioRing builds upon an optical blood flow inspection approach. These artefacts may be neglected by considering the accelerometer data provided by the ring. In the tested system, this already has been implemented. However, it decreased the number of measurements and the availability of current heart rate data.

The Lego assembly scenario itself exhibits motion, in order to accomplish the given task. Therefore, another consequence of this initial test could be to change the point of time where the stress level of a user is evaluated. In case there is a short pause in between two different tasks, the heart rate could be evaluated and compared to previous measurements during pausing situations. In general, the evaluation

Fig. 6.15 Burger shop game to simulate occupational stress

revealed the importance of the appropriate point in time for measuring the stress level of a user with the BioRing. Another topic of improvement considered at that time concerned the measuring frequency of the BioRing. In other words, instead of measuring 4 s every 10 s, data of humans should be measured continuously.

The initial findings triggered further investigations related to the applicability of the BioRing. On the one hand, the firmware of the ring was modified to continuously provide measurements, on the other hand an additional algorithm calculating the heart rate based on the measurements has been implemented. Aside from technical improvements, the application scenario has been modified, in order to avoid movements of the left hand and the left forefinger on which the BioRing typically resides. The new testing scenario applied a BurgerShop game (see Fig. 6.15) in which a player has to produce different types of orders for customers in a certain amount of time to move to the next level. Overall, the deadline to reach the top level in 20 min has been defined to challenge test persons.

Within this scenario, an approach similar to the previously one has been taken:

- Introduction (10 min)
- In the introduction, the test subjects get an overview of the tasks they have to accomplish. This overview includes a short explanation of the sensor setup and the game to be played.
- Equipping the test subject (5 min)

- Test subjects wear the Polar H7 chest belt and the BioRing on the forefinger of their left hand. In order to protect the privacy, the individual subject will be asked to fix the Polar Belt H7 on his own at a separate room. The observers guide the participant equipping with the BioRing.
- Time of adjustment (5 min)
- Baseline data of individual subjects are collected in calm state for 5 min.
- Playing the burger shop game (20 min)
- The subjects play the game exactly for 20 min. The remaining time is shown in front of the PC on a large info wall. The goal is to reach level 10 within the 20 min. In order to avoid noise w.r.t. measurement, the subjects are encouraged to keep their left hand calm and control the game via their right hand and the mouse.

Altogether 12 subjects were tested, whereby the measurements of two of them were considered invalid a priori. The reason for that was the fact that the BioRing seems to have severe issues when measuring a human with cold hands. The data resulting from such a measurement exhibit a constant heart rate of zero beats per minute. Furthermore, the width of a finger has an impact on the quality of measurements. It has been observed that skinny fingers influence negatively the quality of the measured blood flow signal. In the tests, for one subject the measurement with the BioRing did not work at all. The measurement failure was irreproducible for the testing team (neither cold or skinny finger, nor technical issues in terms of battery or service availability). Thus, only the measurements for nine subjects provided a usable data for the analysis. Subsequently, the results are described in more detail.

In the case of subjects 157, 160 and 158, the Polar H7 only provides measured data for 15 min and in case of subject 160 only for 10 min within the human physiological database. However, this phenomenon contradicts the fact that the app continued to measure and the Polar H7 HR was shown on the display. This may be caused by network/server issues or even by service disruptions.

Overall, there were nine measurements that provided suitable data for further processing. The evaluation of these data was conducted by employing two distinct ways of calculating the HR, i.e. the old and the improved and novel algorithm. For five subjects, the new way of calculating the HR worked out properly. Properly means that the BioRing HR approximately conforms to the HR retrieved by the Polar H7. For the remaining four data sets only the original HR could be calculated. The reason for this discrepancy could not be determined.

The measured values regarding the polar belt show that the HR of the nine subjects changed during the experiment. The recorded HR varies around ±5.52 b.p.m on average. In fact, the data of all subjects exhibit a constant up and down of the HR. However, subject 154 displayed a significant increase of 28 b.p.m. above baseline compared to the average increase of 5.52 b.p.m. It has also been observed that at the end of the experiment the HR of subject 156 and 157 increased slightly by 5 b.p.m. above the average increase of 5 b.p.m, whereby, the HR of subject 158 and 159 increased significantly by 15–25 b.p.m. The reason for this rise may be the increased stress the subjects experienced at the end of the 20 min interval.

In summary, the experiences gained with respect to sensing stress based on heart rate show that system designers and implementers need to carefully take into account the measured data provided by human sensors. Dedicated software needs to analyze and correct wrong measurements before considering any behaviour change of an automated system based on heart rate. Finally, we can recommend involving users in system adaption based on their physiological states. This increases the awareness of users and avoids unexpected behavioural changes of the systems.

6.2.3.2 Findings with Respect to Adaptive S-BPM Processes

In the laboratory case, the sensor integration has been implemented by custom refinements for evaluating stress levels. Thus, customized Java programme code was written to evaluate the sensor data stored in a database. This approach requires developers to investigate algorithms for stress measurement based on heart rate and encode them within the models. With respect to reusability, modularity and flexibility, a middleware for human physiological data management would be beneficial. This middleware could be implemented as message bus (cf. Bernstein et al. 2009) that notifies interested processes when, e.g. changes in stress levels or location occur. Given such a middleware, it could be applied in dedicated subject behaviours of adaptive S-BPM processes. Guidelines for designing such processing systems are derived subsequently.

The related work on adaptive systems described above and multiple process developer discussions within the SO-PC-Pro project inspired the formulation of design guidelines for adaptive S-BPM processes. These findings are summarized in the following, in order to provide a reference point for process analysts, designers and implementers. The related work (cf. Sect. 6.1) revealed two important aspects when designing adaptive systems:

- Means for context perception and assessment, and
- Means for adapting different workplace elements adequately

The former refers to the presented triggers of adaptation, whereas the latter refers to the taxonomy of adaptations. In the LEGO assembly scenario, the measurement of physiological attributes of an operator has been investigated as enabler triggering system adaptation based on different stress levels. The simple test model uses the subject "Stress measurement" to continuously perform both checking and evaluating heart rate data for a person based on data stored within a central database.

Thus, the "Stress measurement" subject needs to pro-actively check and evaluate. Even if this approach worked within the laboratory setting, a re-active approach might be an alternative in productive settings (reduction of traffic, running processes, number of requests to the DB...). Re-active means that the S-BPM process is notified from an external "human-sensing" middleware in case of changes (e.g. stress low, stress high...) and does not continuously check for changes itself. This middleware could also manage the sensors used to measure human data (e.g. single measurement by one sensor, multiple sensors providing same values).

Aside from monitoring operators via sensors to trigger adaptation, operators may also pro-actively trigger adaptations, e.g. by dedicated functionalities like request job rotation, pause or task offloading. For this reason, the triggering behaviour needs to be modelled within the internal behaviour of the subjects.

By enabling the integration of PLC behaviour and sensors in S-BPM processes also environmental states at a smart workplace like lighting, temperature or table height may be observed and applied to trigger process changes.

Spatio-temporal aspects (time, location) may also be considered in process designs. Time may either be considered in timer-events, measurement of times takes for certain operations. Location may be provided manually via user input, automatically via GPS or scanning of worker RFID tag.

System triggers and task/mission triggers may be directly encoded in S-BPM models (in transitions, rules). Thus, monitoring of the process progress, e.g. via KPIs or current process state, allows to check an S-BPM processing system state.

Adaptation may affect function allocation, task scheduling, interaction and content. In S-BPM, functions are performed by certain subjects or processes. A modeller may define dedicated roles and users at design time and thus allocate humans or machines in advance to performing the behaviour at runtime. This would correspond to static function allocation. In case a process designer wants to implement a dynamic allocation of humans and machines to subjects at runtime two means may help: (i) selection of an actor out of a list of actors assigned to the role and (ii) dynamic process binding in case different behaviours (e.g. machine behaviour vs. human behaviour) may be triggered when a certain task needs to be accomplished.

Scheduling of tasks in S-BPM may be realized via a dedicated Scheduling subject (either human or machine, or both) which instantiates processes, prioritizes them, defines aimed target duration, monitors tasks completion and modifies schedule based on operation outcomes. In an S-BPM process *Timing* relates to the point of time where a task/process is initiated. This timing may be affected by manual process instantiation, instantiation upon message receipt or system triggered instantiation.

Duration refers to the time a task takes. In S-BPM, task durations of individual subjects may be monitored and KPIs defined to support the management via the indication of deviations. Furthermore, S-BPM-based simulation models could be used gain insight in potential system behaviour before adapting/rescheduling operations. Aside duration, *Priorization* of tasks may be encoded in S-BPM processes in dedicated Business Object fields that are evaluated at runtime.

Another element affected by modifications within adaptive systems represents the interaction among users and machines. S-BPM processes may be tailored to different user groups. Furthermore, recent developments (Kannengiesser et al. 2016) allow customizing user interfaces according to different types of users. In close relation with the interaction, developers need to consider the content to be displayed to users. In S-BPM a designer would need to consider different codalities, levels of abstraction and the quality within the related business objects. This would allow for device- and user-specific shipping of content.

With respect to the taxonomy of adaptive systems, the following generic types of subjects may be derived (cf. Fig. 6.1).

Generic context assessment subjects

- Task identifier

    - Who (man or machine) is doing what?

- Human property sensing

    - What is the current value of relevant human properties (e.g. stress level, state of exhaustion...)?

- Human state inference

    - What is the current state of a human (e.g. working, pausing, running...)?

- Machine property sensing

    - What is the current value of relevant machine properties (e.g. power consumption, acceleration, speed...)?

- Machine state inference

    - What is the current state of a machine (e.g. idle, standby, producing...)?

- Environmental property sensing

    - What is the current value of relevant environmental properties (e.g. humidity, temperature, illumination...)?

- Environmental state inference

    - What is the current environmental state (e.g. hot and humid, daylight, artificial lighting...)?

Generic adaptation subjects

- Task allocation—refers to the above given concept of "Function allocation" and considers who (human or machine) is responsible to perform a certain function or task. This may be encoded in static rules within the process models or dynamically decided during runtime based on the current work distribution among humans and machines

- Task scheduling—such a subject defines the interface among a scheduling software focusing on (timing, duration, prioritization) and the processes to be triggered or dynamically reallocated

Dedicated subjects for adapting interaction and content are not recommended. Regarding the adaptation of interaction, the defined interaction logic resides in S-BPM within the defined subject interactions and the exchanged messages. Thus, dedicated models need to be created with respect to different interactions and provided for execution support. Regarding content adaptation, one could model a dedicated "content broker" that provides for different types of consuming subjects adequate content, e.g. in terms of quantity, or granularity. Alternatively, dedicated content-provision subjects could be defined for each type of content consumer.

Based on the individual project, the given subjects and intended behaviour may be considered by process designers to implement adaptive S-BPM processing systems. The assessment subjects are split-up into subjects sensing concrete values and subjects responsible for inferring a certain state. Thereby, multiple sensors could provide data on relevant properties and the inference subjects may consider them. This separation also allows interested subject to independently request current values of certain properties and inferred states. Furthermore, subjects aggregating the different states of humans, machines and the environment may be modelled in future process development projects since these dimensions typically need to be carefully aligned.

6.3 Conclusive Summary

The worker and his or her well-being is regarded a crucial part of manufacturing situations. Designing and implementing adaptive systems considering human properties to identify disturbances, monitor crucial states and tune workplaces a.t.l., in order to fit human needs gained interest in diverse research areas, such as human factors engineering, pervasive computing, Industry 4.0 or factories of the future.

Advances in the area of wearable sensors proclaim that sensing human properties within manufacturing settings is technically feasible. Thereby, sensing human properties, such as the level of comfort or stress, may be used to adapt system behaviour in manufacturing situations. In this chapter, S-BPM's capabilities to design a human-aware assembly scenario have been investigated. Thereby, related work from adaptive systems design addresses dimensions and triggers for adaptation. We could derive relevant design aspects and set up a laboratory environment at the Johannes Kepler University Linz for testing measurements and adaptation designs. The developed system architecture and the respective S-BPM models can be used for further projects due to the generic integration approach of S-BPM with sensors via Web Services and the OPC Unified Architecture (cf. Neubauer et al. 2015).

Although measuring human physiological data in work situations is technically feasible, designing such systems requires ensuring the availability and reliability of human sensor data. The laboratory test revealed that even commercially available sensors like the Polar H7 chest belt may fail in terms of delivering no measurements due to lack of contact with the skin. Hence, for certain work situations it is recommended to investigate suitable sensors and their applicability within the given work environment. Furthermore, we could observe that the quality of the BioRing measurements differs among test subjects. Influencing factors like finger temperature or width of fingers cause different quality of heart rate measurements. Therefore, a "one-sensor fits them all" mentality is not appropriate. We rather recommend evaluating the appropriateness of certain sensors with individual humans in concrete work settings.

Adaptive processing systems can be implemented utilizing S-BPM concepts and technologies. Adaptation may either be triggered explicitly by humans or implicitly via sensors. Certain machine states, environmental or spatio-temporal states may trigger adaptation. Triggers may cause changes in task allocation and task scheduling. Finally, the interaction between users and the system, as well as the content provided may be adapted. Possibilities to considerer the triggers and types of adaptations in S-BPM models have been discussed in this chapter. They shall serve as starting point for future developments targeting adaptive sensor-based S-BPM processes initiating changes at runtime.

References

Bernstein, D., Ludvigson, E., Sankar, K., Diamond, S., & Morrow, M. (2009). Blueprint for the intercloud-protocols and formats for cloud computing interoperability. In M. Perry, H. Sasaki, M. Ehmann, G. O. Bellot, & O. Dini (Eds.), *The Fourth International Conference on Internet and Web Applications and Services ICIW 2009* (pp. 328–336). IEEE. doi:10.1109/ICIW.2009.55.

Boblin, G. (1976). Delayed habituation of the electrodermal orienting response as a function of increased level of arousal. *Psychophysiology, 13*, 345–351. doi:10.1111/j.1469-8986.1976. tb03088.x.

Feigh, K. M., Dorneich, C., & Hayes, C. C. (2012). Toward a characterization of adaptive systems: A framework for researchers and system designers. *Human Factors, 54*(6–12), 1008–1024. doi:10.1177/0018720812443983.

Jacobs, S. C., Friedman, R., Parker, J. D., Tofler, G. H., Jimenez, A. H., Muller, J. E., et al. (1994). Use of skin conductance changes during mental stress testing as an index of autonomic arousal in cardiovascular research. *American Heart Journal, 128*(6), 1170–1177.

Jouven, X., Schwartz, P. J., Escolano, S., Straczek, C., Tafflet, M., Desnos, M., et al. (2009). Excessive heart rate increase during mild mental stress in preparation for exercise predicts sudden death in the general population. *European Heart Journal, 30*, 1703–1710.

Kannengiesser, U., Heininger, R., Gründer, T., & Schedl, S. (2016). Modelling the process of process execution: A process model-driven approach to customising user interfaces for business process support systems. In *International Workshop on Business Process Modeling, Development and Support* (pp. 34–48). Springer International Publishing. doi:10.1007/978-3-319-39429-9_3.

Kelsey, R. M. (1991). Electrodermal lability and myocardial reactivity to stress. *Psychophysiology*, *28*(6), 619–631. doi:10.1111/j.1469-8986.1991.tb01005.x.

Lawler, K. A. (1980). Cardiovascular and electrodermal response patterns in heart rate reactive individuals during psychological stress. *Psychophysiology*, *17*(5), 464–470. doi:10.1111/j.1469-8986.1980.tb00185.x.

Lundberga, U., Granqvistb, M., Hanssonc, T., Magnussonc, M., & Wallind L. (1989). Psychological and physiological stress responses during repetitive work at an assembly line. *Work & Stress: An International Journal of Work, Health & Organisations*, *3*(2).

NASA Langley Technical Report. Retrieved July 20, 2016, from http://ntrs.nasa.gov/archive/nasa/casi.ntrs.nasa.gov/20010067614.pdf.

Neubauer, M., Krenn, F., & Majoe, D. (2015). Towards an architecture for human-aware modeling and execution of production processes. *IFAC-PapersOnLine*, *48*(3), 294–299.

O'Gorman, J. G., & Homeman, C. (1979). Consistency of individual differences in nonspecific electrodermal activity. *Biological Psychology*, *9*(1), 13–21. doi:10.1016/0301-0511(79)90019-X.

Scerbo, M. W., Parasuraman, R., Di Nocero, F., & Prinzel, L. J. (2001). The efficacy of psychophysiological measures for implementing adaptive technology. NASA/TP-2001–211018.

Steinhauser, N. B., Pavlas, D., & Hancock, P. A. (2009). Design principles for adaptive automation and aiding. *Ergonomics in Design*, *17*(2), 6–10.

Taelman, J., Vandeput, S., Spaepen, A., & Van Huffel, S. (2009). Influence of mental stress on heart rate and heart rate variability. In J. Vander Sloten, P. Verdonck, M. Nyssen, & J. Haueisen (Eds.), *4th European Conference of the International Federation for Medical and Biological Engineering, IFMBE Proceedings* (Vol. 22, pp. 1366–1369). Berlin: Springer.

Van der Klink, J. J., Blonk, R. W., Schene, A. H., & Van Dijk, F. J. (2001). The benefits of interventions for work-related stress. *American Journal of Public Health*, *91*(2), 270–276.

Open Access This chapter is distributed under the terms of the Creative Commons Attribution-NonCommercial 4.0 International License (http://creativecommons.org/licenses/by-nc/4.0/), which permits any noncommercial use, duplication, adaptation, distribution and reproduction in any medium or format, as long as you give appropriate credit to the original author(s) and the source, provide a link to the Creative Commons license and indicate if changes were made.

The images or other third party material in this chapter are included in the work's Creative Commons license, unless indicated otherwise in the credit line; if such material is not included in the work's Creative Commons license and the respective action is not permitted by statutory regulation, users will need to obtain permission from the license holder to duplicate, adapt or reproduce the material.

Learnings

7

Chiara Di Francescomarino, Chiara Ghidini, Mauro Dragoni,
Udo Kannengiesser, Richard Heininger, Dennis Majoe,
Lubomir Billy, Pavol Terpak, Nicola Flores, Franco Cesaro,
Alexandra Totter, David Bonaldi, Matthias Neubauer
and Christian Stary

Abstract

This chapter reports on learnings gained from the industrial cases (Chaps. 4 and 5) and on a more general level on learnings related to sensing. Doing so, the generic steps and stakeholders involved within the two different cases are described and for each activity bundle respective learnings are reported. Aside from the procedural reflection, learnings from the regional consulting partners within the cases are described on a general level. In addition to the case learnings, learnings with respect to sensing human and machine properties are reported. As such the

C. Di Francescomarino (✉) · C. Ghidini · M. Dragoni
Fondazione Bruno Kessler, Trento, Italy
e-mail: dfmchiara@fbk.eu

U. Kannengiesser · R. Heininger
Metasonic GmbH, Pfaffenhofen, Germany

D. Majoe
MA Systems and Control Limited, Southampton, UK

L. Billy · P. Terpak
Centire, Bratislava, Slovakia

N. Flores · F. Cesaro
Cesaro&Associati, Fumane, Italy

A. Totter · D. Bonaldi
ByElement GmbH, Schindellegi, Switzerland

M. Neubauer · C. Stary
Department of Business Information Systems – Communications Engineering, Johannes
Kepler University Linz, Linz, Austria

© The Author(s) 2017
M. Neubauer and C. Stary (eds.), *S-BPM in the Production Industry*,
DOI 10.1007/978-3-319-48466-2_7

chapter is intended to inform practitioners about crucial aspects to be considered, lessons learnt in the different activities of the cases and suitable method support or enrichment regarding the different S-BPM activities.

7.1 Learnings from the Industrial Cases

The industrial cases presented in Chaps. 4 and 5 reported on the application of S-BPM in two different settings. The first one focusses on digitizing the production process in a vertically integrated manner, whereas the latter supports employee involvement in workplace improvement. However, both cases applied a similar project approach which will be discussed and reflected with respect to learnings in this section (Fig. 7.1).

The case implementations represented an international and multidisciplinary endeavour. Stakeholders of the cases included

- Case Companies (management and employees/workers)
- Regional consulting partners
- R&D department of technology providers (S-BPM tool provider, MoKi collaboration tool provider)
- Sensor developer
- Human-centred design and evaluation consultant
- Process management researcher
- Funding agency (European Commission)

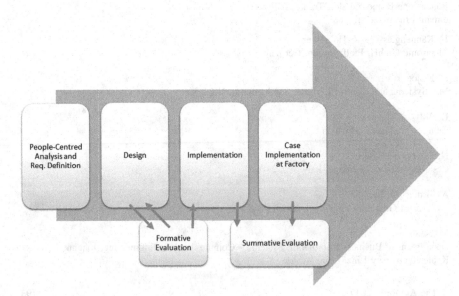

Fig. 7.1 Generic steps taken within the industrial cases

Subsequently, learnings within the different activity bundles are reported. Furthermore, observed interdependencies are discussed in this section. Finally, general learnings from the cases are presented.

7.1.1 People-Centred Analysis and Requirements Elicitation

The cases aimed to gain deep insights into work practices and needs of people at their workplace in order to enable respective solution design. Thus, a procedure has been applied which builds upon accepted frameworks and models in the field of human-centred design (cf. Maguire 2001), Requirements Engineering (cf. Paetsch et al. 2003; Dean and Don 2003) and Subject-Oriented Business Process Management (cf. Fleischmann et al. 2012).

Basically, the procedure consists of three activity bundles—(1) Analysis of organizational improvement potentials, (2) Use case definition, (3) Requirements elicitation—that may be conducted iteratively in order to elicit and design appropriate solutions for future production workplaces (Fig. 7.2). Within the initial analysis, on-site observations and interviews with employees have been conducted to gain knowledge about the as-is situation and first insights into desired to-be situations. Aside, a brainstorming session with the management of each industrial partner has been conducted to identify suitable use case candidates and opportunities for organizational improvement. Use case candidate descriptions comprise involved stakeholders and workplaces, the motivation and opportunity and initial improvement ideas from workers and management. Each potential improvement has been assessed along several dimensions: Process automation, people-centredness, management impact, production efficiency, application potential of S-BPM for communication and execution support and level of involvement of the project partners. These assessment dimensions stem from overall, high-level project goals, topics relevant to the funding agency and company needs.

Learnings related to the analysis of organizational improvement potentials are

- Encourage open-minded ideation
- Carefully observe workplace context to identify relevant influence dimension for solution development (e.g. culture, environment, social interdependencies, …)

Based on the knowledge gained from the initial analysis, in a second step a concrete use case has been derived. Such a use case description is composed of, according to Kliem et al. (1997): (1) Motivation and Opportunity, (2) Goals and Objectives and (3) Scope of the case, including boundaries to stakeholder and related systems. Additionally, the description has been enriched with a high-level S-BPM process model to illustrate the involved actors and their collaboration. The case definition was supported by the use case dimensions given above. Especially

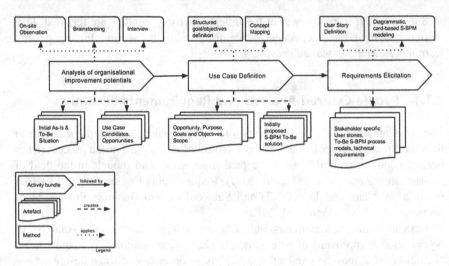

Fig. 7.2 Generic elicitation and design approach in the industrial cases

the goal and objective definition with multiple stakeholder from different fields turned out to require support for the structured collection and alignment of use case goals and objectives.

Goals and objectives were collected in a table structure by each stakeholder. This step resulted in a set of goals and objectives of different stakeholders. Since the results were overlapping across different stakeholders and the granularity of the different inputs varied, a consolidation of the collected goals and objectives was necessary to reduce duplicates and align different points of view. Thus, Concept Mapping has been applied to identify replications and depict relationships between goals and objectives. Concept maps structure knowledge in the form of nodes and edges. Concepts represent a subject (area) or metaphors and are related to one another by edges. As they represent relationships, each relation needs to be named. The Concept Mapping resulted in a consolidated list of goals and objectives of the respective case.

Learnings related to the use case definition:

- Sole provision of the definition of the terms "goal" and "objective" is not sufficient for a distributed, multi-perspective procedure to collect goals and objectives. A shared understanding related to both terms needs to be developed before in order to reduce diverse levels of granularity. Active discussion of results and synchronous alignment is recommended
- Collaborative, multidisciplinary goal and objective definition requires careful alignment among stakeholders. The consolidation of results needs to be comprehensible for stakeholders

The documentation gained from the first two activity bundles was reformulated by the management and the project team in terms of user stories, in order to specify functional requirements for that case. User stories follow the idea to formulate a requirement in terms of the sentence structure 'who—wants what—why' and they are used to structure implementation tasks in the context of agile software development. To ensure the alignment with the end users, the user stories were validated with them. Additionally, workers were able to formulate further user stories. Based upon these requirements an S-BPM implementation could be developed. The S-BPM models were created by applying a diagrammatic, card-based S-BPM modelling approach in the first step. The card-based modelling does not require IT support and aims for involving process participants in modelling. However, the card-based approach was supported by an S-BPM tool subsequently. Since the resulting models can directly be executed, it could be validated with the end users in a kind of role play allowing the identification of errors or hot spots for further improvement.

Learnings related to the requirements definition:

- User stories represent a simple means to define functional requirements. However, the specification process needs to be moderated and supported in order to ensure an adequate level of granularity
- User stories and S-BPM process specifications need to be aligned. When modelling keep in mind the defined user stories. Furthermore, map user stories to new process designs and perform a consistency check
- The defined and agreed-upon user stories need to be considered as dynamic entities! The current list of user stories should be made available for all stakeholders, in order to encourage active discussion among them
- User stories need to be actively considered in later project stages as baseline for task accomplishment

People-centred requirements elicitation depends amongst others on the context of the requirements elicitation at a specific time, like the dependencies of workers on the ongoing technological developments and the dynamics and changes in management affecting the solution or use case itself. This context should be taken into account to balance the organizational requirements (use case scoping, organizational changes during the project), the elicited functional people-centred requirements and the state of the technical development and requirements over a long development period, as the 3 years of the project in hand.

Hence, an integrated requirements and project management framework is considered to be helpful. Such a framework should comprise existing dependencies between the use case context, the technology development and the people-centred requirements stated by the workers. Its implementation should involve all the stakeholders at key points of the development to monitor the project setting and situation related to the people-centred requirements analysis, in order to ensure that people-centred requirements engineering is not influenced by any managerial, organizationa, or technological issues during the project lifecycle.

7.1.2 Informed Subject-Oriented Process Design and Implementation

The defined use cases for each industrial partner, the identified functional requirements in terms of user stories and the organizational requirements in terms of a high-level to-be S-BPM process model represented the initial reference point for the solution design. In the first step, the development and regional consultant partners created mock-up prototypes for the desired user interfaces. Furthermore, the S-BPM models were refined by the process and development partners.

In order to inform the design process and ensure that the project meets user expectations, formative evaluation activities were conducted. In developer workshops, the development and consulting partners mainly aligned technical issues regarding the design and implementation of the desired solution, whereas the focus groups were intended to receive feedback from the actual users. The involvement of operative stakeholders in the process design and validation contributed to the development of a shared understanding and targeted towards qualifying employees in subject-oriented modelling.

The project team consisted of several stakeholders, in order to collect different know-hows. Management had a holistic understanding of the company and delivered valuable input to optimization potentials, relevant applications and different solutions. In addition to that, the management represented customer needs. Production workers contribute to providing local optimization potential, requirements and feedback on possible solutions from the user perspective. The regional IT consulting partners accompanying the project were responsible for introducing solutions, gathering feedback and ensuring the project implementation on-site at the industrial partners. Research and development partners contributed to innovate solution and evaluation designs.

In general, the project team considered early prototyping and user-led design and implementation as vital for the project's success. Without continuously showing and explaining new technological solutions, it is difficult for people to envision the possibilities of a new solution and to indicate requirements and advices during the development. Thus, early prototyping and tool training are essential for the knowledge transfer. Furthermore, it may serve to showcase the possibilities of the technology to future users in an early stage and to create a common vision.

Informed by the results of the focus groups more advanced prototypes were created for the industrial cases. These prototypes were actually tested within concrete user tests investigating the usability, usefulness and acceptance of developed solutions. Again, the outcome informed the development team within the implementation activities.

Learnings related to subject-oriented (process) design:

- Blending S-BPM models with user interface mock-up prototypes is beneficial for fostering a shared understanding between users and developers

- The generic Metasonic workflow support user interface was deemed too complex to be used by shopfloor workers. Customization of user interfaces enabling the provision of easy-to-use interfaces is vital to stakeholder acceptance
- Modelling S-BPM with actual users needs to be carefully moderated and guided

Although S-BPM comprises a limited set of modelling symbols, it may not be the best or the easiest modelling approach to be used. Its benefits and drawbacks have to be evaluated involving the specific target users and checking the project's purpose (Fig. 7.3).

Learnings related to formative evaluation:

- Clear documentation of evaluation results as well as the definition of consequences and measures for the implementation supports the alignment with user needs
- User involvement contributes to a shared understanding of user needs and adequate solution design
- Formative evaluation activities were observed to be beneficial for:

  - Management commitment
  - Discussion of different support aspects for certain groups of users

- Workshops should provide sufficient time and space for testing and feedback articulation, in order to avoid that participants have only a limited amount of time and do not really engage in evaluation activities

The implementation in both the cases has been tailored to the capabilities and needs of the specific companies. The focus in company A was to digitize the production process and integrate sensors in order to facilitate real-time production state tracking. As such, the implementation required the collaboration of regional IT consultant, the S-BPM tool provider, the hardware developer and the S-BPM research team. Within developer workshops, interfaces and technical issues were aligned within the team. Individual modules, such as location tracking or power

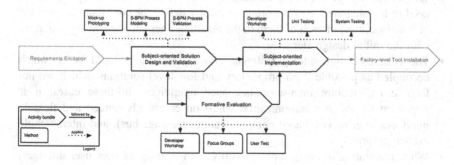

Fig. 7.3 Design and implementation activities

metering were tested within different unit test in order to ensure the provision of appropriate functionality. Furthermore, the integration of the diverse components has been tested within system tests. The implementation also comprised interfacing existing systems of the company. However, company A introduced a new ERP system during the implementation phase. Modified interface definitions and missing interfaces for the required solution delayed the implementation and caused additional alignment effort.

In company A, research prototypes for integrating sensors in S-BPM processes have been applied and tested as part of the implementation (OPC UA template, location sensing service). Furthermore, customizing S-BPM user interfaces has been tested in a productive setting for the first time.

Learnings related to the implementation relevant for company A:

- Process designers and implementers need to understand semantics of sensor data that are used within the process
- Synchronisation between the business process (workflow) engine and the real-time engine needs to be carefully investigated and decided upon a case-by-case basis, e.g. when implementing push or pull notifications
- Customizing user interfaces according to the approach of Kannengiesser et al. (2016) is vital. However, the customization needs to be done by experts and is hardly understood by domain users

In company B, the S-BPM tool provided by Metasonic has been integrated for the first time with the MoKi collaboration platform. The Metasonic tool functionalities for modelling and executing S-BPM process models have been combined with the MoKi functionalities for the collaborative user-friendly modelling of (structured and unstructured) knowledge. The focus in company B was supporting the company's suggestion process, by enabling workers to report issues and provide suggestions about their workplace, managers to provide feedback, analyse data and make decisions and all of them to discuss and keep track of problems and potential solutions.

Learnings related to the Metasonic-Moki integration:

- When two or more existing technologies, possibly providing multiple features, need to be integrated, it is important to clearly define the contribution (in terms of functionalities) of each of them in the resulting integrated technology, starting with the initial design steps
- The communication among different existing software should be as much decoupled as possible from proprietary and low-level solutions, which are not flexible and require intense maintenance operations. In these cases, it is important to design communication based on commonly agreed and flexible interfaces (e.g. service-based communication, message bus), and interoperable exchange formats
- When integrating different tools, possibly each offering its own user interface, users have to be provided with an adjusted or unique interface (e.g. the user

interface of one of the tools, a completely new user interface, or an interface embedding the others), minimizing extra learning effort, and avoiding confusion due to different user interface elements

Learnings related to the solution implementation:

- Involving real users of the implemented tool in the design of the user interfaces is of the utmost importance. Indeed, different devices and user expertise with common usage patterns (e.g. tablet interactions vs classical keyboard/mouse interaction) affect the acceptance
- S-BPM processes that have to be executed, when describing human behaviours, have to be designed in a flexible way to take into account a number of exceptions and errors that can occur when dealing with human procedures (requiring rolling back operations)
- Avoiding duplicate and scatter information in different repositories is fundamental for maintenance and general applicability purposes
- Adopting simple solutions is to be preferred in industrial environments because it allows meeting scalability requirements in a more convenient way

7.1.3 Factory-Level Tool Installation

The factory-level tool installations in company A and B comprised the organizational and technical setup of the solutions developed for the defined cases. These activities were performed by the regional consulting partners and the technology providers. As key take-aways they reported the following observations:

- Always test the system in the actual field with actual users:

  - Network quality, network configurations, email-server configurations, different end-user devices may cause unexpected behaviours when switching from the test to the live system
  - Users do not always behave as developers would expect them to do

- Shop floor conditions may influence asset tracking. For instance, in the case of company A, the configuration of the signal strength with respect to different workplaces was carefully tested on-site
- Ensure an adequate hardware environment for the productive use of the developed technologies, avoiding the usage of outdated test machines

7.1.4 Summative Evaluation

Summative evaluation reported in both the cases on findings related to the outcome of the actual case implementations. For each case implementation, the technology acceptance, the achievement of goals and objectives and the people-centredness of the provided solution were investigated based on an individually developed case evaluation framework. The following key take-aways have been observed by the solution developers, evaluation designers and evaluators:

- Evaluation designers need a clear understanding of the solution provided and the relationship to the case goals and objectives. Hence, close cooperation with solution developers when designing the evaluation framework is recommended
- Evaluation designers need to closely work together with actual (regional) evaluators in order to ensure that evaluators are aware of the evaluation object and the method
- The documentation of the evaluation results should be supported by evaluation designers. Validation of results by multiple stakeholders is recommended

7.1.5 Consultancy Learnings Reported Within the Cases

In addition to the above given case learnings related to the different activity bundles performed, general learnings from the regional consulting partners have been reported and are described in terms of principles to follow in such projects.

7.1.5.1 Learnings Related to Company A
Continuously discuss the project progress with the company management

Company A has, within the project implementation, experienced changes on the management level. Due to the effort to increase the production and efficiency, crisis managers were hired. New managers (in conclusion hired for just a short period) seemed not always to be familiar with the impact the project should create. Therefore, they did not support the project implementation adequately. For future, it is advisable to permanently discuss the project course with management and precisely present the project impact on the current as well as on future production.

Gain feedback from a sufficient number of users to avoid individually customized solutions
Company A experienced changes on different levels of operation within the project implementation. Especially in the last phase of the project the company had to deal with changes of the staff's structure. Some employees have been affected by salary decreases and therefore decided to quit—among them at least three workers previously involved in the solution design. Thus, employees evaluating the developed solutions who were not involved in depth in the project could have missed the complete information on the project aspect—mainly its potential benefits. Those employees may perceive the developed case rather of low additional benefit, and

thus, resistance to the new approach may become evident. Therefore, the involvement of an extended group of potential users (not only 5) is recommended to continuously validate the solution design and implementation.

Engage shop floor workers

A core topic of the case has been "people-centredness". The consulting and industry partners have made a maximum effort to involve all relevant workers, especially shop floor workers. It can be stated that shop floor workers have been involved in the project implementation as originally envisioned. However, the continuous presentation and discussion of the project progress with the shop floor has been observed as a crucial element for project success. To some extent, the communication could have been too focused on the high management, neglecting the workers.

Carefully introduce technologies that might be used to monitor workers

Some of the implemented features can be used for "worker monitoring". When perceived by workers (e.g. power consumption, time monitoring, etc.), such features need to be discussed with them and the usage of the data as well as the security of the data needs to become transparent. Otherwise, resistance towards such solutions could rapidly come up.

Reserve sufficient time for feature testing

Although the project set out enough time for testing, some of the features were not used to an extent enabling conclusions. Moreover, some of the features show their impact and benefits on a long-term basis. Potentially, more time for comprehensive testing and deficiency correction should have been planned, as it could have increased the perception of employees being involved. The evaluation process could have been carried out within the testing process repeatedly, enabling to monitor the employees' perception in time.

Closely cooperate with providers of existing systems and their interfaces

During the project implementation, Company A implemented a new ERP system. Some system features collided with the proposed solutions and, to a certain extent, affected some of the project activities. It would have been beneficial for the regional consulting partner to be involved in the analysis sessions between company A and the ERP provider in order to align overlaps, interfaces and conflicts.

Continuously update and review use cases and solution ideas

In an initial phase, use cases were defined. However, the project design and implementation covered the period of almost 3 years including changes affecting different elements of company A. For instance, management changes, changes in management commitment, staff layoff and economic issues of the company could all have had an effect on the initially envisioned solution. Thus, company requirements must not be considered static, they rather present a dynamic element that needs to be tackled as such to create stakeholder value.

7.1.5.2 Learnings Related to Company B

Involving users from the beginning of the project increases their willingness to participate

The people-centred approach adopted from the initial phases of the project and the involvement of the workers in the analysis and design phases supported the project participation in terms of motivation and commitment. Both, Company B management and workers declared that such an active involvement allowed for the creation of something actually useful and helpful for their daily working experience.

Formative and case evaluations are useful:

Formative and case evaluations are useful for a twofold purpose: (i) supporting the system development and iterative refinement; (ii) user-centredness. On the one hand, they provide an effective means to support the development process, starting from the design of the system up to its iterative refinements as well as actual advantages for the case. Since the perception a developer has of the to-be system is likely to differ from user expectations, early feedback and iterative development supported the alignment between users, the organization and the development. On the other hand, the involvement of workers in the suggestion and evaluation phases, and the importance given to their feedback, increase their understanding of the system as well as their motivation towards the system usage.

Furthermore, the following aspects of the formative and case evaluation activities were observed to be beneficial

- Management commitment
- Discussion of different support aspects for certain groups of users (to develop a common understanding)
- Sufficient time for workshops (thus avoiding that participants have only a limited amount of time and do not really engage in the evaluation activity).

7.2 Learnings Related to Sensing

7.2.1 Human Sensing

The experiences gained within the sensor-related investigation of the authors revealed the fact that when sensors that are worn by workers in order to determine something about their status as a result of physiological measurements, widespread adoption will require that the workers believe that the end objective is not only good for productivity but also good for the work force.

The accuracy rating of data coming from a sensor must be very high if instantaneous changes in a workflow are going to be performed automatically as a function of the sensor data. Since the interrelationship between physiological responses and mental state is very complex, the analytical treatment of the sensor data must also achieve very high classification accuracy if it is to be used in real time.

At this stage it appears that the risk of upsetting workers (privacy intrusion) and the risk of upsetting a workflow (due to inaccurate sensor and data analytics) can be minimized by using data over longer periods of time, in such a way that it can be partly anonymized, inaccuracies can be reduced as outlier, and unacceptably noisy data are removed from the processed data.

Human sensors also need to be treated within the context of the "big picture". The attraction of human sensors is to allow automatic systems to gain some insight into the working life of the employee. As an example, take the case of a good shop floor manager who keeps a close eye on an employee working in production. Applying his intuition, experience and empathy the manager can detect when the employee is stressed and the manager can try to improve the work conditions by changing the workflow or training. The manager does not only see stress in the employee's visage, but also knows the man's experience on the job and his temperament, for example he takes longer to learn but once he does he excels. He knows the jobs the worker is on and he knows they are very difficult to perform.

To match the capability of the manager, the sensors need to be combined with other information so that a full picture is built up. Worker Stress + worker experience + workers current jobs + complexity of those jobs.

Thus the human sensor has its place, inside a large labyrinth of extra data, and to achieve automated high-level semantic conclusions, data from many sources over long time is needed. If not, then only very simple almost trivial analytics will be achievable.

7.2.2 Asset Tracking

Although during the developments of Company A a tag sensor with many inbuilt functions was built, it appears that in the face of diverse applications (ranging from many different types of production method to many different features associated with each asset) tags need to be much more diversified to fit in closely with a given domain or specific product or service.

Certain key electronic functions can be retained as standard such as memory, primary sensing and communications.

However the diversity will come in

- The embodiment of the electronics (for example into packaging)
- The physical way in which humans will probe the tag
- The physical way in which machines will probe the tag
- The tag deployment and recycling infrastructure

- Tag data security
- Cost benefit

In fact it would seem that consultants could create commercial consultancy services purely to address these topics.

From the point of view of the necessary middleware-software systems processing data from sensors, data analytics could be kept very simple with limited need for complex algorithms. Instead databases could simply be generated showing the data and making it available for querying by other applications when necessary. Thus, the software systems could be very light and even adopt an Internet of Things model for scaling up towards many millions of assets.

Probably the biggest benefit of tagging in this way would come from the ability to make sweeping observations about wastage in the process or the organization (e.g. finding out why so many items are perishing from heat or identifying quality failure issues early in the production process). In this case visualization of the big sensor data could allow human decision-makers to identify financial savings.

This concept was considered in a use case related to a bakery where cream cakes were either being over produced or under produced leading to wastage or lost sales. In this use case, very low cost tags could have been used as part of the product packaging. This would allow a fully automatic and accurate real-time stock control to be applied across several retail outlets across a large geographic area. This data could lead towards improved prediction of demand and just in time cake production.

7.2.3 Machine Usage Profiling

While tags on assets can provide status information, there is a limit to which the internal workings of a machine (e.g. a CNC machine) can be inferred or understood by the production modelling system. During the developments it became clear that many production CNC machines do not expose their internal workings, for example by providing status information, by way of a computer connection. Clearly, this will change as such a feature is seen as useful. However, intelligent features may not be provided in all production machines, and there remains a large number of legacy equipment in factories across the EU.

At the same time we realized that energy consumption in factories is an important issue, to be monitored in order to reduce costs. By combining these two ideas, we decided to use the monitoring of power to a machine as a means to infer the status of a machine through the way it uses power in real time as well as the overall level of total power consumed per week or month.

Doing so, a commercial OPC UA-enabled solution for non-invasive power metering was applied. This solution offered Ethernet connectivity and immediate CE approvals which meant they could be deployed on industry machinery with no risk to safety.

What we learnt was that deploying energy sensors in fully up and running factories requires special health and safety considerations that should not be underestimated. In several cases, it was not easy to interfere with the installations and installing the sensors required a multidisciplinary team of electrical and computer staff as well as management with health and safety in the loop.

Interfacing the energy monitors for each of the machines was achieved after relevant data exchange protocols were adhered to, and then real-time data of current consumption could be measured in real time via OPC UA.

The main idea behind energy monitoring is to look at the way the electrical power changes in real time during very short bursts as well as on average. Rotating electrical machines at first takes large amounts of power to achieve the high rotational speeds. Thus, at start up and within a few seconds the power profile is peaked and remarkable. However, with no load except friction the CNC machines reach a steady state of power consumption that is very low. The rotating parts usually have a very high rotational inertia and very high rotational momentum achieved once running at full speed. Therefore, when a tool begins to cut into a metal part at high speed the extra power to achieve the cut is comparatively small and perturbations are also very small having been filtered by the large rotational momentum.

Resistive electrical loads like ovens and boilers provide much simpler energy profiles. General automation based on DC servo motors and frequent load changes also are easier to characterize. Valve solenoids combined with pressured hydraulics or pneumatics are more difficult to model as the electrical pulses and compression system cannot be easily logically related without a clear idea about the different behaviour modes.

In a situation such as our CNC machine use case, while it is possible to detect the run up and run down of the machines, more subtle changes require a very high resolution power detection. Even when providing this information, it is necessary to correlate the energy changes with different workflows.

Therefore, we have learnt that energy power consumption can be used very simply for example to detect if the machine is switched on or off, and when in use. In order to determine more extensive features of the machine's status, it is necessary to be able to detect at high sample rate more subtle changes in the power consumption.

7.3 Conclusion

This chapter reflected on learnings regarding the application of S-BPM in two industrial cases aiming for people-centred production. Concluding, three core aspects of people-centred production shall be highlighted:

- Complexity needs a participatory approach and stakeholder knowledge
- Early participation of stakeholders
- Transparency of solution designs for all stakeholders from top to bottom

The increasing complexity of work demands for highly qualified employees and mutual alignment for task accomplishment. As such employees represent important stakeholders for work design and need be involved in solution design and implementation. Especially early participation when defining workplace requirements seems beneficial for sustainable solution designs. Furthermore, the transparency of solution designs for all stakeholders needs to be ensured from top to bottom in order to avoid resistance and resolve conflicts early. Transparency can be supported by active communication of project results via different channels (face-to-face, presentations, newsletter, social media, …). Transparency of solution designs has also been identified as crucial related to the implementation of sensor technology at workplaces. For humans sensors smack of supervision. Therefore, the "ingredients" of sensor solutions (e.g. usage of data, added value) need to be clear and aligned among all stakeholders.

References

Dean, L., & Don, W. (2003) *Managing software requirements: A use case approach.* Addison-Wesley Professional.

Fleischmann, A., Schmidt, W., Stary, C., Obermeier, S., & Börger, E. (2012). *Subject-oriented business process management.* Berlin: Springer.

Kannengiesser, U., Heininger, R., Gründer, T., & Schedl, S. (2016) Modelling the process of process execution: A process model-driven approach to customising user interfaces for business process support systems. In *International Workshop on Business Process Modeling, Development and Support* (pp. 34–48). Springer International Publishing. doi:10.1007/978-3-319-39429-9_3.

Kliem, R. L., Ludin, I., Robertson, S., & Ken, L. (1997). *Project management methodology—a practical guide for the next millennium.* New York: Marcel Dekker.

Maguire, M. (2001). Methods to support human-centred design. *International Journal of Human-Computer Studies, 55*(4), 587–634. doi:10.1006/ijhc.2001.0503.

Paetsch, F., Eberlein, A., & Maurer, F. (2003). Requirements engineering and agile software development. In *Proceedings of WETICE'03.* Washington, DC: IEEE Computer Society.

Open Access This chapter is distributed under the terms of the Creative Commons Attribution-NonCommercial 4.0 International License (http://creativecommons.org/licenses/by-nc/4.0/), which permits any noncommercial use, duplication, adaptation, distribution and reproduction in any medium or format, as long as you give appropriate credit to the original author(s) and the source, provide a link to the Creative Commons license and indicate if changes were made.

The images or other third party material in this chapter are included in the work's Creative Commons license, unless indicated otherwise in the credit line; if such material is not included in the work's Creative Commons license and the respective action is not permitted by statutory regulation, users will need to obtain permission from the license holder to duplicate, adapt or reproduce the material.

The Future: Obstacles and Opportunities

8

Udo Kannengiesser

Abstract

This chapter discusses the possible future of using S-BPM in production industry, including prospective obstacles and potential opportunities. It commences by proposing a framework representing the fundamental values of S-BPM relevant for its contribution to production enterprises: agility. These values are derived from the agile approach to software development. It is shown how S-BPM supports them in several ways; specifically

1. Individuals and interactions are supported by the notational simplicity in S-BPM
2. Working software is supported by the ability of S-BPM to seamlessly integrate processes along life cycles and value chains
3. Customer collaboration is supported by the widely shared semantics of S-BPM modelling constructs
4. Responding to change is supported by the ability to encapsulate process functionalities by means of subjects in S-BPM

The principal obstacles are identified for the use of S-BPM in industrial practice, in a way to achieve the four agile values. They include a widespread perception of process modelling as a routine task (not a creative activity), security concerns for core production processes, organizational cultures where there is a strong sense of hierarchy and silo mentality, and a desire for global control flow. Based on the size of each obstacle and the degree to which S-BPM is already prepared to address them, the beginnings of a roadmap towards industrial fitness are then developed. For this purpose, the metaphor of a

U. Kannengiesser (✉)
Metasonic GmbH, Pfaffenhofen, Germany
e-mail: udo.kannengiesser@gmail.com

© The Author(s) 2017
M. Neubauer and C. Stary (eds.), *S-BPM in the Production Industry*,
DOI 10.1007/978-3-319-48466-2_8

"compass" is introduced to give orientation to future S-BPM research within a four-dimensional space of opportunities. A specific S-BPM project in the food industry, as part of the SO-PC-Pro project, is presented to show common drivers and challenges of S-BPM implementations for production processes within this four-dimensional space. Finally, the compass is used for identifying further domains that share similar issues likely to be solved using an agile approach supported by S-BPM. The architecture-engineering-construction (AEC) domain is presented as an example of such a domain.

8.1 The Fundamental Values of S-BPM in Production

In order to predict the future potential for S-BPM in the production industry, it is useful to abstract from the specifics of the individual case studies presented in this book. This chapter outlines a framework that proposes four dimensions that characterize the essence of using S-BPM in the production industry. This framework will provide a basis for:

1. Identifying and classifying obstacles for adopting S-BPM in the production industry
2. Directing research activities and practical applications to seize opportunities in production and other, similar domains

How can we derive such a framework? In the previous chapters, S-BPM has been discussed in the context of two overarching goals in production companies: On the one hand, traditional production management needs to be enriched with humanistic aspects, such as worker empowerment and autonomy. On the other hand, production processes need to be automated using decentralized, highly flexible technologies for increased customer satisfaction. These two goals are consistent with an existing notion that has become popular in several industry domains, and is termed *agility*.

Common views of "agility" as such have not much in common with humanistic values. Superficially, this notion is often seen as synonymous to flexibility: the ability of a system to respond to change (Saleh et al. 2003). However, most of the approaches to achieving agility in socio-technical domains such as manufacturing, project management and software development are based on autonomous, local decision-making by individuals (i.e. people). Rather than having to adhere to central control mechanisms, people in agile systems are encouraged to utilize their own knowledge and creativity to respond to the situation at hand, and use communication and collaboration to align their individual decisions and actions with others.

This concept is closely associated with lean production systems, where individual production units (people or machines) communicate with one another via kanbans to streamline the overall flow of work. The connection between lean management and humanistic values has been made most explicit by the notion of *kaizen*. Kaizen implies a cooperative management style. Work is typically aligned among cross-functional, interdisciplinary work groups that collectively decide upon clear work goals and intensively exchange information for work alignment. Consensus among work groups instead of individual top-down management decisions represents a primary goal of Kaizen. Kaizen aims at employees who are highly qualified and who pro-actively and self-directedly contribute to workplace innovation and continuous improvement.

Given the dual nature of agility as a catalyst for producing not only humanistic but also economic value in socio-technical systems, it can potentially provide the basis of a generic framework for S-BPM in the production industry. One of the most known frameworks for agility has been proposed in the domain of software engineering: the "manifesto for agile software development" (Fowler and Highsmith 2001). It includes the formulation of four basic values that are shared across various techniques for agile development:

1. Individuals and interactions are valued more than rigid procedures and tools
2. Working systems are valued more than comprehensive documentation
3. Customer collaboration is valued more than contract negotiation
4. Responding to change is valued more than following a plan

The remainder of this section elaborates the four agile values including the support provided for each of them by S-BPM. This will provide a basis for identifying obstacles and opportunities for future applications of S-BPM in the production industry.

8.1.1   Individuals and Interactions: Support Through Notational Simplicity

Individual people and their interactions are considered as a critical success factor in the development of new systems, including production processes (Yauch 2007; Alves et al. 2012; Brauner and Ziefle 2015). It is the ability of individuals to reflect-in-action (Schön and Wiggins 1992), often through informal communication and self-organized teamwork that can lead to the discovery of new requirements and conceptual solutions, thus leading the design process in new directions (Gero and Kannengiesser 2014). This ability is needed mostly in development projects with high degrees of novelty and dynamics. In contrast, conforming to predefined, rigid processes can stifle the creativity needed for generating successful design outcomes.

IT tools may also turn out to be straightjackets for people, by requiring overly formal representations or by providing functionalities that are too complex and often unnecessary. In addition, most IT tools do not well support interactive, collaborative modes of working. They typically use conventional desktop screens with mouse and keyboard, granting full access to the tool only for a single person at the same time. Some tools provide more sophisticated collaboration features ranging from shared model repositories to virtual reality; however, they are still seen as inferior to collocated, physical human interaction with its rich set of gestures, facial expressions, etc.

If individual creativity and informal interactions are to be supported, there needs to be a way to model production processes in a quick and easy way, without having to conform to many formal modelling conventions or to struggle with complex tool functionalities. The resulting models may be rough sketches "on the back of an envelope" that may even be incomplete or ambiguous. Their main aim is to provide a basis for discussion, reflection and reinterpretation, often among team members in spontaneous, informal meetings. For example, mechanical engineers rarely commence modelling a new product directly using a CAD tool; instead, they commonly produce hand-drawn sketches on paper, whiteboard or other physical surfaces, in order to reflect on their ideas individually or sharing with others. The importance of sketching activities in the conceptual design stages has been pointed out in a number of domains (Schütze et al. 2003; Petre 2009; Eckert et al. 2012).

A minimal requirement for supporting quick and easy sketching of production processes is the availability of graphical modelling languages, based on their ability to facilitate human understanding (Gerber et al. 2014). For example, the IEC 61131-3 standard contains three graphical languages for structuring and programming PLC code specifying low-level process control. A variety of BPM approaches provide graphical notations for modelling on the business process level. However, many of these languages are highly complex with very intricate syntax, requiring specialized modelling tools. On-the-fly sketching of processes, either manually or by low-tech physical tools, would be quite difficult using these languages.

S-BPM provides the notational simplicity required for quick and easy sketching. Since it has only five modelling constructs, their visual syntax can be defined in a way that allows easily distinguishing them from each other. Perceptual discriminability is one of the key factors for the cognitive effectiveness of visual notations (Moody 2009). For example, the syntactic elements used in the sample models of the principal reference book on S-BPM (Fleischmann et al. 2012) are perceptually discriminable based on simple shapes. The S-BPM tool Metasonic Suite uses colour as an additional visual variable to further enhance discriminability between the syntactic elements. Producing five basic shapes or colours for modelling can be done using any common sketching tool, such as pen and paper, whiteboards, flipcharts and post-it notes. In addition, many of these tools support interactive ways of working within teams of modellers, which enhance modelling outcomes by stimulating discussions and learning (Rosemann 2006).

8.1.2 Working Systems: Support Through Seamless Integration

One of the major characteristics of agile projects is the continuous, frequent development of working systems in small increments. The notion of a "working system" here goes beyond being just "bug-free"—the system needs to "work" in terms of being useful for an individual solving a specific task (Bider 2015). One of the reasons for this emphasis on working systems is to shorten feedback loops, thus reducing the risk of developing a system that does not properly address the needs and expectations of its users. Deploying and using working systems in their intended environment is seen as the most effective basis for such an assessment. It allows users actually "seeing" the impact that the new software has on their task processing and problem solving. This can also be considered the foundation of the well-known "Plan-Do-Check-Act" cycle for continuous improvement in lean production (Dennis 2016). Documentation, such as requirement specifications, system models and test reports, can supplement but not replace the first-hand experience of interacting with the running system.

What is required to support the creation of working production systems once a production process has been modelled? Concerning the creation of control software, model-driven development (MDD) (Mellor et al. 2003) is the notion that addresses part of this issue. Here, graphical process models are transformed automatically into a representation that can be directly executed, e.g. by a workflow engine or a PLC. Another notion supporting the creation of running production systems is enterprise integration. A single process execution engine rarely operates in isolation: In most real-world applications there is an existing IT environment that needs to interact with the execution of a process. Examples include ERP systems, databases and other workflow engines, which may exchange various kinds of data with the process. What is needed, is a mechanism for data integration with external systems, preferably using existing interoperability standards depending on the domain.

S-BPM supports the creation of working systems in production companies by seamless integration in the sense of both model-driven development and enterprise integration. Specifically, S-BPM models can be transformed into two types of executable representations: Abstract State Machines (ASM) (Börger and Stärk 2003) for business process execution by subject-oriented workflow engines, and IEC 61131-3 Sequential Function Charts (SFC) (Müller 2012) for real-time execution by PLCs. S-BPM also provides a number of ways to exchange data with external systems, such as ERP (Dirndorfer 2015), MES (Kannengiesser et al. 2016) and PLCs (Kannengiesser et al. 2015).

8.1.3 Customer Collaboration: Support Through Widely Shared Semantics

Closely involving customers in the development phase aims at producing a clear, common understanding of the requirements. The notion of "customer" should be understood in a broad sense, including the concrete adopters of the system or service to be designed. Adopters may be end users or service consumers within value networks. Customer collaboration then implies that adopters are engaged to participate in the specification and design of the system throughout the project. They are viewed not merely as the final recipients of the system but rather as development partners (van Aken 2007). The *kaizen* approach in lean manufacturing makes extensive use of this concept, by encouraging workers to participate regularly in the improvement of processes and their organization (Berger 1997).

The concept of customer collaboration aims at maintaining a shared agreement about the requirements and system features as the development progresses, encourages stakeholder participation during system design and testing, and increases acceptance of the system during usage. Contract negotiation is the opposite approach, because it limits stakeholder involvement to a separate, upstream phase of requirements specification. A requirements document is produced that is treated as a "contract", implying an ultimate character and discouraging any changes after it has been specified. Such a rigid, top-down approach is rarely in line with the dynamics of reality. In addition, its nearly exclusive reliance upon written specification documents can easily lead to misunderstanding.

For all stakeholders, including production managers, engineers and workers, in order to participate effectively in process development, they need a common language. The semantics of such a language needs to be understandable independently of the stakeholders' levels of expertise and domain specialization. The simple semantics of S-BPM drawn from human communication and organizational theory can provide a good foundation for such a language, despite a few difficulties currently remaining in its practical use (see Chap. 7 "Learnings").

For subjects executed by human actors, such a semantics appears intuitive as it matches the individual's perception of organizational reality: One can either do something (represented as function states), send messages (represented as send states), or receive messages (represented as receive states). Even when subjects are executed by software or machines, the cognitive effort needed to conceptualize their interactions in terms of communicative actions can be assumed to be relatively low—using anthropomorphic metaphors is a common human strategy for understanding and predicting an agent's behaviour (Dennett 1987; Wooldridge and Jennings 1995).

8.1.4 Responding to Change: Support Through Encapsulation

Rather than following a fixed development plan, it is often more effective to accept that changes to the plan will occur. Most instances of designing are iterative and frequently involve reformulating requirements and subsequent changes in the trajectory of designing (Gero and Kannengiesser 2014). There are numerous types of design iterations (Wynn et al. 2007). They are driven mostly by the introduction of new business requirements or technical constraints, the discovery of unforeseen design problems, and the emergence of new design opportunities (Schön and Wiggins 1992).

A common way to prepare for change in system design is the concept of modularity. The fundamental idea is to reduce dependencies between system components by structuring them according to distinct functional modules. The result is a loosely coupled system architecture that allows substituting individual modules with no or only limited impact on other modules in the system (Ulrich 1995; Baldwin and Clark 2000). The same idea has been applied to services and processes including production processes (Bask et al. 2010). While the ideal degree of modularity varies according to the specific context of the system (Schilling 2000; Schilling and Steensma 2001), the underlying principle for inducing any form of modularity in a system is encapsulation. Encapsulation allows separating different functionalities among each other as well as from structural components (i.e. physical mechanisms, human or computational agents that provide these functionalities) (Gero and Kannengiesser 2003; Kampert and Epple 2014).

The notion of a subject in S-BPM fits with the idea of encapsulation. Subjects encapsulate different functionalities by exposing only their inputs and outputs (i.e. the messages they receive and send) while hiding their internal behaviour. This allows modifying this behaviour without affecting the rest of the process as long as the inputs and outputs remain the same. Encapsulation in S-BPM is also applied regarding the distinction between functionality and structural components, because subjects are clearly separated from the agents executing them (Fleischmann et al. 2013). As a result, agents can be substituted without changing the process model; only the mapping between subjects and agents needs to be modified.

8.2   Obstacles

The concept of agility is well known in the production industry. Together with its sibling, lean production, it has also been very popular in various other domains. Today many companies claim that they are agile or provide agile solutions. However, at closer inspection their understanding of agility is often quite shallow, limited to providing some form of flexibility in their products and services. As our project could reveal, truly agile values, such as the ones described in this chapter, are rarely lived in the domain of process management, especially in traditional manufacturing firms. What are the reasons for this lack of adoption? Answering this question will directly shed light onto potential obstacles for using S-BPM in production.

In this section we will use the four agile values articulated in this chapter as a framework for identifying and classifying fundamental obstacles for using S-BPM in production.

8.2.1   Process Modelling as Routine Task not Ideation

The predominant purpose of process modelling today is documentation (Kocbek et al. 2015)—which can be presumed to be a routine task that involves rather little creativity. This fits with some of the terms used in literature and practice: Processes are often referred to as being "modelled" or "mapped" rather than "designed". A Google Scholar search in August 2016 returns 27,540 English articles for the term "business process modeling" and only 6,700 for "business process design". Based on the perception of process modelling (or design) as a routine task, highly structured, systematic approaches are commonly preferred over less structured ones such as design thinking. This fits with observations that design thinking techniques have been rarely adopted in enterprise IT despite their popularity in product design (Gartner 2015). This is especially the case for IT in the production industry, where company cultures, organizational structures, and work procedures are oriented rather to traditional engineering approaches.

Understanding process modelling as a documentation or requirements definition method has led to the development of comprehensive process notations such as BPMN that aim to support a high degree of expressiveness. BPMN, today the most commonly used approach in BPM (Harmon 2016), requires a complex syntax that is not easy to be learned and applied (Recker 2010). Since there is a correlation between process modelling competence and the creativity of process modelling outcomes (Figl and Weber 2012), it can be assumed that the lack of adequate BPMN expertise of many practitioners affects their creativity in process modelling negatively. In addition, the complex notation of BPMN requires computational tool support for modelling, which may explain the apparent importance of process modelling tools in BPM surveys (Harmon 2016). It is certainly possible to sketch process models using only a core or subset of the most important modelling elements in BPMN (Recker 2010; Grosskopf et al. 2010). Yet, the resulting models would then have to be interpreted by modelling specialists to manually transform them into more complex diagrams using a more complete subset of the BPMN specification, and using the BPMN modelling tools that many companies already invested in. This approach is error-prone as it bears the risk of misinterpretation.

The widespread view of process modelling as a routine task, reinforced by the current dominance of the BPMN approach that has been declared a standard for BPM, clearly favours procedures and tools over individuals and interactions. This is an obvious obstacle for the adoption of S-BPM, particularly in rather conservative domains such as the production industry.

8.2.2 Don't Mess with My Core Process

Although the seamless integration of production and business processes is the declared goal of numerous research initiatives and standard committees, companies often remain wary regarding this topic. The reason for that is the belief integrating processes also means exposing them, thus making them potentially vulnerable to privacy and security threats. Traditionally, many manufacturing organizations have sought to protect their production processes by disconnecting them from the outside world. This shift especially concerns their IT systems used for lower-level automation control, as these systems are considered to be vital for manufacturing operations. Any malfunctioning of these systems, e.g. as a result of denial-of-service attacks, will directly incur loss of productivity and loss of revenue (Sadeghi et al. 2015). A maximum level of security is therefore preferred, often by physically isolating security-critical systems and "core processes" from the rest of the enterprise. This strategy is known as the "air gap" principle (Lass and Kotarski

2014). Another strategy for keeping core production processes secure has been the use of proprietary systems without standard interfaces, hoping the effort involved in finding and exploiting vulnerabilities of a system will be too high for successful attacks.

To realize the benefits of Industry 4.0 business models, there need to be seamless integration mechanisms that address concerns of privacy and security. Some of these mechanisms are already provided by standard communication protocols such as OPC UA (Hoppe 2014). Yet, they need to be complemented by protective measures on the business process level.

Today S-BPM does not offer solutions to these issues. The degree to which core processes are exposed to external systems is often limited to coarse-grained documentation, whereby simple flowcharts are generally preferred over executable notations such as S-BPM.

8.2.3 Hierarchies and Silos

A wide variety of stakeholders may need to interact at different stages of the life cycle of production systems and production processes. They include mechanical engineers, electrical engineers, software specialists, production managers, product designers, shopfloor workers and sometimes clients. Discussing different process designs in terms and models that can be understood by all stakeholders independently of their education and discipline—namely, by using a common language such as S-BPM—would certainly be advantageous. However, the main obstacle here is that the local work culture in many companies does not encourage collaborative ways of working. For example, it can often be observed that managers take process design decisions without including shopfloor workers in the decision-making process.

In addition, mechanical engineers often devise production systems and processes without consulting with the software specialists implementing associated control systems (Alvarez Cabrera et al. 2010). These two examples refer to cultural issues that can be referred to by the notions of hierarchies and silos, respectively. Companies with a strong sense of hierarchy rarely use management approaches that feature worker participation and empowerment. Silo mentality represents a similar obstacle leading to poor collaboration across disciplines, functional departments and business units.

The ground for S-BPM in production seems to be most fertile where companies already have established lean and open organizational cultures. This finding is confirmed by numerous industry experts viewing Lean Management as a precondition for the successful implementation of Industry 4.0 and smart factories. Regarding process modelling aspects of Lean Management, Kannengiesser (2014) has already shown the consistency of S-BPM with the value stream design (VSD) approach. However, the actual challenge remains for company organizations, namely to keep pace and align with these technical advances and foster a participative, collaborative work culture.

Where work cultures are characterized by hierarchies or silos, a strong tendency exists to minimize and/formalize collaboration across interfaces between functional units. Such a tendency favours "contract negotiation" and discourages open collaboration, establishing a primary obstacle for adopting S-BPM.

8.2.4 The Desire for Global Control Flow

A common human strategy for understanding and analyzing complex systems is to construct simplified models representing them. These models concentrate on the most typical case, ignoring many variations and exceptions that may occur. Complex processes are mapped into linear sequences of abstract activities, even though in reality stakeholders may behave non-linearly and in unpredictable ways. The fact that these models often remain at quite a low resolution and at best provide a snapshot of reality has commonly been accepted as an instance of the Pareto principle: 80 % of the benefits of process modelling stem from 20 % of the process modelling effort. However, as business and production become more volatile and heterogeneous (Sinur et al. 2013), this principle does no longer apply—at least not by focussing on just 20 % of all process variants. Unfortunately, this issue has remained unnoticed by many process managers. For them, process models need to be linear and mostly sequential, preferably from "end to end".

S-BPM does not provide or support such a linear perspective. It conceptualizes processes as interacting subjects that encapsulate behaviour, and thus hide parts of the process. Instead of following a centralized (and thus linear) control flow, the interactions between subjects can occur indeterministically at execution time. The interplay between subjects is not represented as a linear flow of activities but as an unordered network of messages in a Subject Interaction Diagram. S-BPM models are thus oriented towards local autonomy and behaviour of the agents that execute the subjects, and towards the ability to modify individual behaviours without necessarily affecting the whole process system. There is not much work on combining this bottom-up view with a top-down view describing a process from a global system perspective. In such a perspective, the focus is on the desired sequence of tasks to be performed, in order to achieve the system's goals. It may partially explain the ongoing popularity of simple flowcharts and control flow-oriented approaches such as BPMN. Representations capturing a process in terms of an "end-to-end" sequence of tasks have not been in the focus of research in S-BPM till date.

What is missing in S-BPM models to provide a global process view? According to some BPM practitioners, S-BPM lacks constructs that explicitly show the logical sequence of (main) tasks (as, e.g. represented by sequence flow in BPMN), the exact location(s) of the end of the process (as represented by "end events" in BPMN), and the location of key decision points within the process (as represented by gateways in BPMN). These would be models where the order of activation of subject instances during process execution can be defined according to an assumed "happy" (or any other, specifiable) path.

The desire of "following a plan" as suggested by centrally controlled, linear process models is a clear obstacle for applying S-BPM. At present, there are no subject-oriented constructs that can cater to the desire for global control-flow modelling.

8.3 Opportunities

We have elaborated the values and generic benefits of S-BPM as well as its major obstacles in the production industry. Given this situation, what are the opportunities that arise, in terms of areas of research and industry where S-BPM can realistically create an impact? In this section, we try to provide an answer by first developing the beginnings of a roadmap for S-BPM in production, before presenting a case study overcoming some of the obstacles, and examining other fields of application beyond the classical view of "production".

8.3.1 Towards a Roadmap for Using S-BPM in Production

Having identified the various obstacles for adopting S-BPM in the production industry, it is possible to develop a roadmap that may help navigating around these obstacles. In this section, we will outline an initial basis for such a roadmap.

The four agile values are not completely independent of each other. However, for the purposes of building a roadmap, we can treat them as four orthogonal dimensions to provide future research with a frame of reference. Driving research along one dimension means to develop extensions of S-BPM (methodologically or computationally) and/or evaluate these using industrial case studies. Each of these research efforts will face different obstacles as outlined in the previous Sect. 8.2. The size of each obstacle and the degree to which S-BPM research is already prepared to tackle them determines the speed with which research can demonstrate the overall benefits of S-BPM in production. A roadmap may use this information to propose a research agenda that aims at reaching out for the "low-hanging" fruit first and addressing the more challenging issue later.

Figure 8.1 provides an overview of the four research dimensions using the concept of a compass. Contrary to the normal use of a compass allowing two-dimensional navigation, we use this concept to allow navigating in four dimensions. So, in our four-dimensional world, "navigating" towards notational simplicity ("North") does not mean moving away from seamless integration ("South"). Our "compass" is thus an abstract metaphor for navigation to help visualizing opportunities for future research, despite the potential misunderstanding pointed out here.

The circular arrow in Fig. 8.1 represents the sequence in which the four dimensions ought to be addressed for boosting the adoption of S-BPM in

Fig. 8.1 A "compass" for
S-BPM in production industry

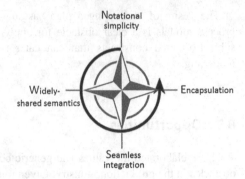

production industry. We chose the indicated sequence based on the amount of effort we perceive will be required for tackling the associated obstacles.

The least amount of research effort is likely to be needed for removing or navigating around the obstacle of "process modelling as routine task not ideation", thus driving research towards the notational simplicity dimension ("North" in the compass in Fig. 8.1). Even in cases where process modelling is perceived a routine rather than a creative task, the benefits of S-BPM in terms of ease of use and stakeholder engagement are immediately obvious, as indicated by a growing number of field studies in various industries (Fleischmann et al. 2015). More of these studies are needed showing these benefits in the production domain.

Work in the SO-PC-Pro project has already started to deliver such case studies, having the potential to serve as reference cases for further applications. Especially in the more technical process domains in production where the BPMN standard had only limited influence so far, there is a good chance that S-BPM may be welcomed more than in traditional business process management domains. This effect may be leveraged by future initiatives aiming to transform S-BPM into a formal standard endorsed by an international standards committee. Another strategy could be to borrow a limited set of graphical elements from the BPMN notation but constrain their use to match the modelling semantics and conventions of S-BPM (Turetken and Demirors 2013; Fichtenbauer and Fleischmann 2016).

The obstacle of "hierarchies and silos" is a slightly trickier one to address, as it is a more general problem. Fortunately, an increasing number of companies are adopting open work cultures. They are the ones S-BPM practitioners can directly target rather than facing an uphill battle with traditional company cultures. The S-BPM approach provides them with a tool that can overcome silos and hierarchies based on its widely shared semantics ("West" in the compass). What still needs to be addressed in more detail, however, is a governance framework answering questions such as: When should a particular stakeholder become involved? To what extent? Should the modelling activity be performed top-down or bottom-up? Such a framework could be used to develop guidelines to help process managers feel more at ease with the S-BPM modelling approach as today it does not answer these practical questions.

The next obstacle to be addressed is the one we call "don't mess with my core process", impeding progress towards seamless integration ("South" in the compass). It is based on the fundamental security, safety and privacy concerns that persist in the production industry and thus keep raising reservations against technologies enabling seamless integration. S-BPM will not be able to dissolve these concerns in the short term, as significant amounts of research as well as tool developments are necessary. S-BPM does provide a sound conceptual basis for this research, as it contains a number of concepts that can be used for enhanced privacy and security control in seamlessly integrated production processes. Particularly, the concept of encapsulation in S-BPM may be used as a basis for effective protection of processes and data from external threats. Such an approach requires the implementation of S-BPM extensions as proposed by Dirndorfer et al. (2012). In addition, sophisticated mechanisms for access control of subjects (Lawall et al. 2015) need to be realized.

Probably the most challenging obstacle to address is "the desire for global control flow" that hampers adoption of the encapsulation idea ("East" in the compass). A number of extensions of S-BPM seem to be necessary. Possible research avenues include modelling incomplete or more coarse-grained subject behaviours, similar to the notion of "normalized" behaviour proposed by Fleischmann et al. (2012). Future work may also require a way to turn communication-based subject relations into more abstract control-flow relations. This enrichment could reduce the "communication clutter" caused by the typically large number of messages in S-BPM models that often reduces readability, and could provide a more condensed visualization of the main functionalities in the process and their (expected or desired) sequence. Another way could be to introduce the notion of a process view: Modellers can define and switch between different views of the same process, depending on the specific purpose (Browning 2009). For example, one may define a view of a Subject Interaction Diagram where only those messages are shown that are associated with the value stream (Kannengiesser 2014); other messages solely aiming at coordinating different subjects would then be omitted. This reduces the number of messages in a chosen view without having to resort to control-flow diagrams. Another view of a Subject Interaction Diagram may use the design structure matrix (DSM) representation of processes (Kannengiesser 2015).

Each of the four dimensions may be elaborated in future work, e.g. by adding specific milestones. This could guide research activities in the sense of a detailed roadmap and would allow measuring their progress.

8.3.2   Practical Application: A Case Study in the Food Industry

The compass introduced in Sect. 8.3 represents the beginnings of a roadmap for research in S-BPM in production, suggesting a sequence in which the four principal issues can be addressed. We can adapt the meaning of this compass to identify the drivers and challenges related to using S-BPM in specific process implementation projects in the production industry. In this section, we show how these challenges were dealt with in a case study in the food industry.

The case study has been implemented for a large manufacturer of baked products based in Mexico. In this chapter we will refer to this manufacturer as Company C. Through participating in SO-PC-Pro, the management of Company C wanted to perform a process improvement project in one of its sales outlets as a pilot for rolling out the solution in other outlets throughout Mexico. The main focus was increasing the profitability of the branch. For this purpose, two value drivers were identified:

1. Loss of revenue because of product returns (i.e. products that need to be discarded as they are no longer fresh (shelf life exceeded))
2. Loss of revenue because of lack of products (i.e. missed sales opportunities)

Targeting these value drivers were the main goals of the case study. As such, the case study can be seen as a Lean improvement project, as it follows the classical principle of the Lean methodology: to smoothen process flow by eliminating various kinds of "waste"; here, the wastes of overproduction (generating unnecessary stock— which in the present case study needs to be discarded after reaching the end of their shelf life) and underproduction (causing consumers to wait for production—which in the case study manifests itself as empty shelves and disappointed customers).

S-BPM was used for developing an improved production and delivery process for baked and frozen goods in the selected sales outlet. This process implements a pull system—a well-known Lean design principle—in addition to the existing push system. This means that production is controlled not only by an upfront schedule or production plan ("pushing" the process) but also by variations in product demand ("pulling" the process). The process was partially automated and integrated in the sales branch. Previously this process was executed only manually, without being enforced or supported by a process execution system.

The four challenges or dimensions identified for S-BPM had various effects on the project.

Notational simplicity: The relative ease of using S-BPM enabled interdisciplinary team of ten people to produce and validate a complete, executable model of the to-be production process within a combined training and modelling workshop that lasted five days. The modelling activity was initially performed using post-it notes, cards and flipcharts, as shown in Fig. 8.2. Most workshop participants were included in these initial stages of modelling, confirming the playful, engaging character of S-BPM modelling. All models resulting from these initial elicitation sessions were later transformed into computational models using the S-BPM tool Metasonic Suite.

Apart from two S-BPM experts in the project team, none of the other team members had modelled with S-BPM prior to the project. However, they were all familiar with flowcharts, and two of them had even worked with BPMN in previous

Fig. 8.2 Initial S-BPM modelling session performed using physical tools

projects. Despite this bias towards the control-flow paradigm, everyone in the team was fairly quickly able to get used to the subject-oriented way of thinking.

Widely shared semantics: Eliciting the production process from the workers in the case study followed a traditional approach using interviews and observations by consultants. Workers were not directly involved in creating, verifying or discussing the process model. It was only through pilot testing of the implemented process with its associated execution support systems that workers had the occasion to experience and comment on the process. The lack of worker involvement during the modelling stage was partially due to the technical character of the project, which mainly aimed at automating tasks rather than establishing a completely novel way of working. The creation of the process model was guided by two S-BPM experts, overcoming the lack of formal frameworks governing the S-BPM modelling activities. They also managed to train the S-BPM novices in the team to conceptualize processes in terms of the five simple constructs: subject, message, function state, receive state and send state.

Seamless integration: For the purposes of the project, processes were not required to be integrated vertically. The only possible integration that was discussed was horizontal: Should the new production process include the upstream processes in the plant providing the raw materials and producing unfinished products? A decision was made to leave these (core) processes out of the scope of this project,

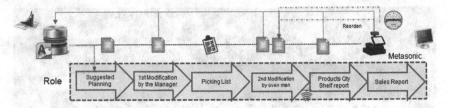

Fig. 8.3 Flowchart providing a simplified, global view of the production process

due to the nature of the project as a research endeavour. Security and similar concerns would have been likely to play a role if this decision had been the other way.

Encapsulation: The outcomes of the initial phase of process elicitation—before the S-BPM modelling approach was applied in the project—were captured using a simple flowchart representation as shown in Fig. 8.3. This flowchart includes icons and basic shapes with fairly open semantics. It was used to represent the production process at a high level of abstraction, without enforcing any formal modelling conventions. This flowchart was helpful in generating a common understanding about the process among project team members. However, when using the S-BPM approach for modelling the same process, the flowchart was no longer used. The change in thinking from control flow towards subject-orientation required some cognitive effort from some team members, which was facilitated by the two S-BPM experts in the team.

The case study demonstrated the strengths and challenges of S-BPM according to the four dimensions. While the implementation and evaluation of the case study is still ongoing, the experiences gained during this study indicate that S-BPM is a promising approach for process improvement projects in the production industry although open research issues remain.

8.3.3 Other Fields of Application: Architecture-Engineering-Construction (AEC) as an Example

The high generality of the compass in Sect. 8.3.1 allows its application in domains not directly related to production but sharing similar concerns including the need for agility. These may be domains situated along the value chain or the lifecycle of produced goods and services (ARC Advisory Group 2001). For example, domains such as product data management (PDM), product lifecycle management (PLM), supply chain management (SCM) and customer relationship management (CRM) may require applications supported by an agile approach to process management. Other domains may be located even further from manufacturing. One of them is the architecture-engineering-construction (AEC) industry. This Section will present AEC projects as an example for the potential use of S-BPM in domains beyond production.

One of the principal concerns in the AEC domain is the planning and execution of construction projects for the built environment. Over the past two decades, there has been an increasing focus on the digitalization of building data to speed up the execution of construction projects. The research concerned with digitalization in this domain is commonly known as Building Information Modelling (BIM). A lot of research and development activities in BIM have been devoted to creating a standard model for building information, called Industry Foundation Classes (IFCs). This standard comprises hundreds of building concepts for all building lifecycle phases (e.g. design, construction, management and demolition). Its aim is to support interoperability across hundreds of software applications and industry domains. Subsets of IFCs, called Model View Definitions (MVDs), can be specified to allow swift access to relevant parts of the data standard.

To facilitate the practical use of IFCs, the approach of Information Delivery Manuals (IDMs) has been developed and adopted as an international standard (ISO 29481-1:2010). IDMs specify how data can be exchanged among different project stakeholders by means of a process model and the types of information to be exchanged. Specifications contained in an IDM are then mapped to relevant MVDs. Specifically, the following artefacts are contained in an IDM:

- Process Map (PM): It is used for defining the industry process to be supported. It should contain a set of activities, roles and the required data inputs and outputs.
- Exchange Requirements (ERs): They specify the information to be exchanged among the contractors.
- Functional Parts (FPs): They allow mapping IDMs to concepts in MVDs.

AEC projects are typically carried out in timeframes of several years (Eastman 2014). As one of the causes for long project durations one can identify the paper-based definition and exchange of IDM artefacts such as PMs, ERs and FPs. The manual work required for interpreting, maintaining and validating these paper documents is error-prone and time-consuming, especially when many parties are involved as typical for AEC projects. The method that best describes this way of working is the waterfall approach. In this approach, projects are structured in distinct phases that are separated by stage gates. The typical phases of an AEC project (with their respective timeframes) are shown in Fig. 8.4.

The waterfall approach allows iterations within a phase but discourages iterations across different phases: Once a document is produced at the end of a phase, it is regarded as a final agreement serving as a "contractual" basis for the subsequent

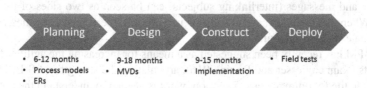

Fig. 8.4 Typical structure of an AEC project (based on Eastman 2014)

phase. Later changes would require not only renegotiation among the parties involved, but also considerable effort to update and validate the consistency of IDM documents.

It is somewhat surprising that most AEC projects rely almost exclusively on paper-based documents, given that the principal motivation for BIM has been the digitalisation of models and model exchange. So far, the benefits of digital information exchange have been realized only for AEC process applications, but not yet for the development process that generates these applications.

One of the obstacles for digitizing data exchanges in AEC projects is the reliance on the traditional view of process modelling that favours extensive documentation over rapid design and testing. This is revealed by the IDM standard that recommends BPMN for defining process maps. However, some AEC researchers are increasingly interested in more agile AEC project approaches. Such research efforts can be categorized according to our four dimensions.

Notational simplicity: Lee et al. (2013) propose a method for IDM process modelling that restricts the use of BPMN for process modelling to a subset of only 22 notational elements. The authors have realized that "IDM development is challenging and error-prone due to an excessive and overwhelming number of BPMN shapes" (Lee et al. 2013, p. 649).

Widely shared semantics: Efforts to reduce the notational complexity of process models for AEC projects are also associated with the need to foster better collaboration between the various disciplines involved in these projects. Engineers, architects, constructors, facility managers, etc. should all be able to create, understand and give feedback on process models representing their roles in a project. This requires a common language, whose definition is the goal of current standardization initiatives such as building SMART (http://buildingsmart.org).

Seamless integration: The method proposed by Lee et al. (2013) tightens the connection between PMs, ERs, FPs and MVDs, to support an integrated, seamless development of process and data models. The use of standardized formats for MVDs, such as the mvdXML format, enhances the validation of IFC files against ERs defined in a given IDM and the corresponding MVD. The seamless integration supported by that work is limited to the initial stages of process development, unlike in production where seamless integration is mostly understood to cover the usage stage (i.e. the execution) of processes.

Encapsulation: Encapsulation in process models is not a well-known concept in IDM-related research. However, the strong interest in representing data flow (often represented in existing IDMs using message flow between separate BPMN pools) in IDMs may provide a fertile ground for adopting this idea. Subjects (i.e. encapsulations) and messages (interlinking subjects) can be seen as two sides of the same coin: Whenever there are several subjects in a process, there need to be messages to coordinate their behaviours.

S-BPM has recently been suggested as a means for increasing the agility of AEC projects (Kannengiesser and Roxin 2016), articulating the strengths of S-BPM with respect to the four dimensions. Yet, more work is needed to understand the potential implications of applying this new approach in the AEC domain.

8.4 Conclusion

This chapter started by extracting the essence of using S-BPM in the production industry, namely as a vehicle for agility in the development of production processes. Borrowing from work on agile software development, four fundamental features of agility were proposed, and it was shown how S-BPM can support them. For each feature, a main obstacle was identified. It provided the basis for a roadmap of research in S-BPM in production, represented as a "compass" in a four-dimensional space of opportunities.

A case study in the food production industry was presented to illustrate the practical implications of using S-BPM in production. Challenges in the case study were classified and described according to the four dimensions of the compass. Finally, the potential usefulness of the framework beyond production was exemplified based on a description of typical shortcomings of architecture-engineering-construction (AEC) projects. The intention of this work was to outline the potential role of S-BPM in tomorrow's factories and give a possible pathway towards its adoption in the manufacturing and other domains. So far, the potential benefits of the subject-oriented approach have been pointed out for production industries mainly on a conceptual level. The case studies presented in this and other chapters are only beginning to demonstrate its practical value. This is one of the reasons, why S-BPM is still rather unknown in the world of production management. However, this situation is likely to change once a larger number of industrial applications using S-BPM are available that go beyond laboratory prototypes and research pilots, and prove its practical value. The conceptual framework established in this chapter can guide the development and evaluation of such applications.

References

Alvarez Cabrera, A. A., Foeken, M. J., Tekin, O. A., Woestenenk, K., Erden, M. S., De Schutter, B., et al. (2010). Towards automation of control software: A review of challenges in mechatronic design. *Mechatronics, 20*(8), 876–886.

Alves, A. C., Dinis-Carvalho, J., & Sousa, R. M. (2012). Lean production as promoter of thinkers to achieve companies' agility. *The Learning Organization, 19*(3), 219–237.

ARC Advisory Group. (2001). *Collaborative manufacturing management strategies.* White Paper, October 2001. Retrieved August 19, 2016, from http://www.arcweb.com/arcreports2001/Collaborative%20Manufacturing%20Management%20Strategies.pdf.

Baldwin, C. Y., & Clark, K. B. (2000). *Design rules: Volume 1. The power of modularity.* Cambridge: MIT Press.

Bask, A., Lipponen, M., Rajahonka, M., & Tinnilä, M. (2010). The concept of modularity: Diffusion from manufacturing to service production. *Journal of Manufacturing Technology Management, 21*(3), 355–375.

Berger, A. (1997). Continuous improvement and kaizen: Standardization and organizational designs. *Integrated Manufacturing Systems, 8*(2), 110–117.

Bider, I. (2015). Agile research in information systems field: Analysis from knowledge transformation perspective. In *Proceedings of 8th IADIS International Conference on Information systems, Madeira, Portugal.*

Börger, E., & Stärk, R. (2003). *Abstract state machines: A method for high-level system design and analysis.* Berlin: Springer.

Brauner, P., & Ziefle, M. (2015). Human factors in production systems: Motives, methods and beyond. In C. Brecher (Ed.), *Advances in production technology* (pp. 187–199). Lecture Notes in Production Engineering. Springer.

Browning, T. R. (2009). The many views of a process: Toward a process architecture framework for product development processes. *Systems Engineering, 12*(1), 69–90.

Dennett, D. C. (1987). *The intentional stance.* Cambridge: MIT Press.

Dennis, P. (2016). *Lean production simplified: A plain-language guide to the world's most powerful production system* (3rd ed.). Boca Raton: CRC Press.

Dirndorfer, M. (2015). ERP integration in S-BPM processes. In A. Fleischmann, W. Schmidt, & C. Stary (Eds.), *S-BPM in the wild: Practical value creation* (pp. 257–268). Springer.

Dirndorfer, M., Handy, B., Schneeberger, J., & Fischer, H. (2012). Subjective security and safety— S-BPM as a base for the description of security and safety objectives. In S. Oppl & A. Fleischmann (Eds.), *S-BPM ONE 2012, CCIS 284* (pp. 214–219). Berlin: Springer.

Eastman, C. M. (2014). Business process re-engineering for BIM: New directions in supporting workflow exchanges in IFC. In *Building SMART alliance 2014 National Conference.*

Eckert, C., Blackwell, A., Stacey, M., Earl, C., & Church, L. (2012). Sketching across design domains: Roles and formalities. *Artificial Intelligence for Engineering Design, Analysis and Manufacturing, 26*(3), 245–266.

Fichtenbauer, C., & Fleischmann, A. (2016). Three dimensions of process models regarding their execution. In *S-BPM ONE'16.* New York: ACM Press.

Figl, K., & Weber, B. (2012). Individual creativity in designing business processes. In M. Bajec & J. Eder (Eds.), *CAiSE 2012 Workshops* (Vol. 112, pp. 294–306). LNBIP. Berlin: Springer.

Fleischmann, A., Schmidt, W., Stary, C., Obermeier, S., & Börger, E. (2012). *Subject-oriented business process management.* Berlin: Springer.

Fleischmann, A., Schmidt, W., & Stary, C. (2015). *S-BPM in the wild: Practical value creation.* Berlin: Springer.

Fleischmann, A., Kannengiesser, U., Schmidt, W., & Stary C. (2013). Subject-oriented modeling and execution of multi-agent business processes. In *2013 IEEE/WIC/ACM International Conferences on Web Intelligence (WI) and Intelligent Agent Technology (IAT), Atlanta, GA* (pp. 138–145).

Fowler, M., & Highsmith, J. (2001). The agile manifesto. *Software Development, 9*(8), 28–35.

Gartner. (2015). *Design thinking can revolutionize your customer experience strategies.* White Paper, November 2015.

Gerber, T., Theorin, A., & Johnsson, C. (2014). Towards a seamless integration between process modeling descriptions at business and production levels: Work in progress. *Journal of Intelligent Manufacturing, 25*(5), 1089–1099.

Gero, J. S., & Kannengiesser, U. (2003). Function-behaviour-structure: A model for social situated agents. In *Workshop on Cognitive Modeling of Agents and Multi-Agent Interactions, International Joint Conference on Artificial Intelligence, Acapulco, Mexico* (pp. 101–107).

Gero, J. S., & Kannengiesser, U. (2014). The function-behaviour-structure ontology of design. In A. Chakrabarti, & L. T. M. Blessing (Eds.), *An anthology of theories and models of design* (pp. 263–283). Springer.

Grosskopf, A., Edelman, J., & Weske, M. (2010). Tangible business process modeling— methodology and experiment design. In *BPM 2009 Workshops* (pp. 489–500). Berlin: Springer.

Harmon, P. (2016). *The state of business process management 2016.* BPTrends Report, Business Process Trends.

Hoppe, S. (2014). Standardisierte horizontale und vertikale Kommunikation: Status und Ausblick. In T. Bauernhansl, et al. (Eds.), *Industrie 4.0 in Produktion, Automatisierung und Logistik* (pp. 325–341). Springer.

ISO 29481-3. (2010). *Building information modelling—information delivery manual—Part 3: Model view definitions.* Retrieved August 18, 2016, from http://www.freestd.us/soft4/2085144.htm.

Kampert, D., & Epple, U. (2014). Outside-in: Simplifying systems by integrating the outside perspective. In *2014 11th International Multi-Conference on Systems, Signals & Devices (SSD), Barcelona* (pp. 1–6).

Kannengiesser, U. (2014). Supporting value stream design using S-BPM. In *S-BPM-ONE—Scientific Research* (Vol. 170, pp. 151–160). LNBIP. Springer.

Kannengiesser, U. (2015). Integrating cross-organisational business processes based on a combined S-BPM/DSM approach. In *17th IEEE Conference on Business Informatics, Lisbon, Portugal.*

Kannengiesser, U., Neubauer, M., & Heininger, H. (2015). Subject-oriented BPM as the glue for integrating enterprise processes in smart factories. In *On the Move to Meaningful Internet Systems: OTM 2015 Workshops* (Vol. 9416, pp. 77–86). LNCS. Springer.

Kannengiesser, U., Neubauer, M., & Heininger, H. (2016). *Integrating business processes and manufacturing operations based on S-BPM and B2MML, S-BPM ONE 2016.* Germany: Erlangen.

Kannengiesser, U., & Roxin, A. (2016). An agile process modelling approach for BIM projects. In *European Conference on Product and Process Modelling 2016, Cyprus.*

Kocbek, M., Jošt, G., Heričko, M., & Polančič, G. (2015). Business process model and notation: The current state of affairs. *Computer Science and Information Systems, 12*(2), 509–539.

Lass, S., & Kotarski, D. (2014). IT-Sicherheit als besondere Herausforderung von Industrie 4.0. In W. Kersten, H. Koller, & H. Lödding (Eds.), *Industrie 4.0: Wie intelligente Vernetzung und kognitive Systeme unsere Arbeit verändern* (pp. 397–419). Berlin: Gito.

Lawall, A., Reichelt, D., & Schaller, T. (2015). Resource management and authorization for cloud services. In *S-BPM ONE'15.* New York: ACM Press. Article No. 18.

Lee, G., Park, Y. H., & Ham, S. (2013). Extended process to product modeling (xPPM) for integrated and seamless IDM and MVD development. *Advanced Engineering Informatics, 27*, 636–651.

Mellor, S. J., Clark, A. N., & Futagami, T. (2003). Model-driven development. *IEEE Software, 20*(5), 14–18.

Moody, D. L. (2009). The "physics" of notations: Towards a scientific basis for constructing visual notations in software engineering. *IEEE Transactions on Software Engineering, 35*(5), 756–778.

Müller, H. (2012). Using S-BPM for PLC code generation and extension of subject-oriented methodology to all layers of modern control systems. In C. Stary (Ed.), *S-BPM One—Scientific Research* (Vol. 104, pp. 182–204). LNBIP. Berlin: Springer.

Petre, M. (2009). Insights from expert software design practice. In *7th Joint Meeting of the European Software Engineering Conference (ESEC) and the ACM SIGSOFT Symposium on the Foundations of Software Engineering (FSE), Amsterdam, The Netherlands* (pp. 233–242).

Recker, J. C. (2010). Opportunities and constraints: The current struggle with BPMN. *Business Process Management Journal, 16*(1), 181–201.

Rosemann, M. (2006). Potential pitfalls of process modeling: Part B. *Business Process Management Journal, 12*(3), 377–384.

Sadeghi, A.-R., Wachsmann, C., & Waidner, M. (2015). Security and privacy challenges in industrial internet of things. In *DAC'15, San Francisco, CA.*

Saleh, J. H., Hastings, D. E., & Newman, D. J. (2003). Flexibility in system design and implications for aerospace systems. *Acta Astronautica, 53*(12), 927–944.

Schilling, M. A. (2000). Toward a general modular systems theory and its application to interfirm product modularity. *Academy of Management Review, 25*(2), 312–334.

Schilling, M. A., & Steensma, H. K. (2001). The use of modular organizational forms: An industry-level analysis. *Academy of Management Review, 44*(6), 1149–1168.

Schön, D., & Wiggins, G. (1992). Kinds of seeing and their functions in designing. *Design Studies, 13*(2), 135–156.

Schütze, M., Sachse, P., & Römer, A. (2003). Support value of sketching in the design process. *Research in Engineering Design, 14*(2), 89–97.

Sinur, J., Odell, J., & Fingar, P. (2013). *Business process management: The next wave*. Tampa: Meghan-Kiffer Press.

Turetken, O., & Demirors, O. (2013). Business process modeling pluralized. In H. Fischer & J. Schneeberger (Eds.), *S-BPM ONE 2013, CCIS 360* (pp. 34–51). Berlin: Springer.

Ulrich, K. (1995). The role of product architecture in the manufacturing firm. *Research Policy, 24* (3), 419–440.

van Aken, J. E. (2007). Design science and organization development interventions: Aligning business and humanistic values. *Journal of Applied Behavioral Science, 43*(1), 67–88.

Wooldridge, M., & Jennings, N. R. (1995). Intelligent agents: Theory and practice. *The Knowledge Engineering Review, 10*(2), 115–152.

Wynn, D. C., Eckert, C. M., & Clarkson, P. J. (2007). Modelling iteration in engineering design. In *International Conference on Engineering Design (ICED'07), Paris, France*, paper no. 561.

Yauch, C. A. (2007). Team-based work and work system balance in the context of agile manufacturing. *Applied Ergonomics, 38*(1), 19–27.

Open Access This chapter is distributed under the terms of the Creative Commons Attribution-NonCommercial 4.0 International License (http://creativecommons.org/licenses/by-nc/4.0/), which permits any noncommercial use, duplication, adaptation, distribution and reproduction in any medium or format, as long as you give appropriate credit to the original author(s) and the source, provide a link to the Creative Commons license and indicate if changes were made.

The images or other third party material in this chapter are included in the work's Creative Commons license, unless indicated otherwise in the credit line; if such material is not included in the work's Creative Commons license and the respective action is not permitted by statutory regulation, users will need to obtain permission from the license holder to duplicate, adapt or reproduce the material.

Index

A
Acceptance, 88, 93, 102, 103, 119, 135, 149
Adaptive system, 168, 188
Agility, 31, 48, 210, 215, 227
Analysis, 70, 114
Architecture-engineering-construction (AEC),
    224
Automation, 9, 30, 169, 171
Automation diabolo, 37, 39
Automation pyramid, 21, 37
Autonomy, 47, 163, 210

B
Behaviour-oriented approach, 87
Building Information Modelling (BIM), 225
Business model, 14, 41, 109, 217
Business-to-Manufacturing Markup Language
    (B2MML), 30

C
Change analysis, 118, 125
Change propagation, 125
Collaboration, 41, 61, 125
Context, 47, 49, 125, 128, 186, 195
Contextual design, 49, 50, 128
Cyber-physical system, 21

D
Digitization, 13

E
Empowerment, 11, 48, 60, 116, 150, 159, 210,
    217
Encapsulation, 40, 46, 88, 215, 221
Error analysis, 158
Error management, 130
Error report, 89, 131

F
Factories of the future, 8, 168
Focus group, 50, 89, 90, 108, 135, 149
Formative evaluation, 88, 122, 149
Function allocation, 170, 188
Functional requirement, 81

G
Goal definition, 74, 116

H
High-Level Control (HLC), 38

I
Industry 4.0, 9
Information exchange, 76
Internet of things, 8
Involvement, 17, 48, 102, 124, 150

K
Kanban, 83, 91, 106

L
Low-Level Control (LLC), 38

M
Mock-up, 50, 89, 111

O
OPC Unified Architecture (OPC UA), 30, 33,
    82, 97, 99, 177, 179, 217
Organizational improvement, 10
Organizational requirements, 119

P
People-centeredness, 102, 154
People-centred production, 13, 207

© The Author(s) 2017
M. Neubauer and C. Stary (eds.), *S-BPM in the Production Industry*,
DOI 10.1007/978-3-319-48466-2

Printed in the United States
By Bookmasters